Socio-Legal Studies in Context: The Oxford Centre Past and Present

D1283679

Edited by
Denis J. Galligan

Blackwell Publishers

ISBN 0-631-19681-1

First published 1995

Published simultaneously as Vol. 22 No. 1
of Journal of Law and Society ISSN 0263–323X

Blackwell Publishers
108 Cowley Road, Oxford OX4 1JF, UK
and
238 Main Street, Cambridge, MA 02142, USA.

British Library Cataloguing in Publication Data
A CIP Catalogue record for this book is available from
the British Library.

Library of Congress Data applied for.

Printed on acid free recycled paper

Printed and bound in Great Britain by Whitstable Litho
Whitstable, Kent.

Contents

JOURNAL OF LAW AND SOCIETY
VOLUME 22, NUMBER 1, MARCH 1995
0263–323X

Introduction

D.J. GALLIGAN*

These essays were specially prepared for a conference held in late 1993 to celebrate twenty-one years of research at the Oxford Centre for Socio-Legal Studies. The conference was also an occasion to mark the retirement of Mr Donald Harris who, as director for most of that time, greatly influenced and moulded the centre and sustained it through difficult times. As well as celebrating, however, the conference had serious academic intentions. The first was to evaluate, in a constructively critical manner, the contribution of the Oxford Centre to socio-legal studies; the second was to reflect on the nature of the discipline itself; the third, to identify the issues and themes which are emerging for the future. Thanks to the attendance and participation of scholars and researchers from around the world, those aims, as the essays here show, were admirably achieved.

SOCIO-LEGAL STUDIES AT THE OXFORD CENTRE

When the Oxford Centre was founded in 1972 by the Social Science Research Council, predecessor to the Economic and Social Research Council (ESRC), the systematic study of law in society did not exist in the United Kingdom. Criminology was well-established and occasional studies of law in its social setting could be found, but the idea of law in all its facets being a serious subject for social science research was novel. The position in the United States of America was different; there, a dynamic law-and-society movement was already in place, a matter from which the founders of the Oxford Centre undoubtedly took inspiration. That interest in the study of law should have been so slow in getting started in the United Kingdom is in some ways easily explicable, in others not. The fact that law departments in universities themselves became widespread only in the sixties and early seventies is the easily explicable part. The result, as Twining points out in his essay, is that the life of the Oxford Centre corresponds to the expansion of the law schools and, therefore, to the development of modern legal education in the United

* *Professor of Socio-Legal Studies, Faculty of Law, University of Oxford, and Director of the Centre for Socio-Legal Studies, Wolfson College, Linton Road, Oxford OX2 6UD, England*

1

Kingdom. The more difficult part to explain is why law seemed to hold such little attraction for social scientists in other departments. Apparently it still does, for according to a recent review, most socio-legal research by far is done in law departments.

It was, nevertheless, a bold and imaginative move to create the Oxford Centre, to give it a wide brief to study law in its social context, and to provide it with sufficient resources to do so. Over the course of the next twenty-one years, the Oxford Centre created socio-legal studies in the United Kingdom. It embarked on a number of major research projects, became a training ground for young researchers who then dispersed themselves around other universities and centres, both at home and abroad, and it served as a focal point for networks, conferences, and collaborations. The result is that, twenty-one years later, the interest in socio-legal studies as a subject for research and teaching is well established. Most law departments now show an interest in building the research into their teaching and many have active researchers within their ranks.[1] But while the subject is popular and secure, it is still in several ways in its early stages. The fact that most of the research is done by lawyers rather than social scientists, while encouraging in one sense, is a major limitation in another. Socio-legal research is essentially social science research and legal academics in the United Kingdom in general have no training in social science. The fullness and depth of insight and analysis which comes from a specific disciplinary tradition, whether psychology, economics or sociology, to name just a few, is often missing. This is not to denigrate the work of lawyers; they have carried the burden of research with imagination and honour. It is to say, however, that the kind of research they do is inherently limited and needs to be matched with hard-core social science.

However, these are matters for the future to which I shall return. Let us first try to form some idea of the making of the subject of socio-legal studies in the United Kingdom, and the Oxford Centre's contribution to it. One way of doing that is to recreate the image of law which must have confronted the founders of the subject and then to examine how that image has been modified as the socio-legal method has flourished. If there is one person with whom a distinct and encompassing image of law can be associated, it is surely Bentham. The essentials are fairly simple: law is a means to the ends of society while the ends of society are determined by utility. Whether the law should intervene in an issue is a matter of utility; where it does intervene, its content should be guided by utility. Decide what actions should be proscribed as criminal, then draw up a clear and simple legal code; if utility requires that factories be regulated in order to secure compliance with standards of health and safety, then enact a code of laws to deal with the problem. The same goes for the protection of the environment, children or endangered species, for the regulation of economic activities, the family or schools, or for the relief of poverty and homelessness. In each case, identify the problem, decide how to solve it, and then pass a set of laws and create a body of institutions for that purpose.

2

Bentham was himself committed to utility as the final measure of all social action, but we need not be utilitarians to subscribe to his view of law as an instrument to social ends. Whatever the ends of law may be, the law itself is simply a means to them; there is no mystery, no uncertainty: laws should be clear, precise, and uniformly enforced. This image of law is indeed powerful and carries with it a number of additional features. First it connotes a distinct image of both the official and the citizen. The official is there to uphold and apply the law in an impartial, even-handed, and dispassionate way; Max Weber's picture of the bureaucrat coldly applying rules according to reason and logic fits well. The citizen for his or her part is, of course, eminently reasonable and rational: the man who used to travel on the Clapham bus, but who now sits in the jury box and might even be a woman. The citizen will obey the law because its normative qualities are accepted, or in the case of the bad man, because of the threat of sanctions. In any event men and women are rational, rule-following agents, capable of knowing the law and complying with its terms.

The second part of the Benthamite vision is that the law will be complete and comprehensive in its terms, and will be enforced. Codes of law should be brief, but they should be complete and without gaps left for the official to fill according to subjective judgements. They must also be enforced, for without general and consistent enforcement, the very basis of the law will be undermined. A third factor is to some extent contained in the first two: the law is not only an authoritative, normative system, it is also distinct and exclusive.[2] Norms of morality, rules of religion, and social conventions of all kinds are separate from law and must give way to it. The judge does not make a decision based on morality or convention or personal preference, but according to the law; officials, in their many guises should, on this view, have adequate legal reasons for their actions and decisions. Fourthly and finally, the law contains and develops its own value system. For Bentham the only value was utility, but in the making and the administration of law, other values creep in from a variety of sources and become legal values. Notions such as reasonableness, fairness, responsibility, and fault all derive from outside the law but come to have a specifically legal meaning and significance. They become terms of art to be understood and applied within a distinctive legal discourse without reference beyond law.

In drawing this picture of the Benthamite vision, I have over-simplified and exaggerated and will undoubtedly incur the displeasure of the master as he sits in his box at University College, London. But a view along these lines is the basis of legal textbooks; it is at the heart of Oxford jurisprudence, has fanned furious debates over the limits of law and the relationship between law and morality, is entrenched in judicial rhetoric, and is reflected in the way legislators each year add recklessly to the statute book. This is the image which confronted the founders of the Oxford Centre and it is little wonder that they were moved to lift the veil, to show that each of its features and the assumptions made about it are not nearly so clear cut; to show,

3

indeed, that what lay behind is both more complex and more interesting than that image suggests.

One of the early and still most impressive studies of the Oxford Centre, the compensation of victims of accidents, challenged a basic assumption of the Benthamite model: it challenged the idea that the law provides a set of rules and standards, together with the necessary institutions, for dealing with certain kinds of problems.[3] The rules for compensating the victims of accidents fit that pattern: the law of torts rests on the simple principle that if A injures B and A is at fault, then A must pay compensation to B. In its study of compensation, the Oxford Centre set out to discover what really happens to the victims of accidents. Amongst many other interesting findings, the research showed that only a small minority of all victims of accidents initiate legal claims and obtain damages through law for their losses. For all accidents taken together the figure was 12 per cent. If the figure is broken down further, the result is even more astonishing: while one in three victims of road accidents gets compensation, fewer than one in fifty of the victims of other main kinds of accidents receive anything. This was the first study of its kind and the first to show how in this area at least the law fails miserably in its purposes. The study became a model for similar research in other countries, not least the United States of America where Congress itself commissioned a similar inquiry.[4] The implications of such research for policy and reform are all too obvious; for while it is important simply to know the facts, facts spill over into other issues: why has the law failed; what are the merits and demerits of fault-based compensation schemes; what is the relationship between legal fault and moral fault, and so on.

Many legal issues are suitable for this kind of deep empirical study. Let me mention just two others. The Benthamite view assumes that where there is an issue in dispute or where one's rights are in issue, the law will provide a set of authoritative standards and the institutions necessary to apply them. For the vast majority of people, however, access to courts, tribunals and other legal bodies, that is to say access to basic justice, depends on legal aid. As the result of a study recently carried out by a former member of the Oxford Centre, we now have good evidence for what many already suspected, that legal representation before tribunals as well as courts makes a substantial difference to outcomes.[5] It is not just a matter of access to justice, but the full process of justice that depends on legal aid. That gives rise to many fundamental questions which have only just become the subject of systematic study: who gets legal aid, how should it be distributed, what should it cover. These are policy issues but they can only be properly settled if basic information about legal aid and the organization of the justice system is known. It may seem astounding that such information does not exist, but economists from the Oxford Centre have now begun to remedy that great gap in our knowledge.[6] Another example concerns the family. Questions about the family are always at the heart of a society's concerns: marriage,

4

divorce, property settlements, the custody of children, and so on. Over many years the Oxford Centre has conducted research into each of these areas. It has provided basic information on such matters as how laws get made, how conflicting policies and ideals are resolved in legislation, what effect the laws have once made, what happens to property after divorce, how the spouses and children fare several years later.[7] Socio-legal research is not primarily directed at policy, but here is a good example of where such fundamental research has had a major impact on policy-making.

The general and consistent enforcement of law is another feature of the Benthamite view. But one does not have to be long in the world to realize that, plain and clear though the law be, the chances of it being enforced are slight. We know that the criminal law is selectively applied, that the police exercise a discretion whether to take any action at all, and that a prosecution should be brought only if it is the public interest, whatever that may mean. But what is well known about criminal law is equally applicable in other areas of law. The complex issues of enforcement have been at the forefront of the centre's research, and as a result of studies by K. Hawkins,[8] B. Hutter,[9] and others,[10] we now know enough about the enforcement process to be able to advance a number of well-grounded theoretical principles. Paul Rock writes of this new science of compliance theory in his contribution to this volume.[11] He records how sociologists at the Oxford Centre recognized early on that while enforcing regulatory laws was a major issue for research, standard notions of policing drawn from criminal law were unsuitable. The Oxford researchers instead took inspiration from developing ideas in interpretive sociology and studied the way officials actually secured compliance with the law. Once that door was opened, researchers were able to enter a rich and complex social world where officials formed intricate working relationships with the very people they were regulating, where both moral and practical considerations shaped those relationships, and where the separation of legal norms from other norms was anything but clear-cut. Within such an environment, strategies of enforcement are worked-out. Keith Hawkins led the way in analysing that environment and in developing a sociology of compliance. His study of the enforcement of anti-pollution standards is a particularly good example in showing how those various factors work in practice and how negotiation and compromise become the keys to compliance.

Research into the enforcement of law points the way to a wide range of issues about decision making by legal officials.[12] Remember the Benthamite model: the law is complete and officials apply it according to reason and logic; licensing authorities, welfare agencies, and government officials of whatever kind are supposed to be simply interpreting and applying the law. As soon as we begin to test that against what happens in practice, the picture looks very different. All sorts of factors and variables influence the process; legal rules compete with other standards and norms, and the clearest set of rules is surrounded by a belt of discretion, whether officially conferred or

5

unofficially assumed.[13] This is not to say that the law has no effect, that anything goes; very much to the contrary. The legal standards are the central point of focus, but around them is woven a tapestry of other patterns and shapes. An understanding of that tapestry, of just how officials make their decisions and exercise their powers, is at the very heart of socio-legal research.

The idea mentioned earlier that the law creates its own values which can then be understood and applied within a distinctively legal discourse, has stimulated some of the most imaginative socio-legal research. Compensation for injury has traditionally been based on fault – fault, that is, as developed in law. Due process and procedural fairness and equality before the law are other examples; others still are notions of proof, standards of proof, and the presumption of innocence. The doctrinal analysis of such concepts is familiar to the lawyer, but to examine them in their social setting presents some interesting and novel issues. One issue is what assumptions lie behind the concepts: proof beyond reasonable doubt, for example, or fault in assessing whether compensation should be paid. Another set of questions concerns the relationship between such legal concepts and similar social and moral concepts. In an important piece of research, Lloyd-Bostock, a psychologist and lawyer, analysed the idea that as a matter of common justice, fault constitutes good grounds for the payment of compensation.[14] She found it did not, although the value of her study is as much in the analysis of the relationship between the two realms as in her conclusion. A final issue is to understand the origins, role, and significance of legal values within the law itself. Where, for example, do ideas of due process come from, what do they mean in law, what practical consequences do they have? McBarnet's classic study of ideas of due process and the rule of law in criminal justice has shown just how revealing a sociologist's analysis of legal concepts can be.[15] By examining the law itself, that is, concepts created and moulded within the law, she was able to show that many of the apparent oddities, even injustices, within the criminal process were not the result of deviant or bad behaviour by officials. She found that, on close analysis, the very substance of the law, the standards and values themselves, explained a great deal of what happened in practice.

From these few examples of research carried out at the Oxford Centre over the last twenty-two years, it can be seen how far we have moved from the simple Benthamite vision of law. In its place has been substituted an image which is many-layered, which shows not just that the application of the law is influenced by its social context but that, in a complex and perplexing way, it is constituted by that social context. But not entirely, for one important lesson is that law is itself in some sense an autonomous element of social reality, constituting as well as constituted by the wider social context. We have also shown what it really means to study law in that context and why the disciplines of the social sciences are indispensable tools for the purpose. Simple common sense and diligence in understanding

6

the social basis of law can take us a long way, but at a certain point it runs dry. That is the point at which the disciplines of social science must be pressed into service, for the precise qualities they bring are the means to penetrate and comprehend social reality at levels beyond common sense and native intuition. Each supplies an additional way of viewing human actions and social situations, and of unlocking facts about them which would otherwise be hidden. The deep understanding of some part of social reality which each discipline makes possible is not fundamentally different from the untutored insights of the layman; but drawing on traditions of observation and generalization, it allows us to delve more deeply, to take a step or two farther in discovering facts and realities.[16]

For these reasons, the commitment to a multi-disciplinary, social-science approach is finally the unique and most significant feature of the Oxford Centre. It has always had a range of disciplines in addition to law - currently sociology, social policy, anthropology, economics, psychology, and social history – on which its research base has been built. Each of these disciplines, together with others like political and administrative science which have not been prominent in the Oxford Centre, has a distinctive contribution to make to the understanding of law and legal institutions. While social scientists in social science departments continue to show such little interest in law, an attitude which is itself hard to comprehend, the importance of maintaining a multi-disciplinary base in the Oxford Centre and one or two other centres cannot be over-stated.

It may be that some of the disciplines within the socio-legal approach have flourished more than others, but all have made a significant contribution to our understanding of law and legal institutions. Ogus suggests in his interesting essay that the economic analysis of law, both at the Oxford Centre and in the United Kingdom generally, has not flourished in the way that had been hoped, although his remarks are perhaps more pertinent to a particular brand of economic analysis rather the subject as a whole.[17] The work of economists in analysing law is certainly greatly valued at the Oxford Centre and their recent work in the economic analysis of the justice system is both significant and timely, and of great potential for further work. Twining comments in his essay on the important insights that psychology has brought to the study of law, while Stephenson argues that psychologists, if they dared, could take a much more positive role.[18] On the other hand, the major achievements of sociology and social policy are clear to see. Anthropology, for its part, is a developing discipline in the work of the Oxford Centre, and it is hoped that political and administrative science will have a greater role in the future. The multi-disciplinary approach is, I suggest, vital to the full flowering of socio-legal studies and will continue to be the hallmark of the Oxford Centre.

A second purpose of the conference was to reflect on the nature of the socio-legal discipline itself. That is a large undertaking which could be approached in several ways. In organizing the conference and arranging speakers, we had settled on the question of whether there was more to socio-legal studies than the sum of its parts. By that we meant to ask whether the great range of specific studies of law and legal institutions could be seen as part of a greater undertaking, an undertaking with its own identity and theoretical foundations. Could we move, in other words, from the particular and local studies of the kind just described to a more cogent and recognizable whole? Just how cogent the question is may itself be debatable, but the point of interest, however best described, was to see whether there is more to socio-legal studies than each discipline applying its methods to a legal phenomenon in order to reveal something more about it.

We should not, however, confuse that enquiry with another, the other being the relationship between empirical research and theoretical generalization. Those who do empirical research are understandably sensitive to the charge that their work is not theoretical, that they are merely supplying knowledge about the bits and pieces of the law. That charge might sometimes be justified, but more often it results from ignorance on the part of the questioner as to the nature of theory rather than inadequacy on the part of the researcher. For good empirical work goes beyond simply reporting facts to generalizing about those facts. Generalization itself occurs at various levels. Take an example from research into the control of water pollution. Studies of a number of inspectors show how heavily they rely on bargaining and agreement in securing compliance with anti-pollution standards. Since it is likely that all inspectors in the field confront similar problems, we might hypothesize, without having evidence for each one, that all rely on bargaining and agreement. But if that is true for inspectors of water pollution, it is also likely to be true of other kinds of officials trying to enforce the law. A number of generalizations might then be offered about the role of negotiation and agreement in legal enforcement. However, to generalize in this way is to theorize; for theory consists in being able to move from the facts particular to one situation to a general claim that the same facts will hold true in another situation. Theorizing at these lower levels, moreover, is not different in principle from high theory at the most grand and speculative levels. At the base of the very grandest theory lies a claim about the world, about the nature of the social reality it purports to describe.

Having cleared the air on that matter, let us return to the issue of the nature of the discipline. Three of the essays are especially relevant here, although it is perhaps only the third that directly takes up the question of an overall framework for socio-legal studies. In the first, 'Horatio's Mistake', Maureen Cain sets out to confirm that the very social context of which law forms part is real and sufficiently autonomous to warrant study. If it is

8

© Basil Blackwell Ltd. 1995

surprising that this should have been in question, the reason lies in certain versions of contemporary theory which insist that no reality exists beyond the text. That idea has become currency among some jurisprudential writers who, according to Cain, have stormed and sacked the citadel of mainstream jurisprudence. Whether that is true is another matter, but these theorists have thrown down a challenge which strikes at the very basis of socio-legal work; for if there is no reality out there to study, the subject of the discipline has disappeared. The challenge, however, is robustly defeated and few are likely to dissent from Cain's conclusion that, despite strands of postmodern theory to the contrary, there is still a social reality to be studied which is not reducible to texts, discourses or pure thought. Apart from the importance of the conclusion, much of the interest of her essay is in the evocative case studies of the colonial experience in the Caribbean and the legal relationships on which it was based.

The second of the three, the essay by Peter Fitzpatrick, 'Being Social in Socio-Legal Studies', nicely complements 'Horatio's Mistake'. For while Cain's essay reasserts the existence of material and social reality, Fitzpatrick delves more deeply into the nature of that reality. Here, the issue is what constitutes society, and the answer given is that the notion of society remains elusive and problematical. But in so far as the notion of society is possible, it is largely as constituted by law. Law as a set of norms, laying claim to both universality and supremacy, becomes the defining characteristic of a society. Against background harmonies of modernism and postmodernism, Fitzpatrick connects the idea of society to a sense of sameness and difference, compliance and deviance, included and excluded. These hallmarks of a society themselves depend on legal norms, while legal norms in turn cannot be reduced into mere social facts. Of course much about legal norms can be explained in social terms – the influence of groups and interests for example – but ultimately law is more than those social forces and has its own nature, logic, and existence. This is a complex essay and I hope I have presented it accurately. It does, however, give considerable encouragement to the socio-legal enterprise discussed earlier; for a common thread throughout that work is the conviction that as much as law is shaped and influenced by the social context, no matter how intricate the relationship between the two, it nevertheless is itself a distinct and irreducible social reality.

The third essay in this group, as we might expect from its title, 'Law and Unified Social Theory', confronts directly the question of whether the different disciplinary traditions can be brought within a coherent whole. Here Robert Cooter first sets out the theoretical basis of economic analysis with particular reference to the analysis of law. He explains the three key concepts of maximization, equilibrium, and efficiency, and then goes on to show how they relate to law. Beginning with a fairly standard account, Cooter then goes on to show the limitations of the analysis and to chart possible directions for the future. The limitation is that economics is based on a thin view of rational self-interest; it assumes that 'the ideal economic decision maker

9

is "perfectly rational", which means utterly instrumental in pursuing explicit ends'. Law and other social sciences, however, recognize a thick conception of self-interest, which is to say that people act for reasons based on social norms rather than pure self-interest. In economic terms, legal actors maximize the effective application of social and legal norms which may be unrelated to any thin sense of self-interest. To take an example, a judge tries to make decisions according to a range of legal and social rules to which he is in some way committed; his thick self-interest consists in the reasonable application of those rules.

The economic analysis of law assumes only thin self-interest and fails to take account of those other dimensions which are fundamental to understanding law. The interesting point is that for other social sciences it is precisely the other dimensions which are the subject of study. Sociology, political science, anthropology, and psychology, are all directed at explaining the creation of social norms, the internalization of those norms by legal actors, and the difficulties of applying the norms in practice. Cooter goes on to show how economic analysis can be brought into partnership with other disciplines to constitute a unifying social theory. The two examples he takes in this essay are the coming together of economics and psychology in understanding the internalization of social norms, and the merger of economics and sociology in analysing the evolution of social norms. This aspect of the essay is of considerable originality and importance, and warrants close study; although somewhat tentative at this stage, it marks the direction future research should take if there is genuinely to be a unification of the social sciences, and in turn a sounder theoretical base for socio-legal studies. Clearly there is still much to be done on the theoretical side and the three essays here are reminders of how difficult but exhilarating the more abstract and speculative side of socio-legal studies can be. The essays are also timely reminders that no wedge should be driven between theory and practice, that the socio-legal undertaking is premised on the union of the two, each informing and being informed by the other.

LOOKING TO THE FUTURE

A twenty-first birthday is a good time not only to assess the achievements of the past and to reflect on the theoretical basis of the subject, but also to look to the future. To what issues should the Oxford Centre and the socio-legal community in general be directing their attention for the next several years? This can be divided into questions of methodology and of substance. On methodology, several important suggestions are made in the following essays. The first is a resounding affirmation of the continuing need for the multi-disciplinary, social-science approach. That point is made clearly and strongly by Faure, Diamond, and Kagan, while Stephenson emphasizes the singular contribution that psychology has to offer. Indeed, the argument

10

put forward by Stephenson is that psychology has been under-employed in socio-legal research. At the same time, he chides psychologists who have studied legal issues for tinkering at the edges of worn-out institutions and practices, such as the adversarial process and the use of juries, rather than demonstrating the need for major changes.

A second point on methodology not often brought out in discussing socio-legal research is the place of comparative work. In his essay, 'What Socio-legal Scholars Should Do When There is Too Much Law to Study', Robert Kagan notes that while comparative legal scholarship can tell us a lot about different legal systems, it is only by taking the further step into a socio-legal approach that the significance of the differences can be judged. He gives a number of examples from his own research of how the comparative method can be put to good effect. The comparative method brings in its wake another characteristic which might almost be seen as a separate aspect of method-ology: that is the collaboration between researchers from different geo-graphical and cultural backgrounds which is a welcome advantage of doing comparative work. After noting that problems of access and interpretation are best handled by natives, Kagan concludes that 'the often startling insights that come from comparison, on the other hand, flow from intensive interaction between two or more sets of natives'.

Talk of comparative work and collaboration as methodology leads us on to matters of substance and to what has emerged as one of the major sub-stantive issues for the future, namely, the globalization of law. In a carefully constructed analysis, Volkmar Gessner explains how the trans-national character of so much law and legal institutions creates issues and problems which are distinctive and increasing.[19] Gessner identifies several different levels of analysis: structural, cultural, theoretical, and normative. Each level can in turn be divided into more specific issues which, taken as a whole, define the global legal environment; taken separately, each might be the focus for further research. To take an example from the structural level, the four points of focus are: the legal actors, who tend to be companies rather than people; the various international institutions; the pervasive role of large, international law firms; and the diversity of national legal systems. The suggestion is that while parallels can be drawn between the global system and the national, the similarities are inexact with the former having its own characteristics and problems. The essay concludes with a number of detailed proposals for future research.

This essay is likely to become the touchstone for future research on the globalization of law. It not only lays out a programme of research, but articulates a theoretical framework within which it should be conducted. It is, moreover, nicely complemented by Stewart Macaulay's essay, 'The Last Word'. Macaulay also stresses the looming presence of trans-national law and emphasizes the role of multi-national corporations, institutions cutting across national boundaries, and the notion of international pluralism. But the flow is not all one way, for as is pointed out in the essay, the pressure

© Basil Blackwell Ltd. 1995

for particularism and localization is also increasing. Particularism and localization here mean concentrating on a national entity, usually marked out geographically and often bound together by language, ethnicity, and religion. Between globalization, on the one hand, and particularism and localization, on the other, there is a sense of competition and tension which might profitably be studied from a socio-legal point of view.

Important as the questions of globalization are, we must not lose sight of the local issues. For socio-legal scholars, the national state has been the traditional hunting ground. And yet, as Kagan plaintively asks in his essay, how are we to cope with so much law? According to some projections, the actions of the state should by now have been wound down, with less law, fewer institutions, and greater spheres of private action. In line with most other confident predictions of the last twenty years, the opposite has turned out to be the case: more law, greater state control, new administrative bodies everywhere you look, and fewer and fewer areas of privacy. And what happens in one state is likely to be more-or-less repeated in other states, with of course the necessary local variations. Given this avalanche of law, what is the small band of socio-legal researchers to do? The patterns of the past have been to select limited areas for close study and then, on the basis of those case studies, to offer generalizations which should hold true in other, similar areas. So, returning to an example noted earlier, from the detailed study of how inspectors secure compliance with legal standards in the area of water pollution, generalizations may be drawn about the problems of enforcing the law. This process of case studies, followed by general hypotheses, tested by more case studies, is the method of any scientific enquiry. Generalization on the basis of selective case studies is respectable and unavoidable, although frustrating in that many areas of law are never subjected to detailed study.

Within that general approach, the questions socio-legal researchers have asked fit into a well designed pattern: how do laws get made; what are the functions of legal institutions; and how do those institutions behave in practice. Kagan suggests that, without detracting from the need for continuing research into these matters, a fourth issue ought to be added: what is the impact of law and legal decisions on social life, on the attitudes, actions, and relations of citizens and officials, and on institutions, both public and private? He is surely right in pointing out that the image of law as dependent on its social context, an image vital to a socio-legal approach, can so overshadow the idea of law as an independent entity in itself that the very idea is lost sight of. The importance of recognizing law as itself a part of social reality and therefore capable of affecting the world around it, was noted earlier in commenting on Peter Fitzpatrick's essay. It may seem surprising that such an obviously vital aspect of law and legal institutions has escaped the research agenda, but it is, nevertheless, true. To take an example, in the context of administrative law and administrative government, where a lot of fine socio-legal work has been done, one will search in

12

vain for any indication of what effect judicial review or the investigations of ombudsmen or the decisions of tribunals have on the bodies subject to them.[20] Now, of course there are exceptions, an outstanding example being some of the work done by members and former members of the Oxford Centre on the impact of family law. The difficulties of assessing the ways that law and legal processes influence their environment are formidable and that might explain why little has been done. However, the claim that this is a serious gap in socio-legal research which should now be filled is surely justified.

The third major idea which emerges from the discussion as suitable for socio-legal research is that of community. In an imaginative essay, Richard Abel paints a rich and many-layered picture of the notion of community.[21] Taking community to mean a shared sense of group membership and mutual responsibility, he shows how it is an essential ingredient of social life and yet 'is morally ambiguous, excluding as well as including, oppressing and fulfilling, degrading and elevating'.[22] Around this central point, a range of questions can be posed: what constitutes a community; how does it form, change, and sometimes disappear; how is membership determined; who is admitted and who excluded; how can communities protect themselves, and what effect does crime have on them? By reflecting on matters like these, we may be able to understand more fully the range and complexity of the social bonds holding groups together, as well as those keeping them apart. Although Abel does not attempt to lay out a research agenda based on these ideas, it is easy to see how a link could be made between the notion of community and many aspects of law. That is well illustrated in Geoffrey Stephenson's essay where he shows how a study of victims might be enriched by examining their place within a community and their perceptions of it. Some might find the concept of community an unsatisfactory basis on which to build analysis and research; it can be diffuse and evanescent, obscuring social realities apparently more substantial. It is, nevertheless, a notion deeply embedded in our consciousness and, as Abel shows, a real and significant social force.

A final set of issues which should be the focus for socio-legal research in the future arises out of societies and legal systems in transition. Here, the immediate subjects are the states of central and eastern Europe in their move from communist rule to the rule of law. Andras Sajo, in his essay, 'On Old and New Battles: Obstacles to the Rule of Law in Eastern Europe', charts the obstacles which have to be surmounted in making the transition. He shows that while it is easy enough to put in place the right laws, there are deeper social factors which will delay and distort the legal transformation. Sajo is particularly interested in the rule of law in a market economy where the object of law is to create and protect rights. He identifies various social factors which curtail the achievement of a rights-based, rule of law system. These are put forward in a number of propositions grouped under three headings: the fear emerging states have of law; dependence on the state;

13

interests in maintaining a distorted market; and cultural factors. The obstacles and distortions which each presents can be overcome, but the transitional process is likely to be long and arduous.

It would be a mistake to think that analysis of these matters is of interest and importance only to researchers working in eastern Europe. For anyone who does fall into that category, the rigorous, analytical framework which Sajo creates will be indispensable. But eastern Europe is not just a local problem for them over there; the issues raised by states in transition should be of interest to us all and there is a strong case for more collaboration and comparative work between researchers in the west and those getting started in the east. The development of collaborative and comparative work of this kind is already a major plank in the Oxford Centre's work and over the next few years will be substantially increased.

There is one final matter which is not directly considered in the essays that follow: that is the relationship between socio-legal research and policy-making. The relationship is of great importance to the future of socio-legal work and should not be ignored. The demand from public as well as private funding bodies that research should have clear and direct policy implications is certainly growing. The consequences are mixed. One is that the long-term research programme, which has been the hallmark of the Oxford Centre, is now in danger of extinction. The danger is augmented by the fact that most research depends on fairly small, short-term grants, where a policy orientation can be insisted on by the funders. On the other hand, there are clearly many pressing policy issues which would be greatly informed by research and there is no reason why socio-legal researchers should not be prepared to contribute to the policy debate. These are matters which call for further discussion, but two general points should be made in concluding this introduction. One is that there simply is no substitute for programmes of research which can be properly and fully executed over a number of years. Good research consists not just in producing a set of data or a bank of figures; it requires a properly constructed theoretical framework within which, through generalization and refining of generalization, real under-standing can be advanced. That is the central and focal sense of research, and research in that sense is as indispensable here as in any other field of endeavour. If good policy is to be made, moreover, it must have that bank of knowledge and understanding to draw on. The second point is that socio-legal research operates at a number of levels, and not all research need be deep or long-term.

CONCLUSION

In this introduction and the essays that follow, it is hoped that the place of the Oxford Centre in pioneering socio-legal research in the United Kingdom has been properly documented. The centre and those who have passed

14

through it since its creation should be given full credit for adding to our understanding of law and legal institutions a dimension which was not only missing but is now rightly considered indispensable. That has been the major achievement of the first twenty odd years and should not be lightly passed over. However, it is the future to which we must now devote our attention and, as the essays here show, the issues for the future are interesting, challenging, and immense. Indeed, those mentioned here are by no means the only ones worth pursuing, and I am sure that each reader of these essays could add several more. Socio-legal researchers, however, must keep their nerve and proceed calmly and methodically to produce the deep empirical studies of the kind mentioned earlier. But, as is again shown in this collection, socio-legal studies, like any area of scientific enquiry, needs a theoretical grounding. Generalization and theorization – and the two really mean the same thing – should be an integral part of all good research. It should not be forgotten, moreover, that a more speculative and higher-level theory, of the kind ably displayed in several of the essays here, is also not only legitimate but of great importance in nurturing to maturity a relatively young discipline.

NOTES AND REFERENCES

1 For a full account of the present state of socio-legal research in the United Kingdom, see ESRC, *Review of Socio-Legal Research* (1994).
2 On this point, see, in this volume, P. Fitzpatrick, 'Being Social in Socio-Legal Studies', (p. 105).
3 The results are published in D. Harris et al., *Compensation and Support for Illness and Injury* (1984).
4 See D. Hensler et al., *Accidents and Injuries in the U.S.: Costs, Compensation, and Claiming Behaviour* (1991).
5 See the study by H. and Y. Genn, *The Effectiveness of Representation Before Tribunals* (1992).
6 This work is being undertaken by N. Rickman and A. Gray and will be published in due course.
7 For examples of such research, see J. Eekelaar, *Regulating Divorce* (1991) and J. Eekelaar and M. Maclean, *Maintenance After Divorce* (1986).
8 K. Hawkins, *Environment and Enforcement* (1984).
9 B. Hutter, *The Reasonable Arm of the Law* (1988).
10 See, also, G. Richardson et al., *Policing Pollution* (1984), and R. Baldwin, *Regulating the Airlines* (1985).
11 See, in this volume, P. Rock, 'Sociology and the Stereotype of the Police', (p. 17).
12 For a review of the sociology of decision making, see K. Hawkins, 'The Use of Legal Discretion: Perspectives from Law and Social Science' in *The Uses of Discretion*, ed. K. Hawkins (1993).
13 Many of these influences are discussed in D.J. Galligan, *Discretionary Powers* (1986).
14 S. Lloyd-Bostock, 'Fault and Liability for Accidents: the Accident Victim's Perspective' in Harris, op. cit., n. 3.
15 D. McBarnet, *Conviction* (1978).
16 See, further, on the indispensability of the social sciences, the introduction in D.J. Galligan, *Readings in Socio-Legal Studies: Administrative Law* (1995).

17 See, in this volume, A.I. Ogus, 'Law and Economics in the United Kingdom: Past, Present, and Future', (p. 26).

18 See, in this volume, G. Stephenson, 'Looking to the Future: A Psychologist's Comments on Richard Abel's *Contested Communities*', (p. 133). However, we should also note Shari Diamond's cautionary note and the importance of psychologists being responsive to the insights of other disciplines: S.S. Diamond, 'The Challenges of Socio-Legal Research on Decision-Making: Psychological Successes and Failures', (p. 78).

19 See, in this volume, V. Gessner, 'Global Approaches in the Sociology of Law', (p. 85).

20 An honourable exception on the last point is J. Baldwin, N. Wikeley, and R. Young, *Judging Social Security* (1993).

21 See, in this volume, R. Abel, 'Contested Communities', (p. 113).

22 It is interesting to compare this notion of community with Fitzpatrick's rather different analysis of society in this volume (p. 105).

JOURNAL OF LAW AND SOCIETY
VOLUME 22, NUMBER 1, MARCH 1995
0263-323X

Sociology and the Stereotype of the Police

PAUL ROCK*

INTRODUCTION

I was asked to contribute to a 'review [of] the work of the Oxford centre within the context of socio-legal studies over the last 21 years . . . [and to] provide an opportunity to explore the current nature and scope of the discipline . . . '. And that is what I shall do.

I have a recollection of attending the inaugural conference of the centre twenty-one years ago. My memory is hazy, but I seem to recall discussion of matters that were of little immediate appeal to one who was then, and still is, a sociologist of crime and deviance, wedded to qualitative methods, to ethnography, and to 'thick description'. There was a propensity to cast the study of law as part of a pre-eminently bookish activity, as a discourse of scholarly ideas about scholarly ideas that floated freely in libraries and seminar rooms. It would have been very easy to continue that drift. After all, it was the authoritative, approved way of talking about law in universities. It sounded impressive. It smacked of philosophy and the history of ideas to which the social sciences in Oxford (and elsewhere) have always been pulled. But that drift was *not* sustained. In its place, some useful and original lines of work appeared, and they appeared, it seemed, almost out of nowhere.

I shall settle on only one or two of those lines of development although others were and are equally important. What is significant, I would argue, is that sociology and socio-legal studies at the centre came to treat the enforcement of law, and of regulatory law in particular, as a complicated, situated, evolving, and interpretive practice whose character could not be divined simply from reading books or from pure reason alone.[1] It was to be treated as empirically problematic, grounded in meaning, negotiated, and emergent, and that was to be illuminating indeed.

* *Professor, Department of Sociology, and Director of the Mannheim Centre, London School of Economics and Political Science, Houghton Street, London WC2A 2AE, England*

I am grateful to Bridget Hutter and Keith Hawkins for their help in commenting on an earlier draft of this chapter.

17

Of course, there were precursors to such an approach. There were the United States legal pragmatists and the first sociologists of the police.[2] There were the United States sociologists of deviance who had presented rule-making, rule-breaking, and rule-enforcement as intertwined symbolic processes.[3] In the United Kingdom, there was Kit Carson who had promised in the early 1970s to direct interpretive sociology towards the work of the factory inspectors.[4] But Carson was virtually alone and he faltered, in part, perhaps, because there was not much of a language or group to sustain him. Instead, it was the centre, founded in 1972 and directed by Don Harris, that promoted research that was not only co-operative but sustained over long periods of time[5] by scholars from different intellectual backgrounds, and the outcome was something of a new intellectual fusion. In Hutter's words, 'the multidisciplinary atmosphere of the centre . . . moved the focus away from something closely related to an enlightened lawyer's approach, to a distinctive subject/discipline, from which some useful and original lines of work emerged . . .'.

THE CENTRE'S REDEFINITION OF THE FIELD

In effect, members of the centre undertook and sustained a classic analytic manoeuvre that is almost always likely to be attended by success. They transposed familiar, established thought to an unfamiliar terrain in which it appeared new and daring. Just as in the 1950s and 1960s, Lemert, Becker, Cicourel, and others had galvanized criminology by transplanting relatively commonplace interactionist ideas about careers, identities, and relations from the conventional realm of medicine, work, and education to the unconventional realm of crime, deviation, and control, disclosing how very conventional the unconventional can be, so, in the 1970s, the centre ferried very similar interactionist and phenomenological theories to yet another territory in which they would again attain a strange character. The centre was dedicated to the new field of socio-legal studies, not to criminology, and it applied the emerging logic of the sociology of deviance, of what some call 'social constructionism', to phenomena in areas of law hitherto neglected, the areas that fell outside what Keith Hawkins called the 'traditional criminological boundaries'.

That emerging logic of interactionism was not quite an orthodoxy in British universities at that time (and is probably not so even now[6]), and it was not taught formally in many places. It was more than a little homespun, the product of younger scholars working sometimes idiosyncratically to fashion their own understanding of what was being said and written in the United States of America. Just as those first British sociologists of deviance, the sociologists of the 1960s, had had to be autodidacts, so the new socio-legal scholars were obliged to teach themselves much of what was to become important. Keith Hawkins, for instance, had been a graduate student at the

18

University of Cambridge Institute of Criminology and he had had to 'struggle to a version of interactionism on my own'. He had been, he said, 'painfully re-inventing the wheel'. The new socio-legal scholars individually and sometimes jointly discovered, extrapolated, and then reformulated a sociology of social control in the work of Peter Manning,[7] Jonathan Rubinstein,[8] Jerry Skolnick, James Wilson,[9] and others. They then proceeded to apply what they had found to what a member of the centre called the 'banal everyday routines' of regulation. In 1989, Hawkins and Thomas were to observe:

> As a theoretical framework having certain methodological implications, the social constructionist perspective is part of the broad tradition of interpretive sociology of deviance, and in many areas of the sociology of deviance, scholars have given much less attention to its potential for furthering our understanding of public policymaking in general and of regulatory policymaking in particular.[10]

It is useful to recall some of the imagery embodied in that 'broad tradition', an imagery whose features I shall exaggerate for purposes of effect, an imagery that was Janus-faced. The sociologists of deviance of the 1960s and 1970s had worked simultaneously to negate an older criminology and to affirm a new. As agents of negation, they been stirred into being by a reaction against an iconography described variously as positivist, correctionalist or administrative. Dennis Chapman remarked at that time how conventional sociology had been bedeviled by a particular stereotype of the criminal (and it is his argument that I have adapted for the title of this paper):

> much of the work done by social scientists in the field of Criminology [he argued] has been unprofitable because it has begun with definitions – stereotypes [of the criminal] – which have determined the course of the inquiry and the conclusions that have emerged.[11]

He argued that such stereotypes depicted criminals as young working-class men 'lacking education, influence and resources', and they removed the crimes of the middle and upper classes from purview. And, it was said (although not by Chapman), those stereotypes also failed to consider motive and meaning and subverted the very possibility of adequate understanding. The interactionists' and radical criminologists' resulting attempt to put matters right led to what Stan Cohen called a 'very radical break from traditional perspectives'.[12]

As agents of affirmation, the new sociologists were preoccupied with the interplay between deviance and regulation and, in particular, with the symbolic and practical incorporation of formal social control into the unfolding deviant gesture. They necessarily dwelt on the doings of people who were visibly at hand; those whom they could effectively study as graduate students and young teachers; the denizens of their own and adjoining social worlds; people who could be found most frequently in public space; the deviants, very often, who engaged in symbolic displays; the people described by Gouldner as 'drug addicts, jazz musicians, cab drivers, prostitutes, night people, drifters, grifters, and skidders, the cool cats . . . '.[13]

19

© Basil Blackwell Ltd. 1995

One such American sociologist mused in 1971, 'after all, we were only talking about ourselves'. Many of the deviants populating the arguments of the new sociology were, in short, those whom Americans would call 'street people'.

When 'social constructionist' sociologists took the next step and explored proscriptions and proscribers as constituents of deviant acts and identities, they had little enough of a research or literary tradition with which to work, they had few economic and social resources to mobilize, and they were committed to the use of direct, ethnographic methods. In the main, they had started with the study of street people, and it was behaviour on the streets that they were inclined to study when they turned to examine rule enforcement in the guise of policing and police officers.

The first anthropological reports of policing typically described how uniformed beat officers strove to maintain order over working-class males in urban space.[14] They were, in essence, accounts of comparatively fleeting, anonymous, and isolated meetings between groups of young men abroad in public: one group, the police officers, being authoritative and powerful, and the other, the working class, possessing very little formal authority at all. Those groups met after rules had been broken, when situations seemed to be running out of control[15] or when there was a contest over the domination of territory.[16] And, when they did meet, their encounters had inevitably to be based on rapidly-formed judgements; on stereotype and pragmatics; on the constraints exercised in public by audiences of strangers;[17] on the use or threatened use of force; and on the ever-present prospect of punishment.

To be sure, the standard portrait of policing was never simple or monochrome. It was qualified by sociologists who insisted always on the situated, nuanced, negotiable, and ambiguous character of social life. Police officers mediated conflict as well as making quick, punitive interventions.[18] They handled much outside the sphere of crime and the criminal law.[19] But there was undoubtedly a clear thesis that much policing should be understood as simple practical activity taking place in a world of oppositions between us and them, the moral and the immoral, the powerful and the powerless, the trustworthy and the untrustworthy, the insider and the stranger, the few and the many, the known and the unknown, the orderly and the chaotic.[20] The police, it was claimed, over-categorized deviants. Deviants were essentialized, reified and depersonalized, quickly reduced to a few core traits for purposes of management.

So vivid and plausible was that picture, so strengthened by the representations of film, news reporting, and drama was it (it is no accident that a number of sociologists of the police are avid watchers of movies), that the uniformed officer patrolling the streets became something of an icon of policing at large, a very personification of the state and its power to coerce, of Matza's Leviathan.[21] The activities of the male, urban beat constable have continued to loom large in the sociology of formal social control. Until very recently, it could be said that there have been very few complementary studies of senior ranks, of women officers,[22] of specialist policing, of rural

20

policing[23] or of police policy-making.[24] It could also be said that there have very few studies of other agents of control, of tax inspectors and customs officers, of the NSPCC and the RSPCA, private police and security staff, bailiffs and tipstaffs. In effect, the gallery of agents of formal social control has been virtually exhausted by the police officer. The interactionist sociology of deviance harboured its own problematic stereotype, and, in turning against it, Hawkins, Hutter, Baldwin, Cranston, and others at the Oxford Centre have done just what the once new criminologists and sociologists of deviance did before them.

They found that, beyond the borders of criminology, in the centre's own special terrain where codes no longer seemed sacred but secular, not moral but technical and instrumental, the older analysis and stereotypy did not work very well. Problems touching on matters of pollution, consumer protection and environmental health, the safety of airlines, railways and nuclear power plants, were certainly controlled and patrolled. They were policed. But they were not policed in quite the same way as that presented by the stock studies of the sociology of deviance.

I remember confronting precisely those problems of fit when, in the 1960s, I was writing my own homespun interactionist thesis on the activities of debt collectors and county court bailiffs. I had to modify and trim analysis to accommodate the special character of a cheap, staggered enforcement system intent on coaxing deviants not conventionally regarded as deviant to co-operate with agents who, for the most part, lacked significant power and legitimacy.[25]

At the centre itself, Hawkins argued:

> What is known about enforcement behaviour has been garnered almost entirely from work on the police, to the neglect of those countless numbers of individuals whose job it is to enforce regulations punishable by the criminal law.[26]

And Hutter has written about people whose:

> presence often goes unnoticed . . . Their work is typically undramatic and largely hidden from the public eye. Yet, these officials are daily making decisions which may be crucial to our general well-being and which, unknown to many, comprise part of our legal system.[27]

Those substantially unnoticed officials may be less dramatic and conspicuous in their actions, they may be less vivid in their symbolization of the state's power to repress (and have not been noticed for that very reason), but they actually control huge swathes of social and economic life. They attend to the collection of debts, taxes, rents, and revenues; the auditing of accounts; the execution of civil writs; the inspection of shops, offices, installations, services, and factories; the work of coroners' courts; and, with increasing effect, the patrolling of private and semi-private space. No accurate census has or possibly could be taken of how many they are and what it is they do (although it has been estimated that the private police alone may outnumber those employed by the state).[28] Were such a census

21

to be taken, it would probably become evident that the citizen's characteristic experience of formal control is not supplied by the uniformed police at all. Rather, it would take the form of a dunning letter or a visit from a government inspector.

COMPLIANCE-BASED ENFORCEMENT

That form differs from the standard model of policing. It is affected, as all enforcement is affected, by the organization of relations and knowledge between controller and controlled. Contrast an ideal-typical police officer, say a constable patrolling an inner-city street, with an ideal-typical regulatory agent, say a factory inspector, county court bailiff or environmental health officer (I shall again exaggerate for purposes of effect): the one enforces rules conceived to carry a clear moral burden, the other does not; the one is confronted by matters of moral culpability, the other is not (or at least not in the first instance);[29] the one often deals with matters after the event, the other with matters that may not yet have occurred at all or are open-ended, continuing, episodic or infrequent; the one has a relatively limited range of enforcement strategies, the other must balance competing strategies, administering an admixture of retribution, prevention, deterrence, exhortation, and mediation over time;[30] the one deals with people who are physically mobile and perhaps even evasive, the other does not necessarily do so; the one's relations can be ephemeral, requiring the quick and authoritative mastery of problematic situations; the other's relations may well be prolonged and require no such instant command; the one deals with people about whom almost nothing may be known, to whom the routine 'cook-book knowledge' of policing will have to be applied;[31] the other is usually somewhat better placed to observe, judge, and learn; the one tends to deal with those held to be morally discredited, the other cannot make any such immediate judgement about credit or discredit; the one may be obliged to rely on a show of force, the other can, in the first instance, frequently assume that it may be possible to rely on appeals to good sense. It is those and other differences, amplified to be sure, that supply the materials for a model of what some members of the centre have called 'compliance-based' enforcement and others 'accomodative enforcement',[32] enforcement that 'follows a serial pattern, a loosely structured but none the less organized process relying heavily upon negotiated conformity, with a gradual increase in pressure being applied to the uncooperative.'[33]

Such enforcement is set in a social, moral, and economic environment, and its structure often has to reflect the resolution of complex, pragmatic, and political questions about what can be done to people whose offending could be construed as a routine part of life in substantial organizations; whose offending could indeed be regarded as a problem of institutions rather than of persons (recall Sutherland's heavily ironic questions about the

22

© Basil Blackwell Ltd. 1995

psychopathology of corporations); who may not so much have done or omitted to do some definitive thing in a past now closed as failed merely to perform an act so far (although any such future performance *could* well put matters right and overturn the significance of acts and actors); whose behaviour, in other words, is phenomenologically open, uncertain as to its precise intention, meaning, and consequence.

Such enforcement has its own internal, recursive forms, its structure unfolding over time; intention, meaning, and consequence becoming revealed chiefly in the evolving pattern of an offender's replies to enforcement, a matter of his or her apparent co-operativeness, respectfulness, and honesty;[34] deviance and conformity being translated, in effect, into forms of contumacy and deference. Attributions of morality and immorality thus become even more emphatically contingent and embedded properties of enforcement careers, responses to responses, the meanings given to patterns of activity elicited in large measure by social control itself.

Compliance-based enforcement tends usually to be discreet and un-observed, confined by circumstance or choice to private or near-private space, waged by people without uniforms or distinctive insignia, who are unrecognizable to most outsiders. Yet it also attains much of its character from the fact that it is permeated by the shared knowledge that, rarely and as a last resort, when the agents' blandishments and threats have ultimately failed, when the offender is indeed defined as beyond the reach of reasonable appeal, the issues in dispute can be rendered formal and public,[35] the courts can be invoked, and the offender can become liable to exposure and punishment.

In all this, compliance-based enforcement seems to work as much informal control works. It resembles, and is probably rooted in, the workings of a more extensive, intricately-figured, as yet little understood but almost certainly highly effective, network of natural surveillance, inspection, and definition,[36] a network of exhortation, mediation, conciliation, and significa-tion that also turns to formal threats of punishment only when other measures fail,[37] a network composed of mundane activity. Much of its success, one may imagine, revolves around the mobilization of informal strategies, and shaming strategies in particular, that are the currency of discipline in everyday life.[38] One may imagine too that it is by exploiting those complementarities, affinities, and connections with mundane methods that compliance-based enforcement produces its chief effects. Whether and how that is so has not yet been investigated with any thoroughness, although such inquiry would be a logical next step for the Oxford Centre.

CONCLUSION

Despite objections from those who still cling tenaciously to the more obvious, punitive model,[39] compliance-based enforcement probably deserves

23

to be taken as the major pattern or archetype of formal social control in Western society. We are certainly told by JUSTICE[40] that it is the most prevalent style of enforcement. However important and interesting it may be, the work of the conventional police officer is actually relatively infrequent and atypical (although it, too, is often, and perhaps most frequently, also 'compliance-based'), one of the last resorts that bring unresolved disputes and problems to view, and, if that is so, we are obliged to take the work of the centre seriously indeed. Although British sociologists of crime and social control do not seem yet to have properly heeded that work, being beguiled still by the strong, theatrical stereotype of the police, the centre's analysis of the criminal sanction demands attention. With Durkheim, it should be asserted that it is restitutive, not retributive, justice that is the representative form of control in industrial society.[41] What now remains to be resolved is not only a more general and schematic analysis of the implications of that work, but also more extensive empirical enquiry into the linkages between compliance-based enforcement and wider nets of informal social relations.

NOTES AND REFERENCES

1 To be sure, as Hawkins and others would concede, some of those arguments may require the qualifying balance offered by Doreen McBarnet, another member of the centre, who reflected that what is written in legal codes does markedly constrain and order practical action. See her 'False Dichotomies in Criminal Justice Research' in *Criminal Justice: Selected Readings*, ed. A.K. Bottomley (1978). The issue is complicated because, as Hawkins argues, 'one of the characteristics of regulatory codes is that they are frequently designed (for all sorts of interesting reasons) in a very vague and spare fashion, thereby granting regulatory officials correspondingly more formal discretion than their counterparts in the police enjoy . . . It seems to me that one of the major empirical tasks for socio-legal studies is to understand the conditions under which legal rules guide and constrain practical action' (letter).

2 Of acknowledged influence were such works as R. Emerson, *Judging Delinquents* (1969); A. Reiss, *The Police and the Public* (1971); J. Skolnick, *Justice Without Trial* (1966); and W. Westley, 'Violence and the Police' (1953) 59 *Am. J. of Sociology* 59.

3 See H. Becker, *Outsiders* (1963), and A. Cicourel, *The Social Organization of Juvenile Justice* (1968).

4 See W.G. Carson, 'Symbolic and Instrumental Dimensions of Early Factory Legislation' in *Crime, Criminology and Public Policy*, ed. R. Hood (1974).

5 Hawkins remarked that 'one of the original rationales for a Centre was that people should be able to engage in empirical research that it might be difficult or impossible to undertake under a conventional university regime. This has been an important feature in enabling a number of us to do quite extensive ethnographic fieldwork.'

6 Although interactionism has a remarkable following amongst criminologists and sociologists of deviance, being the single largest intellectual school to which scholars professed loyalty in a survey of the profession I conducted in mid-1992. See my 'The Social Organization of British Criminology' in *The Oxford Handbook of Criminology*, eds. M. Maguiere et al. (1994).

7 See P. Manning, *Police Work* (1977). The influence of Manning grew as he became involved with the work of the centre, becoming a visiting fellow at Balliol College in 1981 and then a Senior Associate Researcher at the centre itself, working on the regulation of occupational health and safety between 1984 and 1986.

24

8　See J. Rubinstein, *City Police* (1973).

9　See J. Wilson, *Varieties of Police Behavior* (1968).

10　K. Hawkins and J. Thomas, 'Making Policy in Regulatory Bureaucracies' in *Making Regulatory Policy*, eds. K. Hawkins and J. Thomas (1989) 10–11.

11　D. Chapman, *Sociology and the Stereotype of the Criminal* (1968) ix.

12　S. Cohen, introduction to *Images of Deviance* (1971) 19.

13　A. Gouldner, 'Anti-Minotaur: The Myth of a Value-Free Sociology' (1962) 10 *Social Problems* 209.

14　See A. Stinchcombe, 'Institutions of Privacy in the Determination of Police Administrative Practice' (1963) 69 *Am. J. of Sociology*.

15　See E. Bittner; *The Functions of the Police in Modern Society* (1970).

16　See C. Werthman and I. Piliavin, 'Gang Members and the Police' in *The Police: Six Sociological Essays*, ed. D. Bordua (1967).

17　See A. Reiss, *The Police and the Public* (1971).

18　See E. Bittner, 'The Police on Skid Row' (1963) 28 *Am. Sociological Rev.* 699–715.

19　See E. Cumming et al., 'Policeman as Philosopher, Friend and Guide' (1965) 12 *Social Problems* 276–86.

20　See S. Holdaway, *Inside the British Police* (1983).

21　See D. Matza, *Becoming Deviant* (1969).

22　But see F. Heidensohn, *Women in Control* (1992).

23　To be sure, there was the early study by M. Cain, *Society and the Policeman's Role* (1974).

24　Of course, that has begun to change. See, for instance, R. Reiner, *Chief Constables* (1991).

25　See P. Rock, *Making People Pay* (1973).

26　K. Hawkins, *Environment and Enforcement* (1984) xiii.

27　B. Hutter, *The Reasonable Arm of the Law?* (1988) 3.

28　See C. Shearing and P. Stenning (eds.), *Private Policing* (1987).

29　Hawkins observes that 'the issue of moral culpability is interesting and very significant in law enforcement work generally. One of the key distinctions in the regulatory field, however, is that much of the behaviour which is theoretically criminal does not violate moral expectations . . . What happens in regulatory enforcement . . . is that an act is morally screened in the first place and enforcement behaviour (if any) organised accordingly (i.e. a moral frame is applied). If the actor is blameless (a discharge is defined as an accident , a technical problem etc.) the event is framed accordingly, and legal consequences will almost certainly be regarded as inappropriate. Otherwise, the actor becomes a "polluter" and the law is maintained as an option.'

30　See W.G. Carson; 'White Collar Crime and the Enforcement of Factory Legislation' (1970) 10 *Brit. J. of Criminology* 393.

31　See M. Chatterton; 'Police Work and Assault Charges' in *Control in the Police Organization*, ed. M. Punch (1983).

32　Hutter, for instance, regards the word 'compliance' as too broad.

33　Hawkins, op. cit., n. 26, p. 7.

34　See R. Cranston, *Regulating Business* (1979) 169.

35　See L. Mather and B. Yngvesson, 'Language, Audience, and the Transformation of Disputes' (1981) 15 *Law and Society Rev.* 775–821.

36　See, for example, J. Shapland and J. Vagg, *Policing by the Public* (1988).

37　See S. Merry, *Getting Justice and Getting Even* (1990).

38　See J. Braithwaite, *Crime, Shame and Reintegration* (1989).

39　See F. Pearce and S. Tombs, 'Ideology, Hegemony, and Empiricism: Compliance Theories of Regulation' (1990) 30 *Brit. J. of Criminology* 423-43.

40　JUSTICE, *Breaking the Rules* (1980).

41　E. Durkheim, *The Division of Labour in Society* (1964 ed., originally published 1893).

25

JOURNAL OF LAW AND SOCIETY
VOLUME 22, NUMBER 1, MARCH 1995
0263-323X

Law and Economics in the United Kingdom:
Past, Present, and Future

A.I. OGUS*

INTRODUCTION

My allotted task is to review the development of law and economics in the United Kingdom and, in particular, the role played in that development by the Centre for Socio-Legal Studies. The context in which I undertake this task is a sad one. As a consequence of the transfer of responsibility for the centre from the Economic and Social Research Council (ESRC) to Oxford University, there has been a substantial reduction in the number of fully funded research posts. No economist has been appointed to such a post. The centre is, apparently, committed to maintaining law and economics as a central part of its multi-disciplinary mix but it is unlikely to maintain the impetus of former years.

Against that background, let me summarize what I shall be arguing.

(i) Law and economics has made a major contribution to socio-legal studies in the United Kingdom and thus to our understanding of law and its impact; and the centre has played a crucial role in relation to that contribution. Nevertheless,

(ii) Law and economics does not have as firm a foothold in British socio-legal research as other areas of interdisciplinary studies and, in part, this is because its potential at the centre was never fully realized.

(iii) British law and economics *can*, in the future, make a more profound impact if it is able to acquire an identity which hitherto it has lacked. My submission is that such an identity could be acquired if scholars were to focus on the particular characteristics of a legal system which relies heavily on its common law tradition, but at the same time must relate to European institutions and principles drawn from a very different tradition. The seeds for this approach have already been sown by individuals associated with the centre; the tragedy is that the flowers may be unable to grow there.

* *Professor of Law, University of Manchester, Oxford Road, Manchester M13 9PL, England*

I acknowledge, with gratitude, some helpful comments by Denis Galligan.

Law and economics, as that expression is used to describe the application of economic theory to the general body of legal institutions and legal principles, dates from the publication of Coase's seminal article on social costs.[1] Other key publications were Calabresi's treatise on accidents[2] and Posner's general text on the *Economic Analysis of Law*.[3]

Calabresi's work attracted much attention, if also scepticism, on this side of the Atlantic since, at that time, the role of tort in relation to accident compensation was a major topic of debate.[4] But the Coase Theorem and the more general applications by Posner remained in the shadows – the first discussion of their ideas in a leading British legal academic journal seemed to have occurred only in 1977.[5]

The Social Science Research Council had nevertheless recognized the potential of collaboration between economists and lawyers, and two steps were taken in the early 1970s to foster links between them. First, a law and economics workshop series was established but, if my personal memory of them is reliable, not very successfully. The problem of bridging the intellectual gap between the two disciplines was accentuated by the fact that the economists who attended the workshops were not familiar with the rapidly growing American literature which applied economic theory to legal concepts and the lawyers had an insufficient grounding in basic economic theory and methodology.

The second step was to appoint economists to the newly-created Centre for Socio-Legal Studies. It is not difficult to understand why this was slow to bear fruit. In the early years, the goals of the Oxford Centre much reflected the ideas of its first director, Oliver Macgregor, who considered that socio-legal studies should concentrate on the empirical study of particular social problems. In institutional terms, it was a 'melting pot': individuals from different disciplines were thrown together in the expectation that the cumulative effect of their technical skills would provide a rounded analysis of the problems. Thus, economists with only a limited knowledge of the emerging law and economics literature were employed primarily to analyse the data rather than to construct and test theoretical models of the impact of legal rules on behaviour. What emerged was a number of papers which were spin-offs of the larger projects and provided valuable insights on some legal issues, such as the settlement of damages claims,[6] but no organic growth of law and economics as a sub-discipline.

Following Macgregor's departure, the research orientation of the centre changed. There was now a greater recognition that research should be driven by theoretical work; and law and economics became a separate item on the research agenda, along with, for example, ethnomethodology and psychology. Those working at the centre developed a familiarity with the mainstream American literature and sought to apply it to areas of English law. Cento Veljanovski's presence at the centre from 1978 to 1984 – the first (and hitherto only) appointee with academic qualifications in both law and economics – gave a significant impetus to this development. His work, which included important surveys of the literature[7] as well as some major contributions to it,[8] both helped to relate British law and economics to American scholarship and exposed it to a wider audience.

My perception is that, over the last ten years, the focus of the economics work at the centre has drifted away from the main themes of the law and economics literature. I can think of two possible explanations for this. First, as there has been an increasing need to attract money for contract research, so the economic resource has been pushed towards projects with a strong empirical and policy basis and which were not obviously linked to the central theories of law and economics. Secondly, the economists who succeeded Veljanovski at the centre were more concerned than he to relate their work to the 'mainstream' of the United Kingdom economics discipline and that 'mainstream' had, perhaps, been less interested in, or less convinced by, the law and economics literature. Valuable work has emerged from within this constraint, but perforce the coherence of the law and economics enterprise has had to be sacrificed.

AN OVERVIEW OF BRITISH LAW AND ECONOMICS RESEARCH

The task of surveying the output of British law and economics research is not an easy one, not the least because there are problems of defining what is 'law and economics' and of classifying the work. I shall proceed by distinguishing between three broad styles of analysis. My use of examples is necessarily highly selective.

In the first category is work which uses economic theory as an *ordering* device. This has been carried out mainly by lawyers (notably Rob Baldwin, Bill Bishop, Don Harris, Anthony Ogus, Dan Prentice, Chris Whelan), sometimes in collaboration with economists.

Within the parameters of legal doctrine, puzzles emerge concerning the development of legal principles and the relationship between them. The economic perspective provides a framework of analysis which transcends traditional legal distinctions and which can thus lend coherence to the principles. For example, the economic concept of consumer surplus (the utility derived by purchasers over and above the market value of commodities) has been invoked to explain how the law resolves the choice between different remedies for breach of contract.[9] And transaction-cost analysis has been used to explain and rationalize the development of, and choice between, different legal forms of governance where entrepreneurial activity requires co-ordination between labour, capital, and other inputs.[10]

Two imaginative papers by Bill Bishop which fall within this category merit special mention. In one, he demonstrated how the cautious development of principles of liability for negligent misrepresentation could be

28

explained by reference to the need of the law to reach an appropriate trade-off between two different types of misallocation which can result from the provision of information: negative externalities, resulting from reliance on false information; and positive externalities, resulting from beneficial reliance by parties who do not pay for the information.[11] His attempt, in another publication,[12] to address the vexed question of liability in negligence for pure economic loss by reference to the often neglected distinction between pecuniary and technological externalities, constitutes one of the most interesting contributions to the law and economics literature.

In my other two categories, I place the work of economists who, to a lesser or greater extent, have developed a specialism in the economic analysis of law, particularly Roger Bowles, Paul Burrows, Paul Fenn, Hugh Gravelle, Alistair McGuire, David Pyle, Frank Stephen, and Cento Veljanovski. They tend to work in either of two modes, although the dividing line between them is not always clear.

The first of these is positive analysis. Relying on traditional assumptions of, for example, individual utility maximization, models are formulated to predict the impact of different legal rules and institutions on behaviour and therefore also on welfare. Pyle's monograph on the economics of crime and law enforcement[13] exemplifies this approach, as does much of the work of Gravelle. His meticulously argued paper on cost-indemnity rules demonstrates how the contrasting British and American rules impact differently on such phonemena as the probability of settlements, the volume of litigation, and the amount of compensation payable in personal injury actions.[14]

The predictions generated by this form of analysis may, where relevant data can be obtained, be tested by empirical investigation – see, for example, the studies of the effect of solicitors' fees on changes in the regulation of conveyancing.[15] More typically they remain as pure hypotheses. As such, their importance for policy purposes should not be underestimated. In some cases, economic reasoning conflicts with lawyers' intuitions, forcing the latter to re-examine their basic premises. Such premises typically relate to notions of procedural or distributional justice. While notions of justice, and their influence on the law, cannot be ignored, economic analysis demonstrates that resort to them can be simplistic when insufficient attention is given to the consequences. Bowles's early work on questions of currency and interest in relation to damages awards is a good example.[16] Another is the paper by Fenn and others on insider trading: if intuition suggests that insider trading should be controlled because it allows 'unjust' profits to be earned, a more sophisticated analysis can temper that concern by reference to the way in which such trading facilitates information flows and thus benefits all those operating in financial markets.[17]

British economists have been less ready than their American counterparts to engage in my third category: the normative analysis of law. While the identification of allocative efficient solutions, normally by means of the Kaldor-Hicks test, is a valuable input to the policy process, it should not by itself determine policy outcomes. This comes across forcibly in the normative work of Burrows. In his studies of different legal instruments for controlling pollution[18] and of systems of compensating in cases of compulsory purchase,[19] he has been highly critical of the Chicagoan treatment of these subjects which eschews any concern for distributional justice. Bowles's work on professional liability displays a similar sensitivity.[20] Traditional principles of liability *may*, if properly applied, generate appropriate incentives for optimal care but that, by itself, does not necessarily ensure the equitable treatment of the victims of professional incompetence.

THE FUTURE OF LAW AND ECONOMICS IN BRITAIN?

I am reluctant to attempt any overall evaluation of the work which I have described. Some observations are, however, in order. In the first place, the institutional arrangements in Britain, and the career implications of those arrangements, have not been conducive to attracting economists to this field, nor to their commitment to advancing the discipline. Secondly, while the work which has emerged has provided many valuable insights on the institutions and principles of the British legal systems, it has, in general, not advanced the theory of law and economics. It has lacked overall direction and has not provided a contribution to the literature which is distinctively 'British'. In this final section of the paper, I shall, nevertheless, single out some work which constitutes an exception to the general picture. The example is designed to show how analysis of domestic phenomena can be used to extend the theoretical reach of law and economics and thereby make a distinctive contribution to the international development of the discipline.

My chosen example is the piece by Paul Fenn and Cento Veljanovski on regulatory enforcement[21] (a by-product of the centre's empirical work in this area). Enforcement of the criminal law has given rise to a large economic literature,[22] most of it adopting a model of optimal deterrence developed by Becker and others.[23] Under this model, individuals and firms will predictably comply with the law only if the expected cost to them of violation (the sanction and other costs arising from the criminal process, discounted by the probability of escaping detection and conviction) exceed the benefits of violation.

The model has proved to be a poor predictor of enforcement strategy within the area of *regulatory* offences, primarily because British agencies have adopted a policy of persuasion and co-operation rather than confrontation and prosecution.[24] To explain this policy, Fenn and Veljanovski constructed an alternative model under which optimal compliance may be achieved. Firms are subjected to overly stringent standards and, in the event of apprehension, they are motivated to bargain with enforcement officers and to agree to comply with a less stringent standard which may approximate to what is economically desirable behaviour.

30

I want now to develop from this example a research agenda for the future of law and economics in Britain. Legal institutions in Britain have cultural characteristics which distinguish them from their equivalents in the United States of America, the subject of most of the law and economics literature, and even more obviously from those in continental Europe although, as a consequence of British membership of the European Union, we are experiencing some convergence with the latter. This suggests several possibilities; my agenda is by no means comprehensive.

The first is to develop a comparative law dimension to economic analysis. An important strand in the law and economics literature postulates the hypothesis that forces operating within a legal system, particularly litigation and judicial decisions, push substantive principles to allocatively efficient outcomes.[25] That hypothesis can be tested by the comparative method: societies at approximately equivalent stages of economic development and with approximately equivalent sets of citizen preferences might be expected to adopt equivalent resource allocation solutions, notwithstanding apparently significant differences in legal forms. Comparative lawyers have been adept at demonstrating how very different legal structures mask similar outcomes; that approach can be developed within an economics framework.[26]

My second item on the research agenda arises from recent and spectacular developments in the areas traditionally associated with the regulation of natural monopolies. The government policies of privatization and rendering the public sector more accountable have been implemented by new legal forms and by a reinvigorated use of older legal forms. As regards the latter, the ESRC has already a number of research projects on the increasing use of contracts in the public sector. But other devices merit intensive scrutiny. The system of price-cap controls (adopting the RPI – X formula) designed for the privatized utilities purports to be very different from the rate regulation traditionally adopted in the United States of America and much studied there.[27] In particular, the American approach involves the application of economic models which are, to some degree, justiciable, while the British approach confers considerable discretion on the regulators.[28] Then, there are the systems of quality control and performance indicators emanating from the Citizen's Charter and other policy initiatives.[29]

Within more traditional areas of regulation ('social regulation'), the government has introduced a system of compliance cost assessment: government departments must provide, with proposals for new or amended regulations, assessments of the burden that the changes will impose on industry. The system was inspired by, but is markedly different from, President Reagan's famous Executive Order 12,291 which requires regulatory agencies to engage in and submit a fully-fledged cost-benefit analysis of regulatory proposals. The American approach has been intensively studied in an effort to gauge the extent to which cost-benefit analysis can be incorporated within

31

a rational legal framework for regulation, and the extent to which it may bias regulatory outcomes.[30] In contrast, the softer British approach has attracted very little attention from social scientists.[31]

Let me conclude my list with two possible areas of research which stem from the interaction between domestic law and European law. The first of these can be related to cost-benefit analysis of regulatory forms. The European Court of Justice, in examining the validity of instruments designed to implement the provisions of the Treaty of Rome, has applied the concept of proportionality: the means used to achieve a given end must be suitable for that purpose and not go beyond what is necessary to achieve it.[32] There are signs that this notion is beginning to prove attractive to British public lawyers.[33] Whether or not this is the case, the notion clearly has an important economic function – without undue distortion, it can be identified with allocative efficiency – and, as such, is ripe for economic analysis.

The other area of interaction between domestic law and European law is not so easy to describe succinctly, but essentially it relates to the concern that national regulatory regimes should not constitute barriers to intra-Union trade. The choice between, on the one hand, harmonizing national regimes (the 'old' policy) and, on the other, combining minimum such harmonization with provision for mutual recognition (the 'new' policy) raises a host of complex issues, ranging from the degree to which laws should be localized – the economics of federalism debate[34] – to the efficiency implications of encouraging competition between national regulatory regimes.[35]

At the risk of undue repetition, let me underline what is common between these areas and why I am arguing that they should be undertaken by law and economics scholars in Britain. They focus on institutions which, to a greater or lesser extent, are distinguishable from those which apply in North America and which have been subjected to rigorous scrutiny in the American law and economics literature. Some of the institutions are relatively recent and experimental and the need to evaluate them is the more urgent. Economic analysis can make a major contribution to this endeavour and, at the same, time help to give an identity and a coherence to the discipline of law and economics in Britain.

The use of different legal forms for similar policy purposes throws up a major challenge for law and economics. Comparative analysis might, in ways I have suggested, demonstrate the universality of hypotheses generated within a particular institutional or cultural framework. On the other hand, it might lead to conclusions that legal institutions and their impact are in some important sense cultural-specific and that, therefore, the models of law and economics have to be adapted or refined to take account of cultural variables.

NOTES AND REFERENCES

1   R.H. Coase, 'The Problem of Social Cost' (1960) 3 *J. of Law and Economics* 1.
2   G. Calabresi, *The Costs of Legal Accidents: A Legal and Economic Analysis* (1970).
3   R.A. Posner, *Economic Analysis of Law* (1970).
4   Compare P.S. Atiyah, *Accidents, Compensation and the Law* (1970)
5   A.I. Ogus and G.M. Richardson, 'Economics and the Environment: A Study of Private Nuisance' (1977) 36 *Cambridge Law J.* 284.
6   J. Phillips, K.O. Hawkins, and J. Flemming, 'Compensation for Personal Injury' (1975) 85 *Economics J.* 129; J. Phillips and K.O. Hawkins, 'Some Economic Aspects of the Settlement Process: A Study of Personal Injury Claims' (1976) 39 *Modern Law Rev.* 497.
7   C.G. Veljanovski, 'The Economic Approach to Law – A Critical Introduction' (1980) 7 *Brit. J. of Law and Society* 158; C.G.Veljanovski, *The New Law-and-Economics: A Research Review* (1983).
8   For example, C.G. Veljanovski, 'Wealth Maximisation, Law and Ethics – on the Limits of Economic Efficiency' (1981) 1 *International Rev. of Law and Economics* 5; C.G. Veljanovski, 'The Coase Theorem and the Economic Theory of Markets and Law' (1982) 35 *Kyklos* 53; C.G. Veljanovski and C.J. Whelan, 'Professional Negligence and the Quality of Legal Services – An Economic Perspective' (1983) 46 *Modern Law Rev.* 700.
9   D. Harris, A. Ogus, and J. Phillips, 'Contract Remedies and the Consumer Surplus' (1979) 95 *Law Q. Rev.* 581.
10 A.I. Ogus, 'The Trust as Governance Structure' (1986) 30 *University of Toronto Law J.* 186.
11 W. Bishop, 'Negligent Misrepresentation through the Economists' Eyes' (1980) 96 *Law Q. Rev.* 369.
12 W. Bishop, 'Economic Loss in Tort' (1982) 2 *Oxford J. of Legal Studies* 1.
13 D. Pyle, *The Economics of Crime and Law Enforcement* (1983).
14 H. Gravelle, 'The Efficiency Implications of Cost-Shifting Rules' (1993) 13 *International Rev. of Law and Economics* 3.
15 R. Bowles and J. Phillips, 'Solicitors' Remuneration: A Critique of Recent Developments in Conveyancing' (1977) 40 *Modern Law Rev.* 639; S. Domberger and A. Sherr, 'The Impact of Competition on Pricing and Quality of Legal Services' (1989) 9 *International Rev. of Law and Economics* 41; F. Stephen, J. Love, D. Gillander, and A. Patterson, 'Testing for Price Discrimination in the Market for Conveyancing Services' (1992) 12 *International Rev. of Law and Economics* 397.
16 R. Bowles and C. Whelan, 'The Currency of Suit in Actions for Damages' (1979) 25 *McGill Law J.* 236; R. Bowles and C. Whelan, 'Law Commission Working Paper No. 80: Private International Law Foreign Money Liabilities' (1982) 45 *Modern Law Rev.* 434.
17 P. Fenn, A. McGuire, and D. Prentice, 'Information Asymmetry and the Securities Market' in *European Insider Law*, eds. K. Hopt and E. Wymeersch (1991) ch. 1.
18 For example, P. Burrows, *The Economic Theory of Pollution Control* (1979) chs. 4–5.
19 P. Burrows, 'Getting a Stranglehold with the Eminent Domain Clause' (1989) 9 *International Rev. of Law and Economics* 129.
20 R. Bowles and P. Jones, *Professional Liability* (1989).
21 P. Fenn and C. Veljanovski, 'A Positive Theory of Regulatory Enforcement' (1988) 98 *Economics J.* 1055.
22 Compare Pyle, op. cit., n. 13.
23 Notably, G. Becker, 'Crime and Punishment: An Economic Approach' (1968) 76 *J. of Political Economy* 169.
24 For a general survey of the literature on this, see J. Rowan-Robinson, P. Watchman, and C. Barker, *Crime and Regulation: A Study of the Enforcement of Regulatory Codes* (1990).
25 See, especially, G.L. Priest, 'The Common Law Process and the Selection of Efficient Rules' (1977) 6 *J. of Legal Studies* 65, and P.H. Rubin, *Business Firms and the Common Law: The Evolution of Efficient Rules* (1983).

26 For an interesting, exploratory paper in this mould, see U. Mattei, 'Efficiency in Legal Transplants: The Foundations of Comparative Law and Economics' (1994) 14 *International Rev. of Law and Economics* 3.

27 For valuable comparisons between the two systems, see J. Vickers and G. Yarrow, *Privatisation: An Economic Analysis* (1988); C. Foster, *Privatization, Public Ownership and the Regulation of Natural Monopoly* (1992).

28 Compare C. Graham and T. Prosser, *Privatizing Public Enterprises – Constitutions, the State and Regulation in Comparative Perspective* (1991); C. Veljanovski, *The Future of Industry Regulation in the UK* (1993).

29 A. Barron and C. Scott, 'The Citizen's Charter Programme' (1988) 55 *Modern Law Rev.* 526.

30 For example, C.M. Heimann, 'Project: The Impact of Cost-Benefit Analysis on Federal Administrative Law' (1990) 42 *Administrative Law Rev.* 545.

31 Although see J. Froud, R. Boden, A. Ogus, and P. Stubbs, 'Toeing the Line: Compliance Cost Assessment in Britain' (1994) 22 *Policy and Politics* 313.

32 *Bela-Mühle* v. *Grows Farm* [1977] E.C.R. 1211.

33 J. Jowell and A. Lester, 'Proportionality: Neither New Nor Dangerous' in *New Directions in Judicial Review*, eds. J. Jowell and D. Oliver (1988) 51.

34 F.H. Easterbrook, 'Federalism and European Business Law' (1994) 14 *International Rev. of Law and Economics* 125.

35 G. Majone, 'Market Integration and Regulation: Europe After 1992' (1992) 43 *Metroeconomica* 131.

JOURNAL OF LAW AND SOCIETY
VOLUME 22, NUMBER 1, MARCH 1995
0263–323X

Remembering 1972: The Oxford Centre in the Context of Developments in Higher Education and the Discipline of Law

WILLIAM TWINING*

INTRODUCTION

In 1992 A.H. Halsey published a book entitled *Decline of Donnish Dominion*.[1] This chronicles and analyses trends in the British academic profession from about 1970 to 1989. According to Halsey, in this period funding, salary, research facilities, staff-student ratios, public respect, and every dimension of professional status of academics all deteriorated.[2] The first twenty-one years of the Centre for Socio-Legal Studies spans almost exactly the same period, which has been one of this most difficult in the history of higher education – an era in which we moved disjointedly and painfully from a small élite aggregation of institutions towards something approaching a mass 'system'.

The centre was founded in 1972, soon after '1968' and one year before the oil crisis of 1973, two of the great landmarks in Halsey's story.[3] When the history of the centre comes to be written it might appropriately be called 'Don's triumphs in adversity' or 'Don and Co.'. That the centre has survived at all is indeed a triumph; that it has flourished is a near-miracle for which Don Harris, his predecessors, and a remarkable team all deserve great credit.

The purpose of this paper is to set socio-legal studies in the context of developments in higher education and academic law in England since 1972. It is a by-product of a larger project on the discipline of law in England viewed from a largely historical and ethnographic perspective as a peculiar form of academic culture.[4] In this context, the discipline of law refers to that congeries of activities – research, reflection, writing, teaching, learning, and bitching – that are located mainly, but not exclusively, in faculties, departments, and schools of law. I was tempted to call this paper: 'What might law contribute to socio-legal studies?' This is not a frivolous question. I wanted to explore what, if anything, the institutionalized discipline of law has to offer that is unique or special to socio-legal studies as an enterprise

* *Faculty of Laws, University College, 4 Endsleigh Gardens, London WC1H 0EG, England*

35

which is devoted to exploring legal phenomena from a variety of multi-disciplinary perspectives.

In order to make sense of the question and to develop an argument, it would be necessary to adopt at least three different but complementary perspectives: historical, ethnographic, and epistemological. One would need to say something about the modern development of higher education in this country and the place of academic law in that story; second, it would be useful to say something about the culture of law schools from the perspective of the ethnography and sociology of knowledge;[5] and, third, one would need to reconsider some well-worn questions about the nature of 'legal science' and whether we can talk of an autonomous discipline of law in any meaningful sense of the term.[6] Socio-legal studies would require a similar treatment, as a preliminary to exploring whether law-as-a-discipline and its proponents have anything to offer (and, if so what?) that is in any way special or unique beyond some local knowledge.[7] Clearly, this was too ambitious an enterprise for a short paper. So I shall restrict myself here to some brief observations on the first aspect, the historical context of the work of the centre from the point of view of an academic lawyer.

I mention this more ambitious project for two main reasons: first, what follows is part of a larger argument about law as a discipline; second, I intend to take for granted a number of propositions, some of which are controversial. In particular, I shall assume the following:

(i) Many commentators have suggested that, in sharp contrast to the United States of America and some other Western countries, universities in this country are largely post-World War II creations.[8] The same is true of our law schools. For example, the number of undergraduate (internal) law students was just over 1,000 in 1938–9, about 12,600 in 1980–81. In 1991–92 it has been estimated that there were just under 19,000 full-time students registered for single honours law degrees and a further 4,000–5,000 reading for other degrees with a substantial law content.[9] The growth in scale is merely one indicator of a transformation that really only started in the mid to late sixties. The modern British law school is a new and developing form of institution – in many respects no older than the Centre for Socio-Legal Studies.

(ii) The multi-disciplinary study of law could proceed, and has often proceeded, independently of the existence of law schools or of an institutionalized discipline of law; law is too pervasive, important, powerful, and visible a phenomenon to be ignored by any social science or other related discipline.

(iii) Many of the factors that make law a potentially fruitful subject of study for scholars from other disciplines ante-dated or developed independently of its institutionalized study by legal scholars: for example, the rich body of published and unpublished material to be found in the law reports, legal documents, and legal records;[10] the

36

never-ending supply of concrete examples, stories, dramas, and novel real-life problems; and the incredibly wide range of publicly argued and justified decisions.[11] Most of these exist largely independently of the academic study of law, as any medieval or early modern historian can attest.[12]

(iv) Finally, I shall assume that, whether or not it makes sense to talk of any 'autonomous disciplines', law does not qualify as one in any strong sense of that term. I have argued the point elsewhere and do not intend to address it here.[13] I shall, however, at least raise the rather different question whether, given its current diversification and fragmentation, law-as-a-discipline has a recognizable, historically contingent core and, indeed, if it needs one?

REMEMBERING 1972: AN ACADEMIC LAWYER'S PERSPECTIVE

Historians of higher education now tend to place the end of the golden age of the don as early as 1966 or 1967:[14] what is now labelled '1968' had emanations at Berkeley and LSE in 1966; Shirley Williams's 'Thirteen Points', a shot across the bows that was largely ignored by the universities, were published in 1969;[15] the first Rothschild report on government research was published in 1971 and the Advisory Board of Research Councils was established in 1972, but their long-term implications for the dual funding system were not immediately apparent;[16] and there were other signs of impending financial problems. I suspect that in 1972 most academics had not yet seen the writing on the wall and, despite student troubles, were still caught up in the post-Robbins euphoria. Most of the 'plate glass' universities had been founded recently and were in the heady period of their initial development; the polytechnic era had begun; the social sciences were booming; the Social Science Research Council (SSRC) had been set up in 1965; and the Ormrod Committee on Legal Education had reported in 1971.

Within a year of the founding of the centre, the mood changed drastically: for example, 1973 saw the oil crisis and a 4 per cent cut in research council funding; the quinquennial system formally ended in 1975, but the process of undermining forward planning had started earlier.

Thus, from many points of view, the centre could hardly have been born at a less auspicious time. It is not necessary for me to remind you of the dreary chronicle of public events affecting higher education since 1972. But it is relevant to bear in mind that, despite many stops and gos, higher education has continued to expand throughout this period, mainly but not exclusively in the former polytechnics.

The law school story from 1972 to 1993 in many respects parallels that of higher education, but there are a few significant differences. The detailed story is quite complex, but a future historian of the period would need at least to take account of the following:

37

© Basil Blackwell Ltd. 1995

(i)   During the early period of post-war expansion law schools developed in ways that were roughly commensurate with the higher education system as a whole, judged by such measures as numbers of students and staff, and the output of graduates. Law got off to a relatively slow start in the boom period, but accelerated rapidly from about 1968.[17] It has been estimated that first degrees in law in the United Kingdom as a percentage of all university degrees rose from 0.8 per cent in 1965 to about 3.5 per cent in 1980.[18]

(ii)   The British law school is essentially a post-World War II creation in contrast with United States law schools, for which the pattern was set by the end of the last century. University, and later polytechnic, law schools only began to achieve 'critical mass' for the first time in their history after 1970, as is illustrated by the following rough estimates of full-time law teachers in universities and polytechnics in England and Wales:

1909	109
1933–34	130
1963–64	272
1974–75	974
1980–81	1,340[19]
1991–92	1,636 (882 university and 754 polytechnic)[20]

These figures are all approximate. Available statistics for students are more complex and probably even less reliable. But the data suggest that in 1991–92 there were probably at least twenty times more undergraduates studying law in England and Wales than there were just before World War II.[21]

(iii) Traditionally, university law schools had been depicted as poised uneasily between the world of the university and the worlds of the practising profession, looked down on by both and falling between stools in terms of objectives and functions. Today the situation is different, although there are still some fundamental tensions. Academic lawyers may still be referred to as 'the third branch of the legal profession' but, by and large, they are generally treated with somewhat greater respect than they were, and diplomatic relations with practitioners are conducted with greater self-confidence. The image of the law teacher as helot or as failed barrister has almost disappeared.[22] More significantly, during the period 1960-1990, law teachers seem to have become more fully integrated into the academic profession than had been the case in the past. Similarly there is evidence to suggest that, over time, law schools appear to have been accepted as fully part of universities and polytechnics, and indeed to have risen in prestige within academe. They are not, on the whole, treated as independent professional schools on the United States model nor as anomalous appendages which were regarded, to paraphrase Veblen, as no more

38

© Basil Blackwell Ltd. 1995

deserving of a place in a university than a school of fencing or dancing.[23]

The topic is complicated and more research is needed, so let one example suffice: Halsey's 1989 survey suggests that in almost all key respects the profile of academic lawyers very closely resembled the profile of the academic profession as a whole, especially colleagues in the humanities and social sciences.[24] For example, in respect of attitudes to research, productivity, and expectations of promotion academic lawyers seem to be close to the norm;[25] in respect of pay, promotion, and terms of service they seem to be treated much the same as other academics.[26] This may be a reflection of a broader hypothesis: that since World War II nearly all major changes and decisions affecting the discipline of law in universities – on admissions, numbers, gender ratios, staff-student ratios, resourcing, teaching methods, quality assurance, terms of service, and career development of academic staff – have much more closely reflected changes in higher education than in legal practice and the legal system. Except for the post-Ormrod structure, which was a compromise between conflicting interest groups within the legal profession, most debates on legal education seem to have had little impact on its development.[27]

(iv)   During the past twenty years of cuts, squeezes, low morale and steady loss of institutional autonomy, law has been in some important respects one of the better protected disciplines. This is especially true in respect of job opportunities and promotion prospects. Steady demand from both home and overseas undergraduates is no doubt the most important factor, but there are others. There are two important exceptions to this generalization: first, the poverty of students. Law students have probably suffered even worse than most other students, largely because vocational courses in law do not attract mandatory grants and discretionary grants have become increasingly hard to get.[28] Secondly, despite strong representations from heads of law schools about the changing nature of the subject, law, along with politics, is credited or debited, according to your point of view, with having the lowest unit costs of any discipline.[29] The image of law as essentially cheap is a long-established, international phenomenon. Academic lawyers have some justification in thinking of themselves as victims of labelling theory as the nature of their enterprise changes but their funding is based on old formulas, which take little or no account of increases in costs associated with membership of the EC, more labour-intensive kinds of training, new technology, or, indeed, inter-disciplinary research.[30]

(v)   Related to (iv) is a sense that, despite a period of adversity, law as a discipline in this country (as in other relatively wealthy anglophone countries) is generally more diverse, more interesting, and more ebullient than it was twenty-one years ago. Let me hastily deny that this is a complacent statement of the 'you've never had it so good' variety. I share with most academic colleagues a sense of foreboding about the future of our higher education system, especially in respect of research; I am glad that I started my academic career in 1958 rather than 1988; at a time when the growth in scale and the very significant progress in the discipline might have led to a growth in self-confidence, the academic profession as a whole was downgraded in respect of relative pay, status, political influence, and public esteem. Law may have been better cushioned than most, but academic lawyers are now fully part of the academic profession and have shared in the process of downgrading.[31] Staff-students ratios have declined sharply.[32] Furthermore, I have a sense of near-despair about the plight of law faculties in anglophone Africa and other Southern countries.

However, let me remind you of some of the evidence that supports a more optimistic interpretation:

(i) Compare for example the law lists in publishers' catalogues in 1993 with those in 1972 – not only the lists of publishers like Sweet and Maxwell, Butterworth, and Oxford University Press (OUP), but also those of publishing houses that did not exist or did not have law lists. On the whole, the outlets for scholarly legal writing have expanded to accommodate the increased output and the diversity in range and approach is unrecognizably greater.

(ii) Consider the extent to which academic law has been internationalized and de-parochialized in the last twenty years, by no means only in respect of EC law and closer contacts with Continental Europe. Some fields, such as 'Law and Development', African law, and legal anthropology may have been through a rather lean period in the post-colonial era, but they are exceptions.

(iii) Compare the range of courses at postgraduate level in 1972 with those on offer today in Oxford, Cambridge, London, and elsewhere. For example, the number of options listed in the London inter-collegiate LLM has steadily increased, for better or worse, from thirty in 1965 to nearly 150 in 1993, of which about 100 are offered in any one year.[33] I would have found it difficult to name 50 legal subjects in 1972. As most law teachers know, there is a much closer integration of teaching and research at postgraduate than at undergraduate level in law, even in taught courses.[34]

(iv) Compare any standard field as it was in 1972 with its situation today in respect of teaching, research, theoretical sophistication, and quality. My two main fields of interest, jurisprudence and evidence, are un-recognizably different. Take jurisprudence: by 1972 Herbert Hart had revived legal philosophy and Ronald Dworkin had recently succeeded him (Dworkin's inaugural lecture, 'Taking Rights Seriously', was first

40

published in 1970). Law and economics had hardly ventured beyond the University of Chicago[35] – the first edition of Richard Posner's *Economic Analysis of Law* was published in 1972.[36] How many academic lawyers, or legal theorists, in 1972 had conceived or heard of, let alone participated in, critical legal studies,[37] feminist jurisprudence,[38] critical race theory,[39] law and semiotics,[40] the law and literature movement,[41] socio-biology[42] or autopoiesis?[43] A great deal of this intellectual ferment is United States-American and some may prove to have been a mere passing fashion. One might say, by way of counter-examples, that the sociology and anthropology of law and historical jurisprudence have been further marginalized within law schools, despite the contributions of a few individuals.[44] Juristic writing has yet to catch up with developments in the history of ideas.[45] Nevertheless, one might also say that the intellectual ferment in legal theory which began in the fifties never lost momentum, although it has diversified and fragmented in confusing ways.

(v)   There have, of course, been many developments in legal education and training since the Ormrod exercise. I do not intend to comment on these here, except to observe that what we have today could be interpreted as a quite remarkable pluralism which to a large extent fits in with the theme of diversification.[46]

(vi) Finally, there is socio-legal studies. I leave it to others to survey the developments in the field internationally and in this country.[47] Let me restrict myself to a few very general observations about their place in the law school world.

First, if one uses the programmes of recent American Law and Society and SALSA conferences and the recent report by Lee Bridges as indicators,[48] they reflect the themes of diversity, increased sophistication, and confidence.

Secondly, socio-legal studies, even if interpreted broadly, is only one of several significant intellectual trends within the discipline of law. The unempirical nature of most critical legal scholarship has been the subject of much comment (that may be changing). The same is true of most work in normative legal philosophy, law and literature, and other influential movements. Indeed, almost any empirical work on law, at least in law schools, is likely to be classified as 'socio-legal'.[49]

Thirdly, it is my impression that in both research and teaching of particular subjects within law schools, socio-legal studies have moved from barely tolerated marginality, to acceptance, to a relatively high degree of integration. That has been done without imposing a new orthodoxy. For example, what specialist in torts or family law or administrative law or tax or evidence or the administration of criminal justice can afford to ignore the relevant socio-legal work in their teaching or research? Some may do so, but is that scholarly? Socio-legal studies have made significant contributions to the rethinking and reconceptualization of specialized fields of

41

law, both traditional and new.[50] Conversely, more than 60 per cent of research in the United Kingdom that is categorized as 'socio-legal' is currently based in law departments.[51]

Fourthly, in this country, there seems to be a greater receptivity to the contributions of social scientists to the operation of some aspects of the legal system and to policy-making than there was in 1972. To take just two examples: the notorious report of the Criminal Law Revision Committee on Criminal Evidence of 1972 was the work of a body composed solely of lawyers with no visible input from social scientists.[52] At the time some of us criticized the report for its lack of an empirical base.[53] By contrast the recent Royal Commission on Criminal Justice commissioned twenty-two research studies, mainly by social scientists, and took note of existing research on a number of specific topics.[54] Whatever one thinks of its use of socio-legal research or its recommendations or the outcome of the process, at least it had the opportunity to be better informed than its predecessors.[55] Similarly, it is difficult to envisage the Council of Legal Education in 1972 either sponsoring or paying attention to the kind of research that Joanna Shapland and others have done on the Bar vocational course in the last four years.[56]

Next, in respect of law and psychology in which I have a special interest, some of the main themes of this paper are replicated. For example, law and psychology, despite a long history, only became institutionalized on a significant scale in the 1970s. Recent surveys suggest that it is only much more recently that the field has extended significantly beyond jury studies and witness psychology to encompass sustained attention on a much wider range of topics with a much greater focus on cognitive work. For example, the *Handbook of Psychology and Law*, published in 1991, had over twenty chapters reporting on different areas of interest.[57] There is also a growing sophistication on the part of psychologists about the complexities of law and a small, but significant, number of researchers with qualifications in both disciplines. As with other areas of socio-legal studies, there has been disappointingly little general theorizing which might guide research agendas or develop a general 'psychology of law' in contradistinction to the much more fragmented 'psychology in law'. This is disappointing in the light of claims of the kind that one finds at the start of a leading book on social psychology in court:

> Every law and every legal institution is based on assumptions about human nature and the manner in which human behavior is determined. We believe that scientific psychology can help us to understand these institutions and improve them.[58]

There are at least two respects in which trends in law and psychology differ from most other areas of socio-legal studies. First, the most extensive relationships in law and psychology are between practitioners (including academic psychologists providing specific services) with relatively few direct academic-academic relations. A very high proportion of the work involves dealing with specific cases or narrowly focused applied research or quite specific vocational training. Indeed, a great deal of what goes on under the

42

rubric of 'law and psychology' hardly belongs to 'socio-legal studies' if that is interpreted narrowly as being concerned primarily with basic research into the social understanding of law. On the other hand, this is one area in which one institutionalized sub-discipline of socio-legal studies includes a significant number of practising psychologists, lawyers, and judges who participate regularly in conferences, workshops, and other activities. Another striking feature of psycho-legal studies is the extent to which it is dominated by United States-American work and ideas. This, too, is hardly surprising given the relative scale and wealth of United States legal and psychological enterprises (and possibly a culture more receptive to psychology). The dangers of this are illustrated by the *Handbook of Psychology and Law* which very largely treats law and psychology as exclusive to the United States of America.[59] Not only is this parochial in the sense that it makes hardly any reference to non-American sources, but nearly all the contributions take the United States legal system for granted, including such atypical phenomena as the United States Constitution, the civil jury, contingent fees, and the United States version of adversary proceedings. Indeed, in reading United States psycho-legal literature, one needs to be constantly on the look-out for four kinds of cultural assumptions or biases: the distinctive features not only of United States culture, including the culture of law schools, but also whatever is peculiar or distinctive about United States psychology both as an academic discipline and as a practising profession. Despite having had only one psychologist on its staff for most of its life, the Centre for Socio-Legal Studies has played a crucial role in ensuring that British law and psychology has had a distinctive voice. The development of a European network and organization is especially to be welcomed in an area where the interplay between general 'scientific' concerns and specific cultural contexts is particularly complex.

In all of this, the centre has played a key role: very briefly, I would summarize this as follows:

(a) it has been unique in providing a base for social research into law that is genuinely multi-disciplinary, rather than just inter-disciplinary. This extends far beyond particular projects to its being the headquarters of a small, but very significant sub-culture that views almost everything through the multiple lenses of several disciplines;

(b) it has had an important training function not only through postgraduate work, but also in the intellectual development of a significant number of scholars who have spent a period there and then moved on to other institutions;

(c) it has performed an invaluable networking function. For example, the centre's law and psychology workshops which began in 1977, organized by Sally Lloyd-Bostock, were a very important catalyst to the institutionalization of law and psychology as a recognized field in this country.

Of course, some areas have flourished more than others, the impact has been uneven, and there have been some disappointments: I for one would like to see more of a focus on the world order and non-western societies; and rather more of the kinds of theorizing that would involve the critical mapping of socio-legal studies in ways which might produce a more coherent approach to setting agendas for research, so that responses to opportunities and searches for *ad hoc* funding can be set in a broad overview of the state of the field. Naturally, this diversification and pluralism have produced some adverse reactions. Again this is most visible in the United States of America, not least in a recent exchange in the *Michigan Law Review* between Judge Harry Edwards and eighteen respondents.[60] Nevertheless, there is much to celebrate and the centre can take justifiable pride not only in its own specific projects but also in its influence as a catalyst, in research training, and in its influence on the intellectual climate of opinion.

Most of the above generalizations probably represent good news for socio-legal studies. In so far as these generalizations are true it means that in 1993 the size of the pool of potential legal academic researchers is almost four times what it was in 1972, that law schools are generally much more hospitable to socio-legal studies, and that academic lawyers are probably more research-oriented and have a wider range of interests than twenty-one years ago. There is now also a substantial cadre of experienced socio-legal workers in post in a significant number of institutions, a majority in law schools. Thus, even if it were the case that there is little that the discipline of law can offer to the social understanding of law that is unique or even special – a view I may challenge on some other occasion – British law schools are better placed than at any time in their history to offer a stable home for socio-legal studies.

CONCLUSION

(i) Modern British law schools are larger, more sophisticated, more varied, and more self-confident than was the case twenty-one years ago. But they are still a relatively new phenomenon, and major decisions will be made in the next few years that will affect their future direction. One fundamental question is whether law schools will become little more than primary schools for the profession or whether they will diversify into multi-functional institutions with a more varied role and a more diverse clientele.

(ii) One of the major issues facing law as a discipline is whether it can and should have a clearly defined core and, if so, whether that will involve a return to what Judge Harry Edwards, in a controversial recent article, has called 'practical doctrinal scholarship'.[61] If that happens on a large scale and if law schools contract rather than continue to expand in the next phase, there is a danger that socio-legal studies and other recent intellectual developments may become marginalized within them.

44

(iii) There is no room for complacency, but there at least some grounds for optimism. I hope that law schools will continue the trend of being hospitable to socio-legal studies, but not at the expense of the continued development of genuinely multi-disciplinary centres for the social study of law.

NOTES AND REFERENCES

1 A.H. Halsey, *Decline of Donnish Dominion: The British Academic Professions in the Twentieth Century* (1992).
2 id. at pp. 1–2. Halsey's study is based primarily on three surveys of British academic staff carried out in 1964/65 (Halsey and Trow, 1971), in 1976 (Halsey, 1979) and in 1989(Halsey, 1992). Professor Halsey has kindly allowed me to use data about academic lawyers extrapolated from the third survey.
3 The post-war public history of higher education in Great Britain is well-documented. In addition to Halsey's work, I have drawn on W.A.C. Stewart, *Higher Education in Post-war Britain* (1989); J. Carswell, *Government and the Universities in Britain* (1985); T. Becher, *Academic Tribes and Territories* (1989); and P. Scott, *The Crisis of the University* (1984). A striking feature of these excellent studies is that they hardly refer specifically to law, let alone socio-legal studies. This near-invisibility mirrors the attitude of official reports like that of Robbins (1963) and Heyworth (1965). This suggests that law was perceived and treated by those concerned with higher education policy as a not particularly significant or distinctive part of the non-science sector.
4 Some of the themes in this paper, delivered in December 1993, have since been developed, and in some instances modified, in W. Twining, *Blackstone's Tower: The English Law School* (Hamlyn Lectures, 1994).
5 The best ethnographic study of English academics is Tony Becher's suggestive book, op. cit., n. 3. Unlike most modern studies of higher education, this treats academic lawyers as a distinct sub-group, but Becher's sample was too small to be representative.
6 The theme has re-surfaced recently in United States law reviews: for example, R. Posner, 'The decline of law as an autonomous discipline: 1962–87' (1987) 100 *Harvard Law Rev.* 761.
7 On the need for visitors from other disciplines to have local guides, see the discussions in the Cardozo symposium on 'Decision and Inference in Litigation' (1991) 13 *Cardozo Law Rev.* at 295–302, 713–15 (Twining), 783–91 (Anderson). A good example of a type of source material which needs to be handled with care is the law reports. These are a kind of text which are simultaneously overused and neglected, a rich treasure-house and a powerful, dangerous distorting lens. This theme is developed in my 'Reading Law' (1989) 24 *Valparaiso Law Rev.* 1; compare Otto Kahn-Freund's warning: 'Is it not in the nature of the lawyer's work that his mind concentrates on phenomena which are socially marginal? Legal thinking must, I think, be constituted that way – this is the principal difference between law as an academic discipline and other social sciences which are concerned with typical and not with marginal situations. Above all: litigation is a pathological phenomenon in the body politic. The reported cases are cases of the most serious diseases, and the leading cases are often the worst, the least typical of all.' ('Reflections on Legal Education' (1966) 29 *Modern Law Rev.* 121, at 127.
8 For example, 'Americans who have walked through the quads and gardens of Oxford and Cambridge, and who know that Harvard was modelled on a Cambridge college, often think of British universities as immeasurably older than our own. But in fact higher education as a system is much younger in the United Kingdom than in the United States. The U.S. organisational revolution took place 100 years ago, roughly between 1870 and 1910; the emergence of the British system is still underway.' (M. Trow, 'Comparative

45

Perspectives on Higher Education Policy in the U.K. and U.S.' (1988) 14 *Oxford Rev. of Education* 81.)

9   R. Abel, *The Legal Profession in England and Wales* (1988) at 465: 1938-39, 1,515; 1980-81: universities, 8,398; polytechnics, 4,205; total: 12,603, excluding mixed and part-time degrees. The comparable figures for 1990-91 were (old) universities: 11,192 in 1990–91, 12,051 in 1991–92 (J. Wilson, 'A third survey of legal education in the United Kingdom' (1993) 13 *Legal Studies* 143, 146). In 1991–92 there were a further 1,599 reading for mixed degrees (less than 50 per cent law) in universities; the figures for former polytechnics and other higher education institutions teaching at degree level were 6,817 full-time LLB and 2,524 full-time other, excluding Buckingham, external students, and a number of other categories. P. Harris and S. Bellerby, *A Survey of Law Teaching* (1993) (an Association of Law Teachers (ALT) project).

10   The extent, nature, and archival value of, and threats to, the survival of legal records are explored in W. Twining and E. Quick (eds.), *Legal Records in the Commonwealth* (1994). This includes a valuable case-study by Neil Rickman on the use of unpublished data in socio-legal research at the Centre for Socio-Legal Studies.

11   While orthodox judicial and legislative proceedings are generally public and accessible, there are, of course, many areas of significant legal action that are secret or arcane. One theme of Twining and Quick, id., is that there has been a tendency on the part of archivists to equate legal records with court records and to underestimate or ignore the significance of the more arcane, often neglected, records of, for example, arbitration, other forms of alternative dispute resolution, and private sector institutions generally, including multi-national corporations and non-governmental organizations.

12   For example, A. Harding, *A Social History of English Law* (1966) at 7. See, generally, Twining and Quick, id., ch. 2.

13   For example, R. Tur and W. Twining (eds.), *Essays on Kelsen* (1986) introduction.

14   N. Annan, *Our Age* (1990).

15   'Summarised, they suggested reductions or removal of student grants and the introduction of loans both for undergraduates and postgraduates; restrictions on admission of overseas students and progress towards full-cost fees for them; limitations of the range of employment for grant-aided students similar to the pledge for student teachers which had been abandoned ten years before; part-time and correspondence courses; shortening of degree programmes to two years for able students; the option of two-year non-degree diploma courses for less able students; a pre-university year which would discriminate more accurately and would exclude unsuitable candidates; more intensive use of buildings and sharing of staff and facilities between institutions; increases in staff/student ratios; economies in residential facilities, including more home-based students and more loan-financed accommodation . . . the CVCP responded in 1970 giving a cold reply to nearly all of these proposals.' (Stewart, op. cit., n. 3, at pp. 160–1).

16   V. Rothschild, *The Organisation and Management of Government Research and Development* (Cmnd. 4814; 1971).

17   Available statistics are spotty and do not always clearly differentiate between the United Kingdom, Great Britain, and England and Wales. The best collation to date is to be found in Abel, op. cit., n. 9. This can now be supplemented by the third Wilson report and the ALT report by Harris and Bellerby, op. cit., n. 9. The Wilson report gives detailed figures for 1980–81 and 1990–91 for 'old' universities; the ALT study, which is continuing, deals with the former polytechnics and colleges of further education, but omits some categories. In most public policy and statistical documents, law is lumped together anonymously under the social sciences and is to a remarkable extent invisible. It is to be hoped that one outcome of the current review of legal education by the Lord Chancellor's Advisory Committee will be regular statistics.

18   G. Neave, in *Lawyers in Society: Comparative Theories*, eds. R. Abel and P. Lewis (1989) ch. 4, table 4.10, at 188. Other sources suggest that the figures from England and Wales may have been a bit different, varying between approximately 1.5 per cent and 3.5 per cent in a comparable period.

46

19 Source: Wilson, op. cit., n. 9; Abel's figure is 1,282.
20 Wilson, id., gives 882 full-time and 235 part-time (1,115) in 'old' universities in 1991-92 (compared to 784 full-time in 1980-81); Harris and Bellerby, op. cit., n. 9, at p. 13, report a 32.8 per cent increase of staff in the new university sector in the same decade (568 to 754), but a very significant drop in staff-student ratios. There has also been a significant increase in use of part-time staff in both sectors.
21 This estimate excludes part-time students, those reading for degrees in which there is a minor law component and other so-called 'service teaching', all of which are more significant today than formerly.
22 These assertions are, of course, impressionistic, and are only relative to the situation that prevailed until quite recently. My own impressions can be backed by many concrete instances (for example, the creation of academic QCs). A vivid account of the low status of English academic lawyers up to 1965 is to be found in B. Abel-Smith and R. Stevens, *Lawyers and the Courts* (1967) 352–3, 365–75. A well-known example is Harold Laski, writing to O.W. Holmes in 1925, about the Law Teachers' Dinner: 'The judges had, with two exceptions, a most amusing sense of infinite superiority, and the teachers as interesting a sense of complete inferiority.' (*Holmes-Laski Letters* vol. 1 (1953) 763 (13/7/1925); compare id., vol. 2, at 1156.) Some claim that Lord Goff's Maccabean Lecture, 'The Search for Principle', (1983) LXIX *Proceedings of the Brit. Academy* 169, marked the start of a new era of increased status and public appreciation of the contributions of academic lawyers.
23 T. Veblen, *The Higher Learning in America* (1918) 211.
24 Professor Halsey very kindly extrapolated academic lawyers, hitherto invisible, from his 1989 survey. The interpretation of these figures is mine.
25 One major exception is that a significantly smaller percentage of academic lawyers have doctorates than their colleagues in most other disciplines; Halsey's figures suggest that this is not entirely balanced by the number holding professional qualifications.
26 This, again, is in sharp contrast to the United States of America where, among other things, law professors have a significant pay differential, but have to live with quite unfavourable staff-student ratios.
27 One reason for this is that most official reports and public debates focus on the process of professional formation rather than on law schools as institutions. See, further, W. Twining, '"The Initial Stage": Notes on the Context and a Search for Consensus', Lord Chancellor's Advisory Committee (LCAC), Review of Legal Education, first consultative conference, 9 July 1993; LCAC, *Report* (1993) 1–13.
28 For a vivid account of the problems, see P. Thomas, 'The Poverty of Students' (1993) 27 *The Law Teacher* 152.
29 Heads of University Law Schools, *Law as an academic discipline* (1983). The bulk of the report was published in the Society of Public Teachers of Law *Newsletter*, Summer 1984; see also the submissions by the Law Society to the Universities Funding Council and the Polytechnics Funding Council in 1991 (0228R and 0234R), quoted by Thomas, id., at p. 154. From 1993 the unit of resource of fees-only social science students was reduced by approximately 30 per cent (£1,300 compared to £2,770 for laboratory and workshop-based courses) in order to deter expansion of social science departments, including law (Thomas, id.).
30 HULS, id.
31 Halsey, op. cit., n. 1. This is most striking in respect of the relative earnings of law teachers and practising lawyers. For figures in the United States of America (where academic lawyers are better paid than most academics), see D. Bok, *The Cost of Talent* (1993) ch. 8. Compare, however, the possible counter-trend noted above.
32 Wilson, while acknowledging the difficulty of estimating staff-student ratios, indicates that in ('old') universities in England and Wales the average staff-student ratio in law schools declined from 11.4 in 1980/1 to 16.0 in 1991/2 (op. cit., n. 9, at pp. 156–8). An even gloomier picture is painted by Harris and Bellerby., op. cit., n. 9.

47

33 For details, see University of London, *LLM Review: Second Interim Report* (1992).
34 While conducting a review of the London LLM in 1992–93, I was often told by colleagues that the opportunity to undertake postgraduate teaching closely related to their research was one aspect of their job that they valued very highly.
35 On the complex history of the law-and-economics movement, see N. Duxbury, 'Law and Economics and the legacy of Chicago', University of Hull, *Studies in Law* (1994).
36 Recently Posner has ebulliently sought to be re-labelled: see, for example, R. Posner, *Law and Literature: A Misunderstood Relation* (1988); *The Problems of Jurisprudence* (1990); *Sex and Reason* (1992).
37 The first conference of critical legal studies was held in Madison, Wisconsin in 1977; only a very few pre-1977 entries are listed in D. Kennedy and K. Klare, 'A bibliography of critical legal studies' (1984) 94 *Yale Law J.* 461. A significant exception is Kennedy's polemic, 'How the Law School Fails: A Polemic' (1970) 1 *Yale Rev. of Law and Social Action* 71. 'Critical legal studies', so-called, arrived in the United Kingdom rather later, but overtly critical or left-wing legal scholarship arguably has a longer tradition in Europe than in the United States of America.
38 The first use of the term feminist jurisprudence is sometimes attributed to P. Scales, 'Towards a feminist jurisprudence' (1981) 56 *Indiana Law J.* 375.
39 R. Delgado and J. Stefancic, 'Critical Race Theory: an annotated bibliography' (1993) 79 *Virginia Law Rev.* 461. Almost all of the listed entries were published after 1980.
40 B. Jackson, *Semiotics and Legal Theory* (1985); the first volume in the series *Law and Semiotics* (ed. R. Kevelson) was published in 1987.
41 James Boyd White's *The Legal Imagination* was first published in 1973, but a 'movement' did not get under way until several years later. By 1989, thirty-eight United States law schools were reported to be offering 'law and literature' courses. E. Gemmette, 'Law and Literature: An Unnecessarily Suspect Class in the Liberal Arts Component of Law School Curriculum' (1989) 23 *Valparaiso Law Rev.* 267.
42 For example, M. Gruter, *Law and Mind: Biological Origins of Human Behavior* (1991) and the seminars and publications of the Gruter Institute for Law and Behavioral Research in California.
43 G. Teubner, *Autopoietic Law: A New Approach* (1988); symposium in *Cardozo Law Rev.*, March 1992. Overviews of recent currents in mainly American legal thought include G. Minda, 'Jurisprudence at Century's End' (1993) 43 *J. of Legal Education* 27; M.W. McConnell, 'Four Faces of Conservative Legal Thought' (1988) 34 *University of Chicago Law School Record* 12; and M.E. Becker, 'Four Faces of Liberal Legal Thought', id. (Fall, 1988), at 11.
44 For a survey of legal anthropology up to 1987/8, see F. Snyder, 'Anthropology, Dispute Processes and Law' (1988) 8 *Brit. J. of Law and Society* 141; on historical jurisprudence see, generally, A. Diamond (ed.), *The Victorian Achievement of Sir Henry Maine* (1991).
45 See W. Twining, 'Reading Bentham' (1989) LXXV *Proceedings of the Brit. Academy* 97 (the Maccabean Lecture).
46 For an interpretation of the current situation at the academic and vocational stages see Twining, op. cit., n. 27.
47 See, especially, Economic and Social Research Council (ESRC), *ESRC Review of Socio-legal Studies* (1994).
48 L. Bridges, 'ESRC Review Surveys of Socio-Legal Studies' 10 *Socio-Legal Newsletter* (Autumn, 1993) 1.
49 ESRC, op. cit., n. 47.
50 id.
51 Bridges, op. cit, n. 48, at p. 1 (62 per cent of staff engaged in funded socio-legal projects and 71 per cent of respondents claiming an active interest in the area were in law departments). 'Socio-legal' is, of course, a bureaucratic category defined for specific purposes by the ESRC (formerly the Social Science Research Council (SSRC)). For other purposes a wider range of studies might be included.

48

52 Criminal Law Revision Committee (CLRC), *Eleventh Report: Evidence (General)* (1972; Cmnd. 4991).
53 For example, W. Twining, *Rethinking Evidence* (1990) ch. 10.
54 *Report of the Royal Commission on Criminal Justice*, chair, Viscount Runciman of Doxford (1993; Cm. 2263). One member of the Royal Commission, Professor John Gunn, is a forensic psychiatrist.
55 A. Sanders, 'Research for the Royal Commission on Criminal Justice: Implications for Education and Training' (1993) 10 *Socio-Legal Newsletter* 2.
56 V. Johnston and J. Shapland, *Developing Vocational Legal Training for the Bar* (1990); J. Shapland, V. Johnston, and R. Wild, *Studying for the Bar* (1993).
57 D. Kagehiro and W.S. Laufer (eds.), *Handbook of Psychology and Law* (1991/2). The editors consciously organized the book according to 'traditional legal categories', but Shari Diamond notes in the foreword that '[a]lthough social psychology and clinical psychology have probably stimulated the most activity in the last twenty years' there have been notable developments in other branches of psychology, especially cognitive work.' (at v). Compare Sally Lloyd-Bostock's valuable, and more international surveys of the field, for example, *Law in Practice* (1988), and 'Psychology and the Law: their theoretical and working relationship' (unpublished, 1993).
58 M.J. Sacks and R. Hastie, *Social Psychology in Court* (1978) 1.
59 Kagehiro and Laufer, op. cit., n. 57.
60 H.T. Edwards, 'The growing disjunction between legal education and the legal profession' (1992) 91 *Michigan Law Rev.* 34; symposium on legal education (1993) 91 *Michigan Law Rev.* 1921–2219. See, further, Twining, op. cit., n. 4.
61 Edwards, id.

49

JOURNAL OF LAW AND SOCIETY
VOLUME 22, NUMBER 1, MARCH 1995
0263–323X

Law and Unified Social Theory

ROBERT COOTER*

An economist who talks about unified theory to lawyers and social scientists gets welcomed rather like the British expedition to Afghanistan in 1840. The Afghanistanis preferred to fight rather than join the British empire, and many social scientists are similarly disposed towards the economics empire. Like the nineteenth-century British, however, economics imperialism has succeeded remarkably. Economic models of rational behaviour have affected all the social sciences in the last thirty years, as well as history, philosophy, and law. Everyone in social science, whether friend or foe of economics, should want to understand its success.

In this essay, I will try to explain the success of the economic analysis of law, but I will not merely praise the subject. My own feelings are too complicated for that. Like others in my generation of undergraduates, I had a special aversion to materialism. Microeconomics concerns the efficiency of markets, but I was more interested in the majesty of law, the struggle of politics, and the deciphering of culture. My explanation of the successes of economics will reveal limits in models of rational behaviour that insulate economics from psychology and sociology. The correction of these structural deficiencies would unify behavioural theory and overcome limitations in the economic analysis of law.

PROGRESS IN ECONOMIC ANALYSIS OF LAW[1]

Until recently, law confined the use of economics to antitrust, regulated industries, tax, and monetary damages. Law obviously needed economics to answer such questions as, 'What is the market share of an alleged monopolist?', 'Will price controls reduce the availability of automobile insurance?', 'Do the rich pay the capital gains tax?', and 'How much future income do children lose from their father's death?' Beginning in the 1960s, however, the breadth of the economic analysis of law expanded remarkably by its application to property, contracts, torts, crimes, procedure, and constitutional law. Economic analysis addressed new questions such as, 'Will private

* Professor of Law, School of Law (Boalt Hall) University of California, Berkeley, California 94720, United States of America

ownership of the electromagnetic spectrum encourage its efficient use?', 'What damage remedy for breach causes the most reliance on contracts?', 'Does strict liability for consumer product injuries cause excessive precaution by manufacturers?', 'Will harsher punishments deter violent crime?', and 'Does bicameralism increase the discretionary power of courts?' By addressing such questions, economics changed American legal scholarship. At least one economist is on the faculty of every top law school in the United States of America; some law faculties in western Europe also include an economist. Joint degree programmes in law and economics exist in many prominent American universities. Law and economics associations meet annually in Europe, Canada, and the United States of America. Law reviews publish many articles using the economic approach and some journals are devoted exclusively to law and economics. Many law school classes in the United States now include a summary of the economic analysis of the class's subject. An exhaustive study recently found that the major American law journals cite articles using the economic approach more than articles using any other approach.[2] In 1991 and 1992, the Nobel prizes in economics were awarded to Ronald Coase and Gary Becker, two pioneers in the economic analysis of law.

Outside the universities, economic analysis affected law and public policy in various ways. Economic analysis provided the intellectual foundation for the deregulation movement, which dramatically changed the law for regulated industries in several countries. A committee created by the United States Congress in 1984 to reform criminal sentencing in the federal courts (the U.S. Sentencing Commission) explicitly used the findings of law and economics to reach some of its results. Several law and economics scholars have become federal appellate judges, including Richard A. Posner, Frank Easterbrook, Robert Bork, and Stephen Breyer, whose confirmation hearing for the Supreme Court proceeds as I write.

WHY DID THE ECONOMIC ANALYSIS OF LAW SUCCEED?

The economic analysis succeeded more than its most optimistic founders expected. Why? Like the rabbit in Australia, economics found a vacant niche in the intellectual ecology and rapidly filled it. To understand the niche, consider this classical definition: 'A law is an obligation backed by a state sanction.' Lawmakers and adjudicators often ask, 'How will this sanction affect behaviour?' For example, if the manufacturer of a defective product faces liability for consequential damages, what will happen to the product's safety and price?

Lawyers answered such questions in 1960 in much the same way as in 60 BC, by consulting intuition and any available facts. A scientific theory to predict the effects of sanctions upon behaviour, which lawyers lacked, developed from economics after 1960. Just as laws impose sanctions on acts,

51

markets charge prices for commodities. Economists developed price theory, which is mathematically precise and empirically confirmed, to predict how people respond to prices. To economists, sanctions look like prices, because both are tariffs on behaviour. Presumably, people respond to heavier sanctions much like they response to higher prices. Adapting price theory to law allowed economists to predict how people respond to sanctions. To illustrate, suppose that a manufacturer knows that his product will sometimes injure consumers. How safe will he make the product? The answer depends upon the actual cost of safety, which depends in turn upon facts about design and manufacture. In addition, the answer depends upon the 'implicit price' paid by the producer for injuries to consumers, including liability. The producer will need the help of lawyers and other experts to estimate the implicit price. After obtaining the needed information, the rational producer will compare the cost of safety and the implicit price of accidents. To maximize profits, the producer will adjust safety until the actual cost of additional safety equals the implicit price of additional accidents.

I have been discussing sanctions as if they were fixed prices. Some prices, however, are negotiated rather than fixed. Understanding negotiation requires strategic theory. In American football, a player often runs around the right side as a decoy to fool the other team while the player carrying the ball runs around the left side. In contrast, a mountain climber never starts up the south slope as a decoy to fool the mountain while the main party climbs up the north slope. Football is strategic and mountain climbing is non-strategic. In strategic games, each player forms his or her strategy on the assumption that other players form their strategies by anticipating what he or she will do. In non-strategic games, each player assumes that other players form their strategies without anticipating what he or she will do.

Economists apply price theory to law by treating sanctions as prices. Price theory usually assumes that people behave non-strategically. Specifically, each participant in a competitive market expects that his or her own buying and selling will not affect prices. In contrast, game theory analyses strategic behaviour. The rules of a game prescribe the moves that players may make, and the theory of games predicts how people will change their moves in response to changes in rules. Like rules of games, rules of law prescribe how people may interact with each other. When people interact in the shadow of the law, their behaviour often depends upon what each person thinks the others will do. Consequently, rules of law are like rules of games for purposes of economic analysis. Whether people behave strategically or non-strategically often depends upon the number of players in the game. In games with many players, each one may assume that his or her behaviour alone cannot affect what others do, as in a perfectly competitive model. In games that pit a few players against each other, each one may assume that his or her behaviour affects what others do. For example, the two parties in settlement bargaining try to anticipate each other's offers, the principal in a fiduciary relationship drafts a contract that anticipates the agent's reaction, and those

52

who create a nuisance on their property may anticipate their neighbours' response.

The original applications of price theory to law generally treated sanctions as competitive prices, so the models were non-strategic. To illustrate, each criminal assumes that his or her crimes cannot affect the state's schedule of criminal sanctions, each consumer assumes that his or her precaution will not affect the probability of a product's being defective, and each commuter assumes that his or her decision to drive the to work will not affect the decisions of other commuters to drive.

Non-strategic behaviour is simpler to analyse than strategic behaviour. Early in its development, the economic analysis of law found a technique for analysing strategic behaviour as if it were non-strategic. The most famous proposition in the economic analysis of law, the Coase Theorem, asserts that bargaining succeeds so long as 'transaction costs' are low. Thus, the Coase Theorem treats strategic behaviour as a transaction cost. Treating strategic behaviour as a cost facilitated the rapid assimilation of price theory into law. In reality, strategic behaviour does not resemble the cost of oranges, haircuts, or any other good. Calling strategic behaviour a 'cost' postpones analysing it.[3] Game theorists are reworking the economic analysis of law under the assumption that people behave strategically, just as they transformed the study of industrial organization in the 1980s.[4] To illustrate, we now understand better how settlement offers by defendants screen and sort plaintiffs according to the strength of their case. Plaintiffs with strong cases reject a settlement offer and proceed to trial; plaintiffs with moderate cases accept a settlement if offered and go to trial otherwise; plaintiffs with weak cases accept a settlement if offered and drop the case otherwise. The rational defendant uses these facts to compute the settlement strategy that minimizes his or her costs.

Generalizing, we can say that economics provides a behavioural theory to predict how people respond to changes in laws. At the simplest level, where people respond to the sanctions imposed by the state, but not to each other, price theory predicts how changes in sanctions change behaviour. At a more complex level, where people respond to the state and each other, game theory predicts how changes in laws change behaviour. These theories surpass intuition just as science surpasses common sense. In addition to a scientific theory of behaviour, economics provides a useful normative standard for evaluating law and policy. To make public policy, judges and other lawmakers need to know its effects on important values. A member of the California Supreme Court recently presided over a pretend court ('moot court') for law students. After listening to an hour of technical legal arguments, he banged his fist on the table and said, 'What are the policy arguments? This is the highest court in California. I want to know the policy arguments!' To make public policy, judges and other lawmakers need to know its effects on important values. Economics predicts the effects of policies on efficiency. Public officials never publicly advocate wasting money,

53

© Basil Blackwell Ltd. 1995

so efficiency is always relevant to policy debates. Besides efficiency, economics also predicts the effects of policies on distribution. More than other social scientists, economists understand how laws affect the distribution of income and wealth across classes and groups. For example, in one of its earliest applications to public policy, economics predicted who really bears the burden of alternative taxes. In general, economics predicts how laws affect efficiency and distribution, which are two of the most important policy values for lawmakers.

X-RAY VISION VERSUS PERIPHERAL VISION

When I described the successful institutionalization of the economic analysis of law, I did not mention that many law professors in the United States of America say that economics no longer dominates the runway of intellectual fashion as it once did. Some professors even talk about a 'crisis' in the subject.[5] A radio commentator allegedly summarized the evening news by saying, 'The political crisis in Germany is serious but not desperate, and the political crisis in Italy is desperate but not serious.' The alleged 'crisis' in law and economics is not desperate, because its institutionalization continues unabated. Nevertheless, deficiencies in the subject are serious enough to impair the realization of its full potential.

One of the most thoughtful commentators on the economic analysis of law, Robert Ellickson, believes that theory has outrun fact in this field.[6] Ellickson thinks that the economic analysis of law creates too many models and tests too few of them. His remedy is a dose of empirical research motivated by insights more than models, a method exemplified in the 'law and society' movement. My approach in this lecture complements Ellickson's. Theory explains by narrowing attention to recognized causes. Consequently an incomplete theory may prevent a researcher from perceiving all the facts. The economic analysis of law has X-ray vision, not peripheral vision. I believe that incompleteness in economic theory prevents researchers from perceiving facts that psychologists and sociologists regard as central to law. In the next section I explain why.

CORE

Economists usually assume that people maximize something – consumers maximize utility, firms maximize profits, politicians maximize votes, bureaucracies maximize revenues, charities maximize social welfare, and so forth. Theories that assume maximizing have proven useful in predicting behaviour. Economists often say that these models succeed because maximization models rationality and most people are rational. Evaluating this claim requires an understanding of economic rationality. Different people

54

want different things, such as wealth, power, fame, love, virtue or happiness. One conception of rationality holds that rational persons can rank alternatives according to the extent that they give them what they want.[7] Rationality further requires choosing the highest ranking alternative that is available. It would be irrational to do worse by your own standards when you can do better.

Choosing the highest ranking alternative that is available can be described mathematically as maximizing. Just as the person ranks alternatives from worse to better, so the real numbers can be ranked from small to large. To represent the ranking of alternatives mathematically, create a 'utility function' to associate better alternatives with larger numbers. Next, partition the set of alternatives into the available alternatives and the unavailable alternatives. Represent the partition mathematically as a constraint upon the utility function. Choosing the best available alternative corresponds to maximizing the utility function subject to the feasibility constraint. For example, the consumer who goes shopping probably thinks of him or herself as trying to get as much of what he or she wants as can be afforded, and that behaviour is represented as maximizing his or her utility subject to his or her budget constraint.

The maximum of a function is often located where its derivative equals zero, or, in economic jargon, where costs and benefits equalize at the margin. Economists realized this fact when they joined utilitarianism and calculus in the late nineteenth century. The result was the 'marginalist revolution' which gave economic theory its modern form. Subsequent developments have built upon the late nineteenth-century foundations without discarding them. It seems that the marginalists got the foundations right, whereas attempts at mathematical economics before the marginalists went nowhere.

Maximizing suggests that an agent calculates and tries to do the very best that he or she can. Much of what people do that lands them in court, however, is uncalculated or even irrational. Think of rationality as a continuum with irrationality at one end and hyper-rationality at the other. Market competition extracts a harsh price for diminished rationality. Consequently, highly competitive markets approach hyper-rationality, as demonstrated, for example, by applications of the efficient market hypothesis to stock markets. At the other end, some torts and crimes occur when the injurer's rationality has diminished so far that the behaviour seems irrational. Economics has traditionally focused on high levels of rationality. Economic scholars now debate vigorously how to model diminished rationality.

Turning to the second concept in the core of economic theory, no habit of thought is so deeply ingrained among economists as the urge to characterize each social phenomenon as an equilibrium in the interaction of maximizing actors. An equilibrium is a pattern of interaction that persists unless disturbed by outside forces. An equilibrium is stable if the system tends towards it when out of equilibrium. To illustrate, the snow pack in a mountain's bowl is in stable equilibrium, whereas the snow pack on the

55

mountain's side is unstable. Economists usually assume that interactions tend towards a stable equilibrium, regardless of whether they occur in markets, elections, clubs, games, teams, corporations or marriages. An actor who tries to maximize and succeeds has no reason to change his or her behaviour. An interaction is an equilibrium when no one changes his behaviour. Consequently, an equilibrium exists when all actors maximize simultaneously. Conversely, an actor who tries to maximize and fails will change his or her behaviour. An interaction is not an equilibrium when someone changes his or her behaviour. In general, 'maximum' and 'equilibrium' are conceptually connected.

Social theorists often debate the relationship between the individual and society. Sociologists sometimes argue that the group is more than the sum of its parts, just as an animal is more than the sum of its head, torso, and limbs. Many sociologists believe in constructing theory from concepts like 'role' or 'class' that allegedly detach themselves from the goals of individuals and acquire their own life. At the other extreme, some psychologists practice methodological individualism, which reduces the study of groups to the behaviour of individuals. Unlike these approaches, an equilibrium does not detatch from individual behaviour or reduce to individual behaviour. Rather than detaching from individual goals, an equilibrium necessarily allows individuals to attain their goals. Rather than reducing to individual behaviour, an equilibrium cannot exist except in a group. For example, the market price depends upon the interaction of many buyers and sellers, who pursue their own self-interest. So does the unemployment rate or the inflation rate. Economists do not think that they can explain prices, unemployment or inflation until they construct a model of interacting individuals whose equilibrium accurately predicts the phenomenon in question.

'Equilibrium' describes a precise relationship between individuals and society, whereas popular metaphors often fail scrutiny. To illustrate, answering the question, 'Is society more than the sum of its parts?' requires comparing two numbers. What is to be added to arrive at the sum? The metaphor seems inappropriate because society lacks a metric. Similarly, comparing the society of bees to an organism makes sense, because genetic identity directs different bees in a hive towards the same goal, much as it directs different cells in a healthy body towards the same goal. However, comparing human society to an organism makes little sense, because people compete intensively with each other. Like bees, people perform roles, but unlike bees, people often subvert roles. Any social theory that omits competition among individuals leaves out the engine of change. Similarly, comparing the roles of bees to the functions performed by the parts of an automobile engine makes some sense, because bees perform their roles rigidly. A worker-bee does not change his mind and become a soldier-bee. In contrast, people commit to roles tentatively and perform them flexibly. A person may quit a job as a worker and become a soldier. A theory of human roles must explain what keeps people in them.

56

A system headed towards a stable equilibrium reaches its destination unless diverted by outside forces. In markets and social life, outside forces often divert an interaction before it reaches equilibrium. Nevertheless, an equilibrium analysis makes sense methodologically. The simplest pattern of interaction to analyse is one that does not change. Tracing out the entire path of change is far more difficult. Microeconomic theories of growth, cycles, and disequilibria exist, but they have received little application to law so far. The basic approach in law is 'comparative statics' in which the equilibrium under one legal rule is compared to the equilibrium under another legal rule.

The core concepts of maximization and equilibrium concern social interaction, not specifically market interaction. These concepts could have been developed in political science or psychology, rather than in economics. Consequently, I think of these two concepts as part of the core of behavioural theory. Turning to the third concept in the core of economic theory, economists often evaluate an equilibrium according to its efficiency. A production process is said to be efficient if it is impossible to produce the same amount of output from fewer inputs, or it is impossible to produce more output from the same inputs. Another kind of efficiency, called 'Pareto efficiency' after its inventor, concerns the satisfaction of individual preferences. A particular situation is said to be Pareto efficient if it is impossible to change it so as to make at least one person better off (in his or her own estimation) without making another person worse off (again, in his or her own estimation). In general, Pareto efficiency asks whether someone can be made better off without making someone else worse off.

DISTRIBUTION

I will suggest, but not fully explain, why 'efficiency' is more central than 'distribution' to the economic analysis of law. Almost everyone agrees that the state should pursue policies efficiently rather than inefficiently, but many people disagree about policy goals concerning the distribution of income. Some people think that government should redistribute wealth from rich to poor for the sake of social justice, whereas other people think that government should avoid redistributing wealth. Like other people, economists disagree among themselves about redistributive ends. Consequently, economists fail to reach a consensus over the measure of distribution to place in the discipline's core. Unlike other people, many economists agree about redistributive means. Most economists who study law believe that redistributive goals can be accomplished better in modern states by progressive taxation than by reshuffling legal rights in such fields as torts, contracts, and crimes.

I can mention only a few of the reasons why economists believe that broad-based taxes are a better tool of redistribution than private or criminal law.[8] First, redistributing a dollar from one group to another uses some of it.

57

Redistribution by courts uses much more than redistribution by taxes. To illustrate, a plaintiff's attorney in the United States of America routinely charges one third of the judgment, whereas an accountant who prepares someone's income tax return charges a small fraction of the person's tax liability.

Second, redistribution by legal rights elicits more unproductive behaviour than redistribution by progressive taxation. People change their behaviour in unproductive ways to avoid the costs of redistribution and secure the benefits. To minimize unproductive responses, public finance economists urge the state to raise revenues from taxes with a broad base. Legal liability corresponds to a tax with a narrow base. To see why, assume that the state wishes to take income away from the owners of capital and given it to people with low income. The state could pursue this goal directly by taxing dividends. Alternatively, the state could pursue its goal indirectly through liability law. To be concrete, consider holding pharmaceutical companies absolutely liable for harmful side effects of medicinal drugs. Taxing dividends or holding pharmaceutical companies absolutely liable will cause people to change their behaviour in unproductive ways. To illustrate, taxing dividends will cause corporations to retain more profits, and pharmaceutical corporations will respond to absolute liability by refusing to market some drugs or by transferring production to partnerships. The principles of public finance predict that absolute liability of pharmaceutical companies will cause much larger, unproductive changes in behaviour than taxing dividends at the equivalent level.[9]

Third, the actual redistributive effects of adjusting legal rights may not be the anticipated effects. To illustrate, imagine that the state enacts a law imposing absolute liability on pharmaceutical companies in order to transfer wealth from stock holders to consumers. The legislators hope that increased tort awards will be paid by the owners of pharmaceutical stocks. In reality, the pharmaceutical companies may shift these costs to consumers by increasing the prices of drugs, rather than lowering dividends.[10] In general, predicting the redistributive effects of liability law depends upon unraveling complex causal linkages.

Fourth, redistribution through legal rights may involve excessive 'leakage'. Leakage occurs when some rich people obtain part of the funds intended for redistribution to poor people. In general, leakage occurs because the law cannot exclude unintended beneficiaries. To illustrate, assume that drivers are richer than pedestrians on average. Noting this fact, lawmakers decide to redistribute income from the relatively rich to the relatively poor by holding drivers strictly liability for accidental harm to pedestrians. However, some cases will arise in which the pedestrian is wealthier than the motorist, in which case the liability rule will redistribute income from the relatively poor to the relatively rich. This problem arises because liability correlates imperfectly with income.

58

These three basic concepts – maximization, equilibrium, and efficiency – are fundamental to explaining behaviour in institutions that co-ordinate interactions among people. Nevertheless, critics of economic analysis doubt that these concepts can explain law. They ask, 'Isn't it better to describe psychology than to prescribe rationality?' 'Why stress equilibria instead of change?' 'Isn't the aim of law justice, not efficiency?' Quine observed that the core of a science consists of nearly tautological propositions.[11] A tautology, such as 'All husbands are married', describes a convention about how to speak and reason. The core of economics is a formal mechanism of reasoning, with sufficient flexibility to generate alternative models. The alternative models may generate contradictory predictions. Testing contradictory predictions against facts confirms one model and disconfirms another. However, the core of economics, which generated both models, is not confirmed or disconfirmed.

Economists yawn when psychologists announce that empirical research shows that people do not compute their marginal costs and benefits. Like Quine, most economists believe that prediction occurs on the periphery of a science, not in the core. Critics who imagine that their observations disconfirm the core of economics have confused formality and reality. The core of economics should be praised or criticized according to its power to generate predictive models. The relevant question is whether more powerful models come from describing psychology rather than prescribing rationality, or stressing change rather than equilibria, or postulating that law aims for justice rather than efficiency.

Names that refer to some objects can be understood by pointing to them, such as saying 'cat' and pointing to a cat. Other concepts, like 'democracy', 'melody' or 'square root' cannot be conveyed by ostensive definition. Instead, mastering these terms typically involves practising their use, especially mathematical terms like 'square root'. Similarly, you cannot fully understand what economists mean by 'maximization' until you work through some maximizing models. Critics who have never worked through the models typically underestimate the flexibility of the core concepts of economics, rather like a person who knows the dictionary definition of a French word but cannot speak French. Before attacking the core concepts of the economic analysis of law, a critic should go through the intermediate step of understanding them.

Above the core and below the skin of an apple lies its meat. The meat of economics is a collection of concepts concerning what people maximize (self-interest, profits, votes, and so on), the form of the equilibrium (perfect competition, monopoly, strategic, and so on), and the type of efficiency (Paretian, cost-benefit, utilitarian, and so on). In my opinion, the 'meat' of economics lacks some essential nutriments to nourish social science. Specifically, economics 'takes preferences as given' which means that it does not attempt

59

to explain how people acquire their goals. Economics needs a theory of 'endogenous preferences' to explain how people decide what to maximize. The absence of such a theory keeps economics isolated from developmental psychology and theories of social reproduction.

In the next section, I suggest how to begin correcting this deficiency. Economists typically assume that a person pursues his or her self-interest as he or she perceives it. Whatever advances a person's goals serves his or her perceived self-interest. Consequently, self-interest presupposes personal goals, including the central values by which a person defines him or herself. A person acquires values by internalizing them. Internalized values are essential to morality and law. Economics offers no account of how internalization occurs. In other words, economics offers no account of how a person becomes the self in which he or she is interested. I will next discuss how economics might acquire such an account.

THICK SELF-INTEREST[12]

Max Weber argued that protestant Christians regard occupational choice as a religious calling, which causes people to internalize occupational roles. Internalization of occupational roles increases the dedication and creativity with which people pursue business goals. Dedication and creativity enable people to co-operate together in large organizations that apply technical knowledge and achieve scale economies. According to Weber, the protestant ethic brought the discipline of the monastery into the conduct of business, which perfected instrumental rationality as a mode of behaviour and created the industrial revolution.[13]

I restate Weber's claims in the language of modern economics. The need for many people to co-operate in a complex economy creates problems of information and motivation. For example, each employee in a large organization that applies science to production works under the direction of others and gets paid a fraction of the value that he co-operates in producing. The 'agency problem' is to design organizations and contracts to elicit effort and creativity from such workers. Eliciting effort and creativity requires aligning the self-interest of agents with the principal's interests. But, the narrow self-interest of agents never aligns perfectly with the principal's interests. The agency problems become manageable in modern economies because people internalize occupational roles, which broadens their self-interest. When subordinates internalize occupational roles, they require less monitoring by superiors. Less monitoring lowers the transaction costs of contracting and managing hierarchies. Thus internalization of occupational roles is the ultimate form of decentralization, which prevents the constraints of information and motivation from strangling the modern economy.

Internalizing an occupational role involves accepting the norms of an occupation so intimately that they enter the individual's self-conception. As

60

soon as an individual takes norms into his or her self-conception, he or she distinguishes two kinds of self-interest. The simplest self-interest, which I call 'thin self-interest', looks only to objective payoffs in wealth or power. The more complex self-interest, which I call 'thick self-interest', modifies objective payoffs to encompass the subjective value of morality. For example, many lawyers pursue power and wealth through their profession. In addition, some people aspire to be 'good lawyers', meaning people whose work embodies the virtues of the legal profession. The virtues of the profession include both its ethical standards and its technical craft.

Internalizing a role 'thickens' self-interest to include the obligations and goals of an occupation. Thus, the best workers express themselves by showing who they are through their work. Their work shows who they are by reflecting what they have internalized. Contemporary economics has nothing to say about self-expression through work. Self-expressive acts have meaning. The goals and feelings of the actor are the act's meanings for him. Thus, a theory of thick self-interest must be both a theory of behaviour and a theory of meaning. Economists often describe their subject as a 'behavioural science'. Other social sciences have recently returned to interpretivism and hermeneutics. The thick self provides a bridge between behavioural theory and theories of meaning.

ENDOGENOUS PREFERENCES

Psychologists have extensively studied the internalization of norms. Piaget, Kohlberg, and others sketched stages in the development of moral reasoning among children.[14] According to their theories, a child perfects the ability to internalize norms as she or he acquires a capacity for abstract reasoning. Their research makes internalization sound cool and rational. In contrast, 'depth psychology' often traces internalization of morality to irrational processes that are hot and inchoate. According to these theories, internalization of morality ingrains new impulses in a child through emotional experiences. An example is Freud's theory of morality as the 'ghost in the nursery', meaning the repressed memory of parental punishments.[15]

Both types of internalization – accepting reasons and ingraining impulses – create new motives, which can tip the individual's motivational balance. Economic models often view motivation as a calculus of psychological benefits and costs. Internalization can change the sign of the net psychological benefits attached to an act. For example, internalization of morality creates subjective costs to non-co-operation that can shift the dominant strategy in a game from non-co-operation to co-operation.[16] Internalization of norms changes preferences and decisively affects behaviour. However, economic theory cannot explain internalization or predict its occurrence. Filling this gap requires a theory of endogenous preferences linking economics and developmental psychology. A theory of endogenous

61

preferences requires the expansion of decision theory to encompass the choice of who to become. Choosing among selves involves distinctive problems from choosing among commodities.

When self-interest thickens, conflicts arise between the thin and thick selves. For example, a lawyer may feel torn between being a 'good lawyer' and getting rich by shady means. Internal conflict, which is the subject of much psychology and moral philosophy, has only recently found a place in economic models. Economists usually assume that an actor chooses by ordering alternatives from better to worse. When modelling internal conflict, the actor chooses by drawing from a probability distribution over different orderings of the alternatives. One ordering might represent the thin self, the other ordering might represent the thick self, and the probability distribution might be determined by the actor's strength of will.[17]

RATIONAL VERSUS REASONABLE

The focus of economics on thin self-interest creates paradoxes, two of which I will discuss briefly. An independent judiciary is created by providing judges with life tenure, fixed salary, unpredictable promotion prospects, and the duty to remove themselves in cases affecting their material interest. The independence of the judiciary prevents judges from pursuing money, power or other aspects of narrow self-interest. Consequently, an unanswered question in the economic analysis of law is, 'What do independent judges maximize?' As long as economics focuses upon thin self-interest, this question is unanswerable. Instead of maximizing thin self-interest, independent judges typically express their own political and legal vision through their decisions. Their behaviour cannot be explained without a thick theory of a person's interests.

Similarly, voter participation rates in general elections cannot be explained by a thin theory of self-interest. As the number of voters increases, the probably that any one person's vote will influence the outcome of the election approaches zero. But, the opportunity cost of voting, in terms of time and effort, bears little or no relationship to the size of the jurisdiction. Therefore, a theory based upon narrow self-interest would predict much lower rates of voter turn-out in large jurisdictions than actually occurs in democracies. In reality, citizens vote in such elections to express their political preferences, not to gain material advantage. Consequently, the explanation of voting in large jurisdictions requires a thick theory of a person's interests.

The difference between thin and thick conceptions of self-interest relates to a fundamental tension between economics and law. The ideal economic decision maker is 'perfectly rational' which means utterly instrumental in pursuing explicit ends. The ideal legal decision maker is 'completely reasonable' which means that he or she has internalized social morality. The rational actor's self-conception is thin, whereas the reasonable actor's self-

62

conception is thick. Without a thick conception of self-interest, economic analysis cannot answer important legal questions about reasonableness. Adjudicating the reasonableness of professional norms involves weighing the benefits and costs of internalization. For example, how far should a fiduciary go in subordinating his or her interest to the beneficiary's? As another example, most crimes cannot be committed accidentally or by the insane. These crimes presuppose criminal intent or 'mens rea'. To have criminal intent, the actor must know the difference between right and wrong, and choose to do wrong. The contribution of economics to understanding this problem will remain modest until decision theory encompasses psychological conflict between right and wrong.

EVOLUTION OF NORMS

Having discussed the internalization of norms by individuals, I will now discuss the evolution of norms in communities. The modern economy creates many specialized business communities, which may form around a technology, such as computer software, a body of knowledge, such as accounting, or a particular product, such as credit cards. Sociologists since Durkheim have tried to explain how the division of labour binds people together and facilitates co-operation, rather than fragmenting workers and promoting industrial strife. The answer concerns the way business communities generate norms. People develop relationships with each other through repeated interactions in a community, and norms arise to co-ordinate their interaction. The formality of the norms varies from one business to another. Self-regulating professions, like law and accounting, and formal networks like Visa, promulgate their own rules. Voluntary associations, like the Association of Home Appliance Manufacturers, issue guidelines. Informal networks, such as the computer software manufacturers, have inchoate ethical standards. (Elsewhere I refer to all such norms of business communities as the 'new law merchant'.)

Sociologists sometimes use 'norm' to mean 'typical' or 'modal' behaviour, but I use the term to mean 'obligatory behaviour'. For a community to have a customary norm, the obligation must achieve a minimum level of control over the behaviour of the community's members. Otherwise, the community does not have the customary norm in question. A customary norm affects behaviour when people internalize it. Internalizing a norm changes preferences in ways that I described as the 'thickening' of self-interest. Consequently, a customary norm emerges in a community when it is internalized by enough of its members.

Why do some games evoke a sense of obligation in the players concerning the strategies that they follow? I can only sketch an answer here.[18] Imagine a sequential game involving two players and two moves. The first player invests or does not invest. Subsequently, the second player co-operates or appropriates. The first player will not invest unless he believes that the second player will co-operate. Therefore, the second player wants the first player to believe that she will co-operate, regardless of what she actually plans to do. Consequently, the second player will endeavour to signal 'co-operation'.

Now, embed this two-person game in a market with many participants. The participants consist of many 'first players' who want to invest, and many 'second players' who want to find an investor. All second players endeavour to signal 'co-operation'. Since everyone follows the same signalling strategy, the game has a 'pure signalling equilibrium'. A signal represents a player as following a particular strategy. A player who represents himself as following one strategy may actually follow another. Specifically, a player who represents herself as co-operating may actually appropriate. In a 'mixed equilibrium', some players co-operate and others appropriate. The people who co-operate form enduring relationships and secure a modest pay-off in most rounds of the game. The people who appropriate form temporary relationships (the investors exit immediately after appropriation) and secure a large pay-off in a few rounds of the game. Appropriators receive no pay-off in most rounds while they search for an investment partner. In equilibrium, both strategies earn the same average rate of return.[19]

More co-operation in the investment game will elicit more investment, which is productive and benefits all the players. Such external benefits, which all players enjoy, can be called 'local public goods'. Thus, the investment game has an equilibrium in which the players signal that they will supply a local public good. The community benefits from local public goods, so people concerned with its welfare will want to increase the supply. These people will say that everyone ought to co-operate. Saying that everyone ought to co-operate, including yourself, will become part of the way that a person signals necessary co-operation. As explained, everyone signals co-operation, including the appropriators. Consequently, a consensus will arise in the community that people who play the game ought to follow a co-operative strategy. This consensus will convince some people to internalize the obligation and inculcate it in young people. Thus a norm will arise. Generalizing, I formulate the alignment theorem: a social norm will evolve in a community when private incentives for signalling align with a local public good.

An interesting fact about the game, which I cannot explain here, concerns how internalizing the norm increases the supply of local public goods. People who internalize a norm typically cause the equilibrium to shift so that more people conform to it. However, the equilibrium does not shift because the person who internalizes the norm conforms to it. Rather, the equilibrium shifts because the individual who internalizes a norm typically becomes willing to enforce it on others.[20]

This account of the evolution of norms can address important questions in sociology, which I illustrate by two examples. First, consider Lévi-Strauss's application of Durkheim's ideas about social solidarity to tribes.

64

Tribes expand the scope of co-operation by creating cross-cutting and over-lapping systems of kinship.[21] Kinship provides a framework for repeated interaction, which can be modelled as a repeated game. Repeated games enable co-operation, such as solving the prisoner's dilemma, whereas the corresponding one-shot game has a non-co-operative solution. Furthermore, repeated games often satisfy the conditions for the emergence of norms as specified above in the alignment theorem. Kinship and the state are substitutes in the sense that both provide a framework for co-operation and normativity.

Secondly, consider the domination of one group by another. Domination often results in economic exploitation. For example, the dominant group may form a cartel to suppress labour market competition from the subordinate group. By suppressing competition, the cartel can pay subordinate workers less than the competitive wage. Economic studies have long revealed the instability of cartels. Cartels are unstable because, while the cartel benefits all sellers as a whole, each individual member of the cartel gains an advantage from defecting.[22] Norms backed by sanctions are required to prevent defection from cartels. This is true in business or social life. This is why domination typically requires support from internalized social norms, rather than being based upon pure power. For example, the domination of women by men probably requires most men and some women to believe in the rightness of patriarchy.

According to the theory of norms developed here, the group dominating ethical debate and moral education must sustain a consensus about the public good in order to stabilize its position. The account of norms developed here can help explain how the dominant social group can stabilize itself through the evolution of appropriate norms. Sustaining a consensus requires a game with a pure signalling equilibrium. The signalling equilibrium loses its purity when someone gains an advantage by signalling defection from the norm. Once the signalling equilibrium loses its purity, the norm may decay and the cartel may unwind. In these circumstances, the norms required to sustain domination will not persist spontaneously, so the dominant group cannot sustain its position without backing by state power.

Economists are often accused of ignoring social power, partly because no one has the power to affect prices in perfectly competitive markets. In general, game theory predicts how people act when they have the power to influence each other. A tension sometimes develops between the competitive market approach and game theory as economists increasingly analyse organizations and institutions. Tension develops because the competitive market approach emphasizes the optimality of private interaction, whereas game theory sometimes finds multiple, sub-optimal equilibria. Multiple equilibria inject arbitrariness into outcomes, and sub-optimal equilibria invite intervention by state authorities. To illustrate, the corporation can be regarded as a nexus of perfectly competitive contracts, in which case the state's proper role is to enforce the private contracts. Alternatively, the corporation can be regarded as a principal-agent game with market failures,[23] in which case the state may impose regulations to correct the failures. As another example, the 'new utilitarians' like Ellickson see social norms as tending towards efficiency in small groups, whereas many feminists see social norms as tending towards subordination of women.[24]

CONCLUSION

I have suggested how to thicken the concept of self-interest in order to encompass the internalization of norms and the endogeneity of goals. Doing so will bring together economics and developmental psychology. I have also suggested now developing a theory of the evolution of norms based upon the positivist tradition in legal theory. Doing so will bring together economics and sociology.

Unification requires acknowledgment of core concepts used to explain all interactions. The concepts of maximization and equilibrium form part of the core of behavioural theory. While all social sciences should recognize the core of behavioural theory, each of the social sciences should retain its specialized theory. The assumption of exogenous preferences is special to economics. This assumption must be ejected from the core of unified social theory. In general, the unification of social science requires the separate disciplines to abandon their sovereignty, but not their identity. The model of unity is a federal system like the evolving European Community, not imperialism and not separate sovereignties.

NOTES AND REFERENCES

1 This section is based upon ch. 1 of R. Cooter and T. Ulen, *Law and Economics* (2nd ed., 1994).
2 W.M. Landes and R. Posner, 'The Influence of Economics on Law: A Quantitative Study' (1993) 36 *J. of Law and Economics* 385–424.
3 R. Coase, 'The Problem of Social Cost' (1960) 3 *J. of Law and Economics* 1.
4 D. Baird, R. Girtner, and R. Picker, *Game Theory and the Law* (1994).
5 This loose talk is hard to document. The study that I mentioned earlier found some indication of a slowing in the exponential growth of citations to articles applying economics to law. See Landes and Posner, op. cit., n. 2.
6 R.C. Ellickson, 'Bringing Culture and Human Frailty To Rational Actors: A Critique of Classical Law-and-Economics' (1989) 65 *Chicago-Kent Law Rev.* 23–55.
7 Hence the joke: Economist arrives at her office. A colleague asks, 'How's your husband?' She replies, 'Compared to what?'
8 For a model of why the state should not pursue distributional goals through civil law, see L. Kaplow and S. Shavell, *The Efficiency of the Legal System versus the Income Tax in Redistributing Income* (Harvard working paper no. 130, 1993).
9 The distortionary effect of a tax depends upon the taxed good's elasticity of supply and demand. The broader the base, the lower the elasticity. Drugs with harmful side effects for some people are a narrower base than dividends. Also note that dividends are a

66

narrower base than income, which is why most economists prefer for the state to raise money by a tax on all income. To keep the comparison fair, we must compare taxes on different bases that raise the same amount of revenue for the state. The phrase 'at the equivalent level' refers to the level that raises equivalent amounts of money for redistribution. For an exposition of the principles of public finance, see P. Musgrave and R. Musgrave, *Public Finance in Theory and Practice* (1976).

10 Note that capital must earn the same rate of return in all forms of investment in the long run, so consumers will assuredly pay for higher liability awards against companies through higher prices for products in the long run.

11 W. von Quine, 'Two Dogmas of Empiricism' in *From a Logical Point of View* (1953) 20–46.

12 This section is based upon my lecture, 'Prices and Obligations' at the *Seminar D'Actualitat Juredica: 'Dret, Economia i Empresa Juridica'*, Justice Department of Catalonia, Barcelona, 17 March 1994.

13 M. Weber, *The Protestant Ethic and the Spirit of Capitalism*, tr. T. Parsons (2nd ed., 1976).

14 L. Kohlberg, 'Moral Stages and Moralization: The Cognitive-Developmental Approach' in *Moral Development and Behavior: Theory, Research, and Social Issues*, ed. T. Lickona (1976) 31–53; L. Kohlberg, 'Stage and Sequence: The Cognitive-Development Approach to Socialization' in *Handbook of Socialization Theory and Research*, ed. D.A. Goslin (1969); L. Kohlberg, *The Philosophy of Moral Development: Moral Stages and the Idea of Justice* (1981); L. Kohlberg, 'Appendix. The Six Stages of Moral Judgment' in *The Philosophy of Moral Development: Essays on Moral Development*, vol. I (1981) 409–12. Flaws in Kohlberg's approach have generated much criticism from feminists, notably Carol Gilligan, *In a Different Voice: The Psychology of Women's Development* (1982) 8 and 16–17.

15 In Freud's account, morality is the repressed memory of punishment and threats from the father. In technical terms, the super-ego emerges when the child represses his Oedipal fears. See S. Freud, *The Ego and the Id* (1962), tr. J. Riviere, revised and edited by J. Strachey. A clear discussion of these ideas is provided by R. Wollheim in 'The Last Phase', ch. 7 of his *Sigmund Freud* (1971).

16 See R. Cooter, 'Structural Adjudication and the New Law Merchant: A Model of Decentralized Law' (1994) 14 *International Rev. of Law and Economics* 215–31.

17 A model with citations is found in R. Cooter, 'Lapses, Conflict, and Akrasia in Torts and Crimes: Towards An Economic Theory of the Will' (1991) 11 *International Rev. of Law and Economics* 149–64.

18 For a more complete development of this game, see Cooter, op. cit., n. 16.

19 By definition, an evolutionary equilibrium exists when all strategies actively played earn the same average rate of return.

20 In equilibrium, the strategy of conforming to the norm receives the same expected pay-off as the strategy of violating it. Consequently, a person who stops violating the norm and starts conforming to it will cause someone else to stop conforming and start violating. The net effect is nil. However, a person who starts punishing other people who violate the norm will cause the expected pay-off to fall for violators. To restore an equal expected rate of return to violators and conformers, the number of violators must fall.

21 A good review of how Lévi-Strauss extended Durkheimian ideas of social solidarity to kinship is in M. Harris, *The Rise of Anthropological Theory* (1968).

22 To illustrate, the oil-producing nations benefitted as a whole from a cartelized world price for oil, but each individual oil producing nation benefitted even more from secretly discounting oil prices below the level set by the cartel. Individual nations benefit from offering secret discounts because the volume of their sales soars. Consequently, the OPEC cartel unravelled.

23 To contrast these two theories, see L.A. Bebchuk (ed.), *Corporate Law and Economic Analysis* (1990): for example, contrast F. Easterbrook and Daniel R. Fischel, 'The corporate contract' pp. 182–215 with H. Hansmann, 'Ownership of the firm' pp. 281–313.

24 R.C. Ellickson, *Order Without Law: How Neighbors Settle Disputes* (1991).

JOURNAL OF LAW AND SOCIETY
VOLUME 22, NUMBER 1, MARCH 1995
0263–323X

Horatio's Mistake:
Notes on Some Spaces in an Old Text

MAUREEN CAIN*

INTRODUCTION

This paper is based on the discovery of an old course outline and booklist, a discovery forced by my terror at being asked to review a field (socio-legal studies) from whose literature and debates I had been separated for seven years.

What I discovered in this archive of how I interpreted the field in 1974 were three immense silences. First, the reading of jurisprudence was sociological. I invited the students to consider how these ways of thinking law would impact on the beliefs and practices of lawyers and judges. Such an approach side-lined the legal texts. Secondly, there was nothing on women or gender. Not a single book authored by a woman was recommended and the only book about women[1] was used as an example of pressure group politics: a gender-blind analysis in the context of an androcentric theory.

Finally – and this time the absence was total – there was nothing on the underdeveloped world. What I taught my students, about was so called 'primitive' peoples: the Barotse, the Ifugao, and the Tiv.[2] Of course I did it in a way which romanticized their practices, and of course I criticized the anthropological approach for constructing closed systems, bubbles of ideally untouched 'primitivism' within an irrelevanced colonial context. But the fact remains that the voice of the modern third world was not heard. I did not even note its non-existence. As I shared the progressive romantic's mourning for the loss of primitive innocence, the possibility that modern, up-to-date, relevant knowledge could flow from the 'them' to the 'us' did not occur to me.

This paper looks very briefly at the ways in which the first two of these gaps have been filled, before moving to an extended discussion of the implications of including the less developed world. Most crucially, the

* Professor of Sociology, University of the West Indies, St. Augustine, Trinidad, West Indies

I wish to acknowledge the value in making this formulation of a discussion sparked off by my colleague Brian Alleyne.

68

jurisprudential gap has been filled by a postmodern reading of texts. The gender gap has been filled with feminist arguments, most importantly in this context involving debates about alternative epistemologies and how to change relationships when the main weapon available is words. Both these new knowledges have fed into my former students' own efforts to formulate an ontology and epistemology which are adequate to the task of making socio-legal sense from a third-world and downsider perspective, a task which is necessary because existing theories are demonstrably inadequate. In the fourth section of the paper, I attempt to demonstrate that inadequacy and, in conclusion, I attempt to move forward theoretically in a way that builds on both postmodern and feminist insights, while identifying and acknowledging the limitations of these positions.

AFTER FOUCAULT: POSTMODERNISM AND THE STUDY OF LAW

In the United States of America, the Harvard-based Critical Legal Studies Group identified early mentors in such diverse anti-positivists as Foucault, Derrida, and Unger[3] and by 1982 was confident enough to forge an alliance with those who might be happy to be called unreconstructed progressive lawyers.[4] Long-standing concerns with the ways in which established classes and powers manipulate the law to disempower or control the downsiders were able to cohabit comfortably, it seemed, with the efforts of the Harvard group to demonstrate both the autonomy and the infinite malleability of the text.

The postmodern condition came much later to British law schools. Moreover, the failure to institutionalize socio-legal studies in social science faculties meant an absence of that concern with social relationships which defines sociology, at least, as a discipline.

Goodrich, Jackson, Douzinas, Warrington and McVeigh, and, to a lesser extent, Fitzpatrick reveal more the influence of later postmodern theorists, such as Lyotard whose position feeds this lack of concern with structure.[5] Lyotard not only shared with his predecessors and with feminist sociologists of the same date[6] an abhorrence of the totalitarian powers of totalizing discourse, preferring diversity, disagreement, and tolerance; he also claimed ontological primacy for speech and text:

> . . . I choose language games as my general methodological approach. I am not claiming that the entirety of social relations is of this nature – that will remain an open question. But there is no need to resort to some fiction of social orgins to establish that *language games are the minimum relations required for society to exist.*[7]

In the discontinuous and various beginnings there is only the word. I wish to engage with this later in this paper by arguing from another place. Here, however, let us note the contradiction involved in a claim for primacy from any non-hierarchic, pluralistic, postmodern position.

69

Douzinas and colleagues put it this way in the introduction to their book:

[Post-modernism] refuses to accept that there is a 'real' world or legal system 'out there', perfectly formed, complete and coherent, waiting to be discovered by theory.[8]

I have given the whole quotation in fairness to the authors but the second half is polemical rather than theoretical. However, many social scientists do believe that there is a real world out there, albeit unknowable with certainty.[9] Nobody, of course, thinks of the 'world out there' as static or finished or necessarily coherent. And very few people, these days would conflate the 'world out there' with any *knower's* human, historical, discursively restricted and constructed knowledge of it.[10]

In sum, then, postmodern jurisprudence has sidelined the former central question of jurisprudence: 'what is law?' Instead, we are invited to consider how texts may be or should be read. This has centralized the previously absent texts of the law as objects not only of jurisprudential but also of sociological and socio-legal investigation. However, the primal ontological status accorded to texts (or discourses) in these works needs revision before the other gaps can be filled.

WOMEN'S KNOWLEDGES OF THE LAW

Within feminist analyses, postmodernism has been both influential and non-hegemonic, in part because feminist socio-legal scholars have commonly gone beyond the legal texts to consider also the discourses deployed by members of powerful ocupational groups such as lawyers, social workers, and prison officers.[11] In the exploration of such occupational discourses the relational nexus in which speaker and hearers are enmeshed never loses its importance. The context makes the discourse possible, and also shapes what it is heard to say by both participants and analyst.

The clear political purpose of much feminist scholarship has encouraged both transgression of disciplinary boundaries and a refusal to restrict analysis to a pre-determined set of texts.[12] Perhaps the most important explanation for the plurality of feminist methods within socio-legal studies has been the fact that postmodernism fed into a set of concerns that had happened without it, and a practice born of a political/theoretical need. Thus, it was welcomed[13] because of an already present practical insistence among women on mutual acceptance within women's groups, raised to a theoretical level by bell hooks, and Stanley and Wise.[14] The debate within feminism has been between rival pluralistic conceptions of how knowledge is to be produced. Do we emphasize the privilege or necessity of a downsider perspective, or do we buy in to the full postmodern package as a way of dealing with the differences within the downsider group?[15] This non-prescriptive philosophy has freed women 'on the ground' to be inventive and open both theoretically and technically. This is why feminist socio-legal

70

studies are in a healthier state than masculinist ones: broader based and seeking to learn from rather than to destroy those arguing a different position. Thus women themselves have filled to overflowing what was a mere gap in my 1974 curriculum.

ENTER THE DOWNSIDERS: POSTMODERNISM AND THE THIRD WORLD

European colonialism was invented in the Caribbean, and I will argue that exploring legal aspects of this colonial experience points up the absurdity of a choice between prioritizing text and prioritizing context in an attempt at understanding. Before approaching this question from a theoretical point of view, I shall here discuss it by means of three short empirical examples.[16]

In Trinidad, in 1849, the police were given powers to 'seize and carry away any drum, gong, tambour, bangee, or chac chac in use at any dance or assembly at any time on a Sunday or after 10 o'clock in the evening of any week day'.[17] It was allowed to play European instruments after this hour. Indeed, from 1654 when song and dance assemblies were banned in Martinique, to the turbulent years of the sugar crisis in the 1880s, there was a succession of such ordinances. In Trinidad, in 1883, ordinance no. 11 made:

> every Owner or Occupier, or their Agents responsible for the Rogues, Vagabonds, and such like, assembling in their yards or premises and singing or dancing to the music of drum, chac chac, or any other instrument.[18]

Both Rohlehr and Trotman explain this legislation on the grounds that the European population and the middle classes feared that drum playing and related festivities, whether among slaves or later among the free African and East Indian populations, provided occasions for meeting and fomenting trouble and rebellion.[19] According to Rohlehr both the 1739 rebellion in South Carolina and the 1816 uprising in Barbados started in just this way.

My second example concerns the Mohurram massacre of 1884. Mohurram is a festival in which events leading to the death of Mohammed's two grandsons are re-enacted. In Trinidad the occasion was celebrated by the East Indian population who had been arriving as indentured labourers since 1845. By the 1880s the festival was 'a mixture of piety and profanity'[20] involving not only the Muslim population but also Hindus and Africans. The latter group often helped to carry the brilliant Tadjah (ceremonial tombs) and joined in the drumming. Hosay was becoming popular as a national working-class festival. However, in 1882, an ordinance to control Indian festivals was passed. The regulations declared, among other things, that 'No other than an immigrant or the descendants of immigrants shall take part in any such procession'.[21]

In 1884 the customary march to launch the Tadjah into the sea at San Fernando assembled. The police barred the way to the town, and read the

71

© Basil Blackwell Ltd. 1995

Riot Act which the largely non-English-speaking, drum-beating participants either did not hear or did not understand or, in any event, ignored. The police fired. The official report indicated fourteen killed and another four or five 'likely to die'.[22] Singh explains the tragedy instrumentally, first in terms of the growing political and economic power (through strikes) of the East Indians on the sugar estates. But the Hosay processions posed no direct threat to the plantation owners. Rather, Singh continues, their concern was with the multi-racial and multi-ethnic character of the festival. A united working class would have posed a real threat. Hence the denial to Africans of the right to participate, an example, Singh argues, of the social construction of racism in Trinidad.[23]

However, in both these cases something else was happening too. There was more to the policing of culture than the response to a political or economic threat. Rohlehr's entire six hundred pages document the 'struggle by the "respectable" and "decent" class of people to impose what they considered to be a "proper" style on what they termed the fanaticism, noise, or discord – the Afro-based style'.[24] The official report on the Mohurram massacre explains:

> They came on waving their sticks and yelling . . . Those in front were dancing and leaping in a most diabolical manner.[25]

What appears to be insistently present in both cases is a nameless rage at the sheer difference of the sounds and movements, at their incomprehensibility, at their otherness which could only be made sense of by the denial of full humanity to their creators. So these other noises were outlawed. Thus, the police were 'unfortunately required to fire' at thirty yards on the Mohurram procession.[26] The non-sense of others makes sense of the police action, and the debate can proceed as to whether or not the firing was 'as moderate as possible'.[27]

Without a postmodern understanding of these sounds and movements as powerful in themselves, as presenting an ontological challenge to the European which did not depend on a relational nexus for its potency, this persistent pattern of culture policing throughout the region cannot be adequately explained. Indeed, the challenges could only be explained away, as politics or as economics, whereas they need to be grasped in their own right as a statements of alternative identities: uncaused and integrally powerful.

So, the Caribbean needs postmodernism. But the acute labour shortage which brought the East Indians to Trinidad after emancipation also produced quite directly its own crop of ordinances. After emancipation the 'habitual idlers' ordinance' was used to harrass back to the land 'every person wandering abroad'.[28] After indentureship began in 1845, frequent disputes over the terms of this new relation led to the imprisonment of 987 East Indians between 1849 and 1854, breach of contract being conceived not merely as a civil wrong. And so on until the British warships came to 'supervise' the oil-field workers' strikes of a century later.[29]

72

Plainly, then, sense needs to be made of some aspects of colonial law and law enforcement in the time-honoured, instrumentalist way. There was a need for labour. The state – legal rules, courts, police, prisons – was harnessed to assist capital in meeting that need. The discourse may have been legal, but the relational underpinning seems here to over-determine the text. In the Caribbean, therefore, it does not make any kind of sense to choose either the one mode of explanation or the other. Both are needed, which is to say that apparently incompatible ontologies must needs be reconciled.

HORATIO'S MISTAKE

In resolving the conundrum of needing two ontologically opposite positions in order to make adequate sense of law in the Caribbean region, I have leaned heavily on feminist insights and, in particular, on my own feminist reading of Foucault.[30] It is necessary to argue, with Foucault, that knowledge – discourse – text – culture are (a) uncaused and (b) integrally powerful. Knowledges cannot be explained as 'caused' by relationships. Indeed, any search for origins such as causes is itself methodologically inappropriate.[31] Foucault also argues that discourses constitute and embody their own, inherent powers: they do not depend for their powerfulness on the structural locations of their spokespeople. Foucault also argued, however, that the articulations of discursive relations with both primary, extra-discursive relations, and secondary relations needed to be mapped.[32]

Mapping non-causal articulations is difficult because mapping is itself a knowledge process, and extra-discursive relations exist in a different onto-logical plane, forever itself, which is not and never can be knowledge. It is a truism today that there is a radical separation between knowledge and what can be known. This is the case whether what we are trying to know is a text or an extra-discursive relationship. Representation is not possible: theoretical knowledge is so many signifiers in search of a signified (which they will eventually constitute as external to themselves). The kind of realism which is adequate to an understanding of the past and present of this one small Caribbean nation must be sufficiently sophisticated to take all this for granted. But there was more to enslavement than the fact that the slaves did not understand the traders' speech and purposes nor they the slaves'. In that sixteenth-century African silence, there was at work a relational power. The vision (discourse) to which this power was harnessed, which was con-tinually shaping it, was not known in the terror and loss of the capture: nor did the captors know the culture of the stolen. That unknowingness on their side has persisted for five hundred years. The downsiders, perforce, have had to learn their captors' thoughts; and they have built up relationships within which and from which their own discourse can now be heard to be uttered.

That was a story. Let us return to the rational mode, and explore the two fallacies of epistemological primacy and epistemological privilege. The

73

fallacy of epistemological primacy was Horatio's Mistake. He believed that nothing existed in heaven and earth that could not be thought of. Epistemological primacy is the position about which Lyotard reserved judgment: the notion that human knowledge calls the world (or in weaker versions, just the social world) into being. This reduces reality to what is or may be known. In spite of its rhetoric, it achieves the same conflation of the signified with the signifier as empiricism, only in reverse fashion. Instead of privileging ontology and arguing for the immediate knowability of the externally real, it privileges epistemology and argues for the reduction of the externally real to knowledges and their products.

In a weaker version, epistemological primacy is reserved only for social relationships. Because human knowledge enters into their production, relationships are deemed to be capable of being conflated with that knowledge as it and they are continuously re-known.

Epistemological privilege argues that since the world, including the social world, is not presentable in discourse, it has no potency outside of discourse. Therefore all struggles for power can be interpreted as (and reduced to) discursive struggles. Because knowledge enters into the production and use of beliefs, the power of the bullet is the same as or arises from the power of its signifier.

I take issue with this arrogant placing of human knowledge at the centre of the universe, and argue instead for an autonomous existence for the material world, in which I include not only untouched stars and virgin forest, artefacts with a knowledge component such as houses, fields, cakes, gardens, radios, bicycles, and income tax forms, but also social relations. My argument hinges on the inherent powerfulness of social relations as well as of other artefacts. I agree that some relationships have impacted powerfully upon people before they were available to discourse/knowledge.[33] The examples I always use are drawn from Harding's account of how sexual harassment as a pattern of relationships preceded its naming, and from the identification of the near universal female experience of pressurized sex by Kelly and her research subjects.[34] Relationships with the power to cause discomfort pre-existed knowledge/discourse of them. Now that they are 'known' they may be changed, but that is another theoretical story.

This attempt to challenge empirically the fallacies of epistemological primacy and epistemological privilege has often been experienced by my socio-legal friends as an embarrassing lapse, as if perhaps I was not familiar with post-Derridean arguments. So, for those who cannot accept an empirical argument about unthought and unspeakable relationships which yet have (so much) power, let me now discuss relationships of which we can think.

Here too the argument is that a social relationship is no more capable of being represented in discourse than any other reality. Why should the theory of representation be preserved in ancient aspic for this one aspect of the extra-discursive world? Rather, we need an ontology which recognizes that social relationships have a status independent of discourse, although the way we speak them articulates with how we live them. Sometimes social

74

relationships refuse to fit our discourse. This is quite common with marriages in the United Kingdom, it seems. For girls these frequently turn out to be less than their magazines had led them to expect: more, indeed, like the extra-discursive relationships in which they observed, with puzzlement and incoherence, their mothers to be enmeshed.[35]

Let me summarize these three claims.

(i) Social relationships have a being, an ontological status, independently of discourse.
(ii) Social relationships integrally involve in their very constitution relational powers, just as discourses integrally involve discursive powers.
(iii) Relations and their powers are not caused or called into being by discourse. Such a search for causal origins is no more useful in understanding relationships than it is in understanding discourse.

All this is to say that like discourse, social relations exist powerfully in a state of radical and uncaused autonomy. What is needed, therefore, methodologically, is a mapping of the articulations between relationships and knowledge/discourse or, if you will, between discourse and the extra-discursive. How can such a mapping be done if we acknowledge no representational possibilities for language? One aspect of such a post-scientific scholarly methodology will be non-causal theory.[36] We will also need techniques for the 'discovery' of hitherto unthought relations. Such scholarly strategies may form yet another contribution of the Caribbean to world culture, for it is here, as we have seen, that the dualistic conflict within western ontology most obviously needs to be transcended.

IN CONCLUSION

At home in Trinidad, I argue the need to embrace postmodern insights so that it will be possible to move beyond instrumentalism, and explain resistance and selective acceptance, as well as the 500-year-long oppression.

In the Metropole, I have the opposite case to make. I have to argue that even at the end of the twentieth century, there is more to the social world than we know, and that this will always be so because the social world is itself and our knowledge is only our knowledge. I have to argue that the texts of the law are powerful and demanding of archaeological and genealogical analysis, but that for an adequate genealogy, two or three other things are essential: a theory of the extra-discursive in general; particular theories of those extra-discursive relations which articulate with the legal text(s); and an ontology and a methodology which allow us to speak, albeit with humility and uncertainty, of social relations and their powers. Genealogy needs a sociology, as sociology has needed to understand the autonomy and power of the text.

NOTES AND REFERENCES

1 K. Hindell and M. Sims, *Abortion Law Reformed* (1971).
2 M. Gluckman, *The Judicial Process Among the Barotse of Northern Rhodesia* (1958); L. Hoebel, *The Law of Primitive Man* (1964); P. Bohannan, *Justice and Judgment among the Tiv* (1957).
3 M. Foucault, *Archaeology of Knowledge* (1972); M. Foucault, *The History of Sexuality, Volume 1: An Introduction* (1978). J. Derrida, *Grammatology* (1974); R. Unger, *Knowledge and Politics* (1975).
4 D. Kairys (ed.), *The Politics of Law: A Progressive Critique* (1982).
5 P. Goodrich, *Reading the Law: A Critical Introduction to Legal Method and Techniques* (1986); B. Jackson, *Seimiotics and Legal Theory* (1985); C. Douzinas, R. Warrington, and S. McVeigh, *Postmodern Jurisprudence* (1991); P. Fitzpatrick, *Mythology of Modern Law* (1992); J.-F. Lyotard, *The Postmodern Condition: a Report on Knowledge* (1984).
6 L. Stanley and S. Wise, *Breaking Out* (1983).
7 Lyotard, op. cit., n. 5, p. 15.
8 Douzinas et al., op. cit., n. 5, p. x.
9 For example, see R. Bhaskar, *The Possibility of Naturalism* (1979); M. Cain, 'Realism, feminism, methodology, and law' (1986) 14 *International J. of the Sociology of Law* 384; M. Cain, 'Realist philosophy and standpoint epistemologies OR feminist criminology as a successor science' in *Feminist Perspectives in Criminology*, eds. L. Gelsthorpe and A. Morris (1990); T. Woodiwiss, *Social Theory After Postmodernism* (1990).
10 Foucault's position is also capable of an interpretation which allows autonomy and potency to the extra-discursive: see, especially, Foucault, op. cit. (1972), n. 3, pp. 46 ff. See, also, M. Cain, 'Foucault, feminism, and feeling: what Foucault can and cannot contribute to feminist epistemology' in *Up Against Foucault*, ed. C. Ramazanoglu (1993).
11 H. Allen, *Justice Unbalanced* (1987); M. Eaton, *Justice for Women* (1986); M. Fineman, 'Implementing equality: ideology, contradiction, and social change' (1983) *Wisconsin Law Rev.* 789. A. Worrall, *Offending Women: Female Law Breakers and the Criminal Justice System* (1990).
12 In addition to works cited at n. 11, see also, for example, P. Carlen, *Women's Imprisonment* (1983); M. Cain (ed.), *Growing Up Good* (1989); M. Chesney-Lind, 'Judicial paternalism and the female status offender' (1977) 23 *Crime and Delinquency* 121; S. Noonan, 'Theorizing correction' (1992) 30 *Alberta Law Rev.* 719; C. Smart, *Feminism and the Power of Law* (1989); C. Smart and S. Sevenhuijsen (eds.), *Child Custody and the Politics of Gender* (1989)
13 In particular, see D. Haraway, 'Situated knowledges: *The Science Question in Feminism* and the privilege of partial perspective' (1988) 14 *Feminist Studies* 3.
14 b. hooks, *Ain't I A Woman: Black Women and Feminism* (1982); Stanley and Wise, op. cit., n. 6.
15 J. Flax, 'Remembering the selves: is the repressed gendered?' (1987) 26 *Michigan Q. Rev.* 92; S. Harding, *The Science Question in Feminism* (1986); S. Harding, 'Conclusion: epistemological questions' in *Feminism and Methodology*, ed. S. Harding (1987); M. Hartsock, 'The feminist standpoint: developing the ground for a specifically feminist historical materialism' in *Discovering Reality*, eds. S. Harding and M. Hintikka (1983); M. Nicholson, (ed.), *Feminism/Postmodernism* (1990).
16 The generic term 'downsiders' is taken from V. Kerruish, *Jurisprudence as Ideology* (1991). More extended examples are available in M. Cain, 'The policing of culture in Trinidad and Tobago and the Caribbean: Transcending the "modern" vs "post-modern" divide' (paper presented to the Law and Society Association, Phoenix, Arizona, June 1984).
17 C.R. Ottley, *An Historical Account of the Trinidad and Tobago Police Force from the Earliest Times* (1964) 38.
18 G. Rohlehr, *Calypso and Society in Pre Independence, Trinidad* (1990) 35.
19 D. Trotman, *Crime in Trinidad* (1986); Rohlehr, id..

20 K. Singh, *Blood-stained Tombs: The Mohurram Massacre of 1884* (1988).
21 Sir H.W. Norman, *Correspondence Respecting the Recent Coolie Disturbances in Trinidad at the Mohurrum Festival with the Report thereon by Sir H.W. Norman KCB* (1885).
22 id., p. 37.
23 Singh, op. cit., n. 20.
24 Rohlehr, op. cit., n. 18, p. 13.
25 Norman, op. cit., n. 21, p. 11.
26 id., p. 49.
27 id.
28 Trotman, op. cit., n. 19, p. 208.The strategy was used throughout the Empire; see, also, J. Wills, 'Thieves, drunkards, and vagrants: defining crime in colonial Mombasa, 1902-32' in *Policing the Empire*, eds. D. Anderson and D. Killingray (1991).
29 S. Craig, *Smiles and Blood* (1988).
30 M. Cain, op. cit. (1993), n. 10.
31 See Foucault, op. cit. (1972), n. 3.
32 id., p. 46.
33 See Cain, op. cit. (1990), n. 9.
34 S. Harding, 'Why has the sex-gender structure become visible only now' in *Discovering Reality*, eds. S. Harding and M. Hintikka (1983); L. Kelly, *Surviving Sexual Violence* (1988).
35 S. Lees, *Losing Out* (1988).
36 See Cain, op. cit. (1990), n. 9.

77

JOURNAL OF LAW AND SOCIETY
VOLUME 22, NUMBER 1, MARCH 1995
0263-323X

The Challenges of Socio-Legal Research on Decision Making: Psychological Successes and Failures

SHARI SEIDMAN DIAMOND*

Socio-legal research covers a rocky and varied terrain as it attempts to map out and analyse what Lawrence Friedman has aptly described as the 'loose, wriggling changing subject matter' that is law.[1] The challenges and value of interdisciplinary thinking about socio-legal concerns are nowhere more evident than in studies of legal decision making, a focus of particular interest to psychologists, sociologists, anthropologists, and others. Although much impressive research conducted squarely within those separate disciplines has informed our understanding of legal decision making, the most powerful contributions have been largely the work of researchers or teams of researchers educated in the academy or by independent study in approaching questions without disciplinary blinkers.

I do not mean that every informative piece of socio-legal research must be a United Nations production, mounted by a representative research team consisting of one sociologist, one economist, and so on. I do mean that our understanding of legal phenomena deepens when researchers take into account how scholars in other disciplines would approach the questions they are asking and the evidence for the claims they are making.[2] In the following analysis of research on legal decision making, I use my own disciplinary background in psychology to illustrate the particular challenges of socio-legal scholarship and the benefits that accrue from an interdisciplinary research perspective. I also consider the unfortunate consequences that psychologists studying legal decision making may encounter when their traditional discipline leads them to ignore social context and limits their attempts to understand how legal decisions are made.

THE PROTOTYPE STUDY OF DECISION MAKING

Whether a researcher is studying potential offenders, police, prosecutors, judges, or jurors, a standard approach examines the variations in decisions

* American Bar Foundation, 750 North Lake Shore Drive, Chicago, Illinois 60611, United States of America

that are associated with variations in the elements of the case or potential case that the decision maker is considering. Thus, is a prosecutor more likely to file charges when the defendant has a criminal record of violence than when the defendant has no previous record? Is a jury more likely to convict a defendant who does not testify than one who does? Is a citizen less likely to drink and drive if a law is passed mandating a minimum sentence for drunk driving? Do criminal sentencing guidelines eliminate inconsistency in judicial sentencing decisions? As the discussion below will demonstrate, such deceptively simple questions are not only difficult to answer but may also be answered incorrectly if the researcher addressing them fails to consider influential aspects of the decision making process.

LEAKY FUNNELS: COURT DECISIONS AND CASE SELECTION

Legal activity resembles a very leaky funnel: few entries that enter the formal legal system at the top make it out of the trial spout at the bottom. The events that disappear out of the sides of the legal funnel are likely to be quite different from those that stay. Yet, court outcome data are often the focus of research on legal decision making, in part because published results of court cases are more readily available than most other traces of legal decision making. There is a particular irony in this focus for studies of federal trial court decisions in the United States of America. Despite the mass of paper production associated with court activity, many federal courts publish only 60 per cent of their decisions. As Peter Siegelman and John Donohue have shown, the unpublished cases can differ substantially from those selected for publication.[3]

Even when no publication filter covers the spout of the legal funnel, leaks in the sides affect the outflow. The vast majority of civil filings are settled or dismissed before trial. In the criminal justice process, at least in the United States of America, most criminal charges are dismissed or disposed of with guilty pleas. The selection of cases that go to trial is not random. At the simplest level, guilty pleas are routine for some offences, less common for others. Similarly, characteristics of the evidence and the defendant along with accurate and inaccurate expectations about the particular decision maker (for example, the judge's reputation, beliefs about how juries react to doctor-defendants) affect settlement and plea agreements.

The complex selection pattern that leads to trial or sentencing has important implications for the traditional study of court decision making. In the prototypical study, the researcher examines the cases that survive to trial or sentencing and asks whether, for example, age affects the outcome for the defendant. Comparing the outcomes for defendants of various ages and statistically controlling for other characteristics, the researcher measures the effect of age. But selection affects the sample of cases being analysed and this chop-and-slice approach of looking only at cases available at sentencing can produce a substantially misleading picture.

79

Suppose, for example, that young defendants who co-operate with the prosecution are more likely than older defendants to have their cases dismissed so that the sentencing pool retains most of the older defendants but only the uncooperative young defendants. Unless the pattern of selection can be modelled by identifying and adequately measuring the determinants of selection, it will not be possible to adjust for these differences in evaluating sentencing decisions. As a result, what appears to be an effect (or lack of effect) of defendant age on sentencing outcome may be merely an artifact of the selection process. If the data are collected at the sentencing stage only, it is particularly likely that the appropriate measures will be unavailable so that the necessary statistical adjustments can be made. The outcome of this deficiency is that slice-and-chop studies leave more than their share of uncertainty.

The holes in the sides of the funnel divert even more if the funnel's potential catch includes disputes or injuries that may or may not mobilize the legal system. A recent survey in the United States of America questioned a sample of 1,706 citizen of whom just under 200 felt that they had received unsatisfactory medical care.[4] Not one had filed suit. As the landmark Oxford study of compensation and support for illness and injury was one of the first to show, successful mobilization of the legal system is a rare event indeed.[5] Harris and his colleagues, in a survey of over 12,000 households involving 35,085 members of the general public, identified 1,711 accident victims, only 12 per cent of whom obtained damages. It is not surprising that researchers rarely take on the task of tracing the progress of these potential claims from their informal roots to the rare formal disposition: it requires an unusual commitment in both time and resources.

CONTROLLED EXPERIMENTS ON LEGAL DECISION MAKING

Psychologists most often opt to avoid the costs of longitudinal research and the danger of attributing decisions to spurious factors by using the controlled experiment, conducted in a laboratory or field environment, in which all factors except the presumed cause under study can be held constant, or equally distributed across groups.[6] At their best, such studies can provide unambiguous tests of causal influence and insights into the process that cannot easily be obtained in other ways; often, they omit crucial aspects of the social context and produce a misleading picture of decision making.

The appropriate role for statistical evidence in decision making is the subject of an active debate among legal scholars in the United States of America and the United Kingdom.[7] Psychologists have accumulated a large body of research on judgments that reveals an under-use of base-rate information[8] and the preference of decision makers for clinical versus actuarial evidence despite the fact that the actuarial evidence provides more accurate predictions.[9] This research suggests that failures in rational use of

80

probability data are ubiquitous. It might come, then, as no surprise that legal systems generally preclude so-called 'negative statistical evidence' even when it apparently provides probabilistic evidence that exceeds the usual preponderance of the evidence standard required for a verdict in favor of the plaintiff. For example, the colour-blind plaintiff who is injured by a bus on a road where 80 per cent of the buses are green and owned by the Green Company and only 20 per cent are blue and owned by the Blue Company cannot, merely on the strength of those proportions, recover from the Green Company.[10]

Legal scholars have suggested several reasons for the rejection of probabilistic evidence in this case, including that an observer need not accept the 0.8 probability that the bus was green.[11] Gary Wells, a psychologist, in an ingenious set of studies, examined the subjective probabilities and the verdict preferences of respondents exposed to this evidentiary pattern. He found that even when respondents, both lay persons and judges, accepted the probabilities as described, they still resisted finding the defendant liable based solely on naked statistical evidence.[12]

Wells also considered an economic perspective on legal resistance to probabilistic proof. He tested the psychological implications of a suggestion from law-and-economics scholar Richard Posner[13] that the legal system's resistance to statistical proof stems in part from a recognition that adopting such a standard would produce a distortion of outcomes across cases. Applying a statistical probability calculus to each case would defeat the Green Company 100 per cent of the time even though, according to the probabilities, it should lose only 80 per cent of these cases. Wells evaluated this explanation by examining how respondents (again lay persons and judges) reacted to a case in which the probabilistic evidence came from the bus tracks left at the scene. The testimony indicated that if the Green Company was the perpetrator, the tracks would have matched 80 per cent of the time, eliminating the prospect of inappropriately saddling the Green Company with liability 100 per cent of the time if this type of evidence was accepted. Nonetheless, respondents in this study again refused to find for the plaintiff, suggesting that the antipathy of the legal system to explicitly probabilistic evidence as the sole basis for a verdict may have roots that are more psychological than economic.

The Wells studies illustrate the strength of a psychologist's approach to the study of legal decision making, in placing the crucial elements under a microscope and tightly controlling all else. The cost of that control emerges when the researcher fails to recognize, or is unable to include, aspects of the decision making context that would exert a powerful effect on the decision maker's behaviour, modifying the influence of variables that appear to determine decisions in the rarefied experimental situation. An example of this danger arose in one of the early studies of procedural justice. Researchers were interested in the effects of adversary versus inquisitorial systems on the production of evidence. In an elaborate simulation study, the participants

81

playing the role of attorneys were permitted to purchase bits of information. The study revealed that attorneys appointed to represent their clients purchased more information when initial facts were against them than did attorneys who were appointed by the court. The pattern was used to suggest the advantage of the adversary system for more thorough representation of a potentially disadvantaged defendant. Although the simulation included a number of limitations that might have influenced outcomes, two omissions raise some serious questions about the meaning of the results. In the study, the participants were involved with a single case and were given no option of settling or arranging a plea bargain. With no prospect of reallocating resources to more promising cases, as attorneys could have outside the laboratory, the participants were encouraged to invest their efforts in gathering information on the single case they were assigned to handle. Although the study cannot tell us how participants would have behaved if they faced a caseload of opportunities on which to invest their time, it is certainly plausible that alternative opportunities would have affected outcomes.

The controls of experimentation need not entail the sacrifice of context in studies of legal decision making. It is not hard to imagine an experiment, even one in the laboratory, that would simulate a caseload. Such a contextual variable could also be varied so that researchers could assess its ability to affect decisions and modify the effect of other variables.

In some areas, researchers have recognized the importance of attending to context. In creative investigations of public attitudes toward criminal sentencing, Anthony Doob and Julian Roberts, among others, have made context itself the focus of study. In doing so, they have identified some explanations for the public's disapproval of apparent judicial leniency in sentencing and offered some insights on how the public makes judgments about court behaviour. In one experiment, Doob and Roberts provided Canadian citizens with information about a recently sentenced defendant.[14] Half of them read a newspaper account and half read the court transcript. While 80 per cent who read the news account thought the judge had been too lenient, the figure was less than 15 per cent for those who read the transcript. Thus, they were able to show that disapproval all but evaporated when citizens were provided with a more complete representation of the sentencing context than the one that is generally available to the public.

THE INTERNAL FOCUS IN LEGAL DECISION MAKING

Another aspect of psychological research that contributes to an understanding of legal decision making arises from psychology's particular focus on process and individual perception. Objective aspects of the decision making context are transformed by decision makers who may, for example, attribute the defendant's alcohol use to internal or external factors, viewing it as an aggravator or a mitigator. Doob and Roberts' work illustrates the

82

value of exploring the perceptions of decision makers as well as their decisions. Research on judgment indicates that even if the news media accurately portrayed crime and sentencing, we might expect public impressions of criminal activity to be negatively biased because negative and extreme behaviours are more easily remembered.[15] When individuals respond to abstract questions about judicial leniency, as they generally do in public opinion polls, they are likely to think of particular cases and to be influenced by the severity of the cases and the offenders they recall. If recall is negatively biased, those negatively recalled instances should exert a disproportionate impact on impressions. When Doob and Roberts asked respondents who they had in mind when they were asked to evaluate whether courts were too harsh, too lenient, or about right, respondents who indicated that the courts were too lenient in sentencing offenders were more likely to report they were thinking about violent or repeat offenders than were respondents who indicated that the courts were about right.

Although decision makers often are unaware of, and cannot describe, what motivates their behaviour,[16] an examination of their explanations can often yield significant insights with powerful behavioural implications. Research on the psychological foundations of procedural justice reveals that litigants' evaluations of their treatment by the legal system may be determined as much by the opportunity to tell their story to an impartial decision maker as by whether they win or lose.[17] Moreover, Lind and his colleagues found that their perceptions had important behavioural consequences.[18] They examined the perceptions of litigants who participated in court-ordered arbitration. Following the arbitration, the litigants could accept the arbitrator's decision or go to trial. The researchers found that litigants' judgements about the fairness of procedures mediated decisions whether to accept the arbitration directive, and that these procedural justice judgements had a stronger effect on that decision than did either subjective or objective measures of the arbitration outcome.

CONCLUSION

It is relatively easy from a socio-legal perspective to criticize much psychological research purportedly designed to illuminate legal decision making. I have offered those critiques myself.[19] For example, the early jury studies that used student jurors and equated ratings of responsibility or years to be served in prison with decisions about guilt provide an easy target. Yet, the contributions and potential contributions of a psychological perspective to socio-legal research should not be underestimated by a focus on the failures of what is still a relatively new alliance. The failures merely point to the dangers of isolated disciplinary-bound research efforts and the value of the interdisciplinary approach championed by Oxford's Centre for Socio-Legal Studies.

NOTES AND REFERENCES

1   L.M. Friedman, 'The Law and Society Movement' (1986) 38 *Stanford Law Rev.* 763.
2   The Oxford Centre for Socio-Legal Studies has been and continues to be a leader in the kind of interdisciplinary thinking and research that maps the socio-legal domain.
3   P. Siegelman and J.J. Donohoe III, 'Studying the Iceberg from its Tip: A Comparison of Published and Unpublished Employment Discrimination Cases' (1990) 24 *Law and Society Rev.* 113.
4   M. L. May and D.B. Stengel, 'Who Sues Their Doctors? How Patients Handle Medical Grievances' (1990) 24 *Law and Society Rev.* 105.
5   D.R. Harris, M. Maclean, H. Genn, S. Lloyd-Bostock, P. Fenn, P. Corfield, and Y. Brittan, *Compensation and Support for Illness and Injury* (1984).
6   T.D. Cook and D.T. Campbell, *Quasi-Experimentation: Design and Analysis Issues for Field Settings* (1979).
7   L.J. Cohen, *The Probable and the Provable* (1977); D. Kaye, 'The Law of Probability and the Law of the Land' (1979) 47 *University of Chicago Law Rev.* 34; J. Koehler and D.N. Shaviro, 'Veridical Verdicts: Increasing Verdict Accuracy Through the Use of Overtly Probabilistic Evidence and Methods' (1990) 75 *Cornell Law Rev.* 247.
8   A. Tversky and D. Kahneman, 'Evidential Impact of Base Rates' in *Judgment under Uncertainty: Heuristics and Biases*, eds. D. Kahneman, P. Slovic, and A. Tversky (1982).
9   R.M. Dawes, D. Faust, and P. Meehl, 'Clinical Versus Actuarial Judgment' (1989) 243 *Science* 1668.
10 *Smith* v. *Rapid Transit* (1945) 317 Mass. 469, 58 N.E. 2d 754.
11 L.H. Tribe, 'Trial by Mathematics: Precision and Ritual in the Legal Process' (1971) 84 *Harvard Law Rev.* 1329.
12 G. Wells, 'Naked Statistical Evidence of Liability: Is Subjective Probability Enough?' (1992) 62 *J. of Personality and Social Psychology* 739.
13 R. Posner, *Economic Analysis of the Law* (1972).
14 A.N. Doob and J.V. Roberts, 'Social Psychology, Social Attitudes, and Attitudes Toward Sentencing' (1984) 16 *Can. J. of Behavioural Science Rev.* 269.
15 S. Fiske, 'Attention and Weight in Person Perception: The Impact of Negative and Extreme Behaviours' (1980) 38 *J. of Personality and Social Psychology* 889.
16 R.E. Nisbett and T.D. Wilson, 'Telling More Than We Can Know: Verbal Reports on Mental Processes' (1977) 84 *Psychological Rev.* 231.
17 E.A. Lind and T.R. Tyler, *The Social Psychology of Procedural Justice* (1988).
18 E.A. Lind, C. T. Kulik, M. Ambrose, and M.V. de Vera Park, 'Individual and Corporate Dispute Resolution: Using Procedural Fairness as a Decision Heuristic' (1993) 38 *Administrative Science Q.* 224.
19 S.S. Diamond, 'Foreword' in *Handbook of Psychology and Law*, eds. D.K. Kagehiro and W.S. Laufer (1992).

JOURNAL OF LAW AND SOCIETY
VOLUME 22, NUMBER 1, MARCH 1995
0263-323X

Global Approaches in the Sociology of Law: Problems and Challenges

VOLKMAR GESSNER*

INTRODUCTION[1]

The study of global aspects of law and legal institutions with a socio-legal frame of reference and with sociological methods looks overambitious and unmanageable. Scarce resources of our discipline and the marginal position of legal sociologists in the world of big business limit all efforts from their beginning. This explains why empirically little has been done so far and few internationally composed research teams have been successful. Theoretically, sociology of law tends to concentrate on municipal law and eventually to generalize national legal phenomena (legalization, informalization, materialization, decentralization, and so on) without taking global legal interaction between states, between firms, between individuals, or the legal activity of international organizations as an object of analysis. The law of the world society does not appear in our textbooks and is left to highly sophisticated, but sociologically uninformed discourses, among lawyers and economists. Legal sociology sometimes gives the impression that it adheres to a description of the world-system as lawless and spontaneous, not in Ovid's idealizing manner[2] but, rather, in Hobbesian understanding.[3] The hesitation in studying legal practices outside or above the nation state is unjustified, first, because they are becoming more and more important, and second, because from a theoretical, as well as from a political point of view, it seems unreasonable to know so little about them. The following brief remarks point to some peculiarities which have to be taken into account while entering this new field.[4]

* Faculty of Law, University of Bremen, D28339, Bremen, Germany

85

STRUCTURAL DIFFERENCES OF GLOBAL APPROACHES COMPARED WITH THE NATIONAL SETTING

1. *Legal actors*

In the national context, most legal interactions take place (in a horizontal relationship) between individuals and firms on the one hand, and (in a vertical relationship) between those actors and the state. This picture, familiar to everybody reading statistics about legal activities (in the court room, in the lawyer's offices, in state administration), changes dramatically as soon as we leave this context and approach the international arena. States globally appear as actors in horizontal relationships (in conflicts based on international public law and as members of multi-national consortia in large investment projects in conflicts based on private law) as well as in vertical relationships (in migration cases, customs, import control, credit insurance, and so on). Individuals are hardly visible as legal actors, the only exception being some trans-border claims for divorce, child support, and succession. In their role as consumers, they completely refrain from legal action across borders even where a single market (as in the European Union) has been created.[5] Most interesting is the role of big and multi-national enterprises and the banking sector. Although they are, economically speaking, by far the most important actors, they are inclined to put their legal claims into the background and work on the basis of mutual trust or economic dependence. It is then mainly the medium-sized firm which, on the one hand, lacks the dominant position to make law superfluous and, on the other hand, is strong enough to go into the global market and to use all necessary legal means to pursue economic interests. Such firms are the clients of the international law firms who design for them complex contracts, use international arbitration, and eventually even bring law-suits to national courts.

A different mixture of actors and their different use of law as a means of pursing interests has obvious consequences for socio-legal analysis: most nationally-verified hypotheses about actor's choices and preferences are of little value globally. Big firms and international organizations have hardly ever been the objects of empirical analysis in the sociology of law, but they cannot be neglected if global legal developments are to be observed and explained. Since the analysis of state behaviour in conflict-resolution has been left to other disciplines, there is no sociology of international law which deserves this name.[6]

2. *Institutional infrastructure*

Implementation of law is dependent on an adequate infrastructure which is a set of state or non-state institutions shaped by social values and priorities, and therefore different in the various legal cultures. In view of this great variation, it is no surprise that the legal culture of the world society has also

86

developed its characteristic legal infrastructure. Institutions such as the International Court of Justice or the International Law Commission, the European Court of Justice, International Organizations like UNCITRAL or UNIDROT, the International Chamber of Commerce, hundreds of more or less specialized arbitration courts, a network of international banks and insurance companies, consulates and foreign chambers of commerce, state agencies and academic structures rendering legal information about foreign countries, and last but not least, international law firms, offer their services for avoiding or resolving conflicts of public or private international law. The professional background of the staff, their working conditions, and their values differ considerably and exclude analogies with apparently similar national institutions. There is, in particular in the international law firm,[7] a strong common law influence, a proximity to capitalist interests and, correspondingly, a distancing from all kinds of welfare-state orientation. Public control or lay participation are absent, and decision-making, particularly in the arbitration business, is secret.[8]

3. *Stratification*

Whereas in most national studies legal sociology can make use of the class variable in order to explain legal phenomena, this makes little sense on the global level. The class variable can in a certain respect be replaced by north-south or centre-periphery classifications which are a trade-based label.[9] Other classifications in use[10] are income-based, resource-based, quality of life-based or block-based, but are all state-centred and cannot be used in a theoretically fruitful manner for non-state actors. Even for state conflicts, their explanatory power is limited due to the universal activities of multi-national enterprises and financial actors. One is inclined to define the relative weakness of parties for every single case taking into account that parties who are really weak simply do not participate in global legal interaction. But this renunciation of the use of stratifacatory variables would be a self-denial of sociology and should not be accepted too quickly.

In a functional perspective, stratificatory variables define the actor's chances to pursue his or her interests; those chances are obviously unequally distributed in the world of cross-border legal interaction. First one may distinguish between economic and all other interests and, due to the absence of welfare state considerations within the global legal infrastructure, give the former more chance of realization. Within the category of economic interests, it is obvious that the trans-national enterprise which dominates the global markets (its share of world trade being estimated at nearly 50 per cent) also relies to a smaller degree on legal structures than less powerful groups of actors. The relevant stratification for legal behaviour then begins below the multi-national or trans-national enterprise. It is defined as the chance to mobilize or create law through the use of the global legal infrastructure, and in particular the access to one of the big (mainly United States-

87

American) law firms. The legally relevant global stratification is a function of a network between repeat players, where contacts with important banks, diplomats, international law firms, and arbitrators are helpful, just as the success of global criminal behaviour is a function of a mafia network.[11] A fruitful classification would then consist of membership versus non-membership in the international legal network: small firms and individuals are typical non-members, larger firms may become members when they fulfil certain entrance conditions and tests of trustworthiness.

4. *Diversity of legal systems*

In the national context, it is only anthropological studies that are confronted with the problem of legal diversity when they deal with traditional customary law in the new states of Asia and Africa. In other areas of the sociology of law, the conflict of laws has never become a major issue. This will obviously have to change when the global level becomes the object of systematic, socio-legal observations. Socio-legal categories which compare legal systems not only descriptively, but with explanatory power, have to be elaborated. Little can be learned in this respect from comparative law[12] where, after a century of research, nothing is offered for the scientific classification of legal orders in the world other than the concept of legal families,[13] telling us that some legal systems are more related to each other than others. A decisive step forward is taken by those legal sociologists who develop legal indicators for a more informative comparison,[14] but they do not yet generate hypotheses about the behavioural consequences of differences by which legal systems are characterized. Questions like 'What advantages and handicaps brings a German lawyer into global interaction in comparison with a United States-American lawyer?'[15] or 'Why do plaintiffs prefer to sue in Germany instead of suing in their home country?'[16] cannot yet be answered by the legal indicators research. It does not make sense to fight for legal pluralism, as is now in vogue, without entering a discussion of the problems created by the diversity of legal systems. Legal science, at least, is critical about the consequences of legal pluralism and makes enormous efforts in order to unify or harmonize law.[17] It seems plausible that global legal interactions are substantially facilitated by these efforts; but if legal pluralists have good arguments against this position, it would be interesting to hear what they are. Recent research on the problems caused by the dramatic increase of European law within the European Community may be a good start for a discussion around social consequences of the unification or harmonization of national legal systems.[18]

Legal diversity certainly complicates research on global legal interaction, but it will also have a salutary effect on those socio-legal approaches which used to talk simply about 'the law', 'the legal system', 'the legal profession', and so on without taking into account their different shapes in the world. The specific characteristics of laws which come into play and compete with

88

one another in the global arena have to be taken much more seriously than when it is done in the national context.

CULTURAL DIFFERENCES

1. *Diversity of legal cultures*

Due to the dominant national focus and a lack of mental distance from our own national legal traditions, legal sociology has so far not been able to describe specific legal cultures as complex phenomena (or is at best still working with hundred-year-old Weberian categories).[19] Thus it lags behind neighbouring disciplines like psychology (intercultural communication), political science (comparison of political cultures), administrative science (models of public administration and bureaucratic intervention), and economics (business cultures, business environment, international management). In each of these, the specific characteristics of national cultures are compared through approaches which have a certain universalism.[20] As long as the legal cultures of the world cannot adequately be described, the explanation of global legal phenomena by cultural variables remains speculative and arbitrary, and leads some researchers totally to reject culture as an independent variable. This is contrary to tendencies in sociological theory and to socio-legal traditions which take values and the social construction of reality so seriously (in disputing processes, in legal decision making, and so on).

Legal cultural differences which may affect global legal interaction are to be studied on different levels: (i) the normative level, (ii) the level of professional and scientific interpretation of norms (supreme court decisions, legal science), (iii) the level of the implementation of norms by institutionalized actors (lower courts, public administration, interest groups) and (iv) the level of individual actors (lawyers, enterprises, citizens). A comprehensive view of a legal culture as a complex social phenomenon must take all four levels into account,[21] in order to move beyond superficial and inadequate levels of national prejudice. Some legal cultures realize legal objectives on the normative level, others in the phase of implementation, while others leave the regulatory initiatives and the struggle for justice on the level of organized or unorganized actors. It is therefore completely misleading to compare legal cultures only on the first two levels of statutes and professional and scientific legal opinions.[22]

There are good examples of the value of the cultural approach in the field of international lawyering, where often the common lawyer is compared either with the Japanese or with the continental lawyer, who differ in their legal education, societal role, professional regulation, and the cultural values. In situations of cross-border interaction, this often leads to misunderstandings between both groups of professionals. It also leads to the dominance

89

© Basil Blackwell Ltd. 1995

of the former due to their more creative approach in contract-drafting and dispute-resolution.[23]

2. *Global legal culture*

The comparison of different legal cultures around the globe seems to raise more problems that the description of a global legal culture. In studying the behavioural patterns of those few actors who dominate and shape the world market, one detects quickly a less normative orientation, a short duration of binding obligations and legal models in order to adapt to changes in the world market and political environments, and a low identification with particular legal systems or cultures. Norm obedience relies more on the reciprocity principle than on legal sanctions. This developing structure of the world-system has been described by Luhmann as 'cognitive', a behavioural pattern of readiness to learn, to accept the non-fulfilment of expectations, to adapt to new circumstances instead of insisting on contractual stipulations and statutory rules.[24] The complexities of the world require a more flexible and more understanding attitude towards the other than what is usual and adequate on the local or national context.

Legal literature on private and public international relations provides us with abundant data confirming this cognitive legal culture. The *pacta sunt servanda* principle is more and more subordinated to the *clausula rebus sic stantibus*; mediation is preferred to adjudication; flexible rules of the *lex mercatoria* replace national law; legal sanctions are neither offered nor required by the actors; contracts are adapted or simply put aside instead of taken as the basis for legal claims; contracts are in many occasions replaced by gentlemen's agreements in order to clearly define relationships as socially but not legally binding. Economic and political science literature, therefore, puts much more emphasis on problems of negotiation then on legal implementation and enforcement. This developing global legal culture stands obviously in sharp contrast with traditional legal attitudes and legal doctrines which cannot imagine the benefits of cognitive mechanisms and mostly do not recognize the law merchant. Global legal culture is therefore to be seen in a permanent tension with national legal cultures which try to reproduce globally what they conceive as normal and natural behavioural patterns.

THEORETICAL PROBLEMS

1. *World society as point of reference*

The legal regulations for and legal behaviour of international and cross-border exchanges are part of world society.[25] World society is the only conceivable reference point for attempts to explain global regulatory

90

processes and to criticize their results. In a systems-theoretical approach, the international legal system is a functional prerequisite of global inter-action since it provides behavioural patterns and models for decision-making. But world society, although being already a social fact, is poorly conceptualized by sociology.[26] Whereas the majority of social scientists still think of 'extra-societal' matters in terms of international relations, a decisive step forward has been to conceive world society as a stage where not only states, but also migrants, churches, media, merchants, interest groups, and mafias play a role.[27] What is unknown so far is their inter-relationship, their position in a global structure, and their cultural orientations. According to Luhmann, these actors communicate in globally differentiated systems (which has made world society the only possible one, since communication processes have made 'societies' and shared culture obsolete).[28] This position is not shared by Wallerstein who reduces the world-system to the utilitarian preferences of economic actors and to contracts and division of labour as their most prominent forms or goals.[29] Two decades of discussion of Wallerstein's 'economic reductionism' has led to more and more complex sociological approaches,[30] in particular, to the increased use of political and cultural variables and to the consideration of non-economic actors in the process of 'structuration' of the world order.[31] It is clearly this post-Wallerstein sociology which allows legal sociologists to build a global frame of reference for their empirical observations. Global legal actors at all levels create global social structures, but they are at the same time following economic (utilitarian), political (ideological), and cultural patterns which are still (in opposition to Luhmann) of basically inter-societal origin.

2. Normative order of the world society

The perception of the world outside the nation state as being anomic has long been overcome. As within the state, the world society also reveals highly regulated areas as well as areas where a normative order is absent or ineffective.[32] But this observation does not mean that the sociology of law may apply internationally the same models which have proven to have an explanatory power within the state-ordered society. Quite the contrary is true, since nearly everything is different. The differences are as follows.

(i) If, on the national level, state norms (laws) are dominant and autonomously created norms are complementary to them, it is the other way around in the international arena. The most visible and most effective normative order is the law merchant, the *lex mercatoria*.[33] State conventions complement this autonomous order, for example, by offe-ring contracting parties the United Nations Convention on the Inter-national Sale of Goods (Vienna Convention). As a consequence, the 'gap' problem of sociology of law is reversed: self regulation can now be taken for granted and legal sociological curiosity then has to be

91

directed to fields where exceptionally legal rules play an important role in structuring global behaviour.

(ii) The legal rules of the international arena are created in diffuse and non-transparent legislative processes (European Union, European Council, GATT, UNCITRAL, and hundreds of other international organizations) whose interests and political intentions are difficult to reconstruct.

(iii) Due to their decentralized production, many international norms are unknown even to legal institutions and legal professions. They often fulfil only symbolic functions for the reputation of international organizations and legal scientists.

(iv) International rules show a high level of abstraction and can neither be criticized from the point of view of specific interests and social problems, nor evaluated as to their implementation. Their interpretation is intended to be international, which is difficult to achieve due to the absence of a clear conception of a global common good and the welfare of mankind.

(v) Since international rules are generally not adapted to new developments, they soon become obsolete and are replaced by a new set of norms. Due to the frequent disappearance of the object of research, the critical role of sociology of law and its contribution to legal policy is therefore much more limited in world society than in national context.

EMPIRICAL PROBLEMS

1. Statistics

With few exceptions, such as the work load of the International Court of Justice (The Hague) and the European Court of Justice (Luxembourg), there are virtually no official statistics about international legal practice. This is also true for institutions of the law merchant, for example, the numerous courts of arbitration and mediation procedures. Domestic courts generally do not consider international cases as being worthy of special attention[34] and make it very difficult to select them for evaluation. Some published cases rather give a biased picture of their daily practice, in particular as regards the questions concerning the application of foreign law and international unified law.

2. Access to information

Because of their limited function in international matters, the traditional fields of socio-legal research (judges, lawyers, court files) give little information about cross-border legal interaction and no information at all about its

92

above-mentioned cognitive aspects. On the other hand, the infrastructure of the global normative order is administered with such a high degree of discretion (partly due to protection of economic interests and partly due to the illegal activities often involved in international exchanges) that access to data is very difficult to obtain. As a consequence, for example, the international banking sector, as well as international arbitration tribunals, have never been made the object of systematic empirical analysis.

3. *International law firms*

International law firms appear to be more accessible than the rest of the global legal infrastructure. These are characterized by their world-wide networks, their experience in contract drafting, their lobbying capacities with national and international institutions (in particular in the European Commission), and their knowledge of the law merchant and business practices. This key institution of the globalization process will be studied by legal sociologists[35] and may open other institutional channels for research.

THE OTHER SIDE OF THE COIN: THEORETICAL CHALLENGE

The sociology of the world society shows a rapid change within the international social field as it was conceived by Jean Bodin and held true until only recently, namely, a juxtaposition of sovereign states. On the one hand, the relationships between states have developed towards more co-operation within a great number of international organizations, leading to a differentiation of state functions in the global arena, and a loss of the absolute character of sovereignty.[36] On the other hand, a second arena of global interaction which keeps distant from governmental influences, develops its own structures and cultures and sometimes even lacks a territorial basis, has become more important.[37] This division into two (or more) different 'worlds', and the growing importance of stateless (autonomous) structures, has influenced also the normative conception of world order.

In the first half of this century, the general idea was that the world order would, in the long run, be shaped according to the national model of the rule of law ('world peace through law' movement). Since then, expectations rather go in the opposite direction: what we observe on the global level will be the future of national regulatory systems. There will be more cognitive orientation, more decentralized norm creation, more autonomy of political arenas, more cultural competition, hence less stability and less transparency of the normative order. If this holds true, world society is not just another field of socio-legal research, but rather the model for which we have to prepare our theoretical instruments. This is the intellectual challenge of doing global legal research.

93

NOTES AND REFERENCES

1   This article is dedicated to Don Harris for his global perspective in the institutionalization of the sociology of law.

2   Ovid, *Metamorphoses*, nos. 89 and 90: '*Aurea prima sata est aetas, quae vindice nullo, sponte sua, sine lege fidem rectumque colebat*'.

3   Max Weber 'solves' the problem of the historical existence of *Weltreiche* without Leviathan by discovering the cohesive role of prophets, priests, and religions in general, compare his *Wirtschaft und Gesellschaft* (1956) 346.

4   My experience in this field is also very limited. It stems from an ongoing empirical research project on cross-border legal interaction and from the organization of a postgraduate course on this subject in the Oñati International Institute for the Sociology of Law. When I was a practising lawyer, my experience with cross-border conflicts was rather catastrophic.

5   Compare Coopers & Lybrand Europe, *Handling of Cross-Border Consumer Disputes, Final Report for the Commission of the European Communities 1990* (1990). Non-American consumers sometimes take foreign enterprises to (United States) courts in order to claim exorbitant and often punitive damages based on product liability. These cases cannot be used to generalize the role of consumers in the global legal arena.

6   But compare two early works: B. Landheer, *On the Sociology of International Law and and International Society* (1966); V. Gessner, *Der Richter im Staatenkonflikt-Eine Untersuchung am Beispiel des Völkerrechtsverkehrs der Amerikanischen Republiken* (1969).

7   R.J. Goebel, 'Professional Qualification and Educational Requirements for Law Practice in a Foreign Country: Bridging the Cultural Gap' (1989) 63 *Tulane Law Rev.* 443–523; K.C. Crabb, 'Providing Legal Services in Foreign Countries: Making Room for the American Attorney' (1983) 83 *Columbia Law Rev.* 1767–1823.

8   There is only scattered socio-legal information we can refer to in this context, for example, Y. Dezalay, *Marchands de droit – La restructuration de l'ordre juridique international par les multinationales du droit* (1992), and 'The Big Bang and the Law: The Internationalization and Restructuration of the Legal Field' (1990) 7 *Theory, Culture and Society* 1–14; H.P. Glenn, 'Private International Law and the New International Legal Profession' in *Conflits et Harmonisation – Mélanges en l'honneur d'Alfred von Overbeck*, eds. W.A. Stoffel and P. Volken (1990); I. Taylor, 'The International Drug Trade and Money-Laundering: Border Controls and other Issues' (1992) 8 *European Sociological Rev.* 181–93; M. Bach, '*Eine leise Revolution durch Verwaltungsverfahren – Bürokratische Integrationsprozesse in der Europäischen Gemeinschaft*' (1990) 21 *Zeitschrift für Soziologie* 16–30.

9   I. Wallerstein, *The Modern World-System* (1974).

10 Compare L. Sklair, *Sociology of the Global System* (1991).

11 In relation to the last aspect, compare U. Santino, 'The Financial Mafia: The Illegal Accumulation of Wealth and the Financial-Industrial Complex' (1988) 12 *Contemporary Crises* 203–43.

12 Compare R. David, *Les Grands Systèms de droit Contemporains* (1950); R. David and J.E.C. Brierly, *Major Legal Systems of the World Today* (1978); K. Zweigert and H. Kötz, *An Introduction to Comparative Law* (1977).

13 For a critical discussion, compare L. Friedman, *The Legal System: A Social Science Perspective* (1975) 202; R. Abel, 'Law Books and Books About Law' (1975) 26 *Stanford Law Rev.* 175–228; I. Markovitz, 'Hedgehogs or Foxes?: A Review of Westinghouse and Schleider's *Zivilrecht im Systemvergleich*' (1986) 34 *Am. J. of Comparative Law* 113–35.

14 W. Evan, *Social Structure and Law* (1990) 156 ff.; A. Podgorecki, 'Social Systems and Legal Systems – Criteria for Classification' in A. Podgorecki, C.J. Whelan, and D. Koshla, *Legal Systems and Social Systems* (1985) 1-24; S. Krislov, 'The Concept of Families of Law', id., pp. 25–38.

15 The differences between United States adversarial justice and Continental managerial justice described by J.H. Langbein, 'The German Advantage in Civil Procedure' (1983) 52 *University of Chicago Law Rev.* 823–86, lead to very different professional experiences of

94

lawyers in both systems. The greater responsibility of United States lawyers in civil litigation certainly capacitates them more for the complexities of international dispute resolution.

16 This question did occur to us in ongoing research on the handling of international cases in German first-instance courts.

17 R. David, 'The International Unification of Private Law' in the *International Encyclopedia of Comparative Law* vol. II, ch. 5 (1971).

18 Compare V. Gessner, *'Wandel europäischer Rechtskulturen'* in *Lebensverhältnisse und soziale Konflikte im neuen Europa – Verhandlungen des 26. deutschen Soziologentages*, ed. B. Schäfers (1993).

19 It seems fair to mention that some 'exotic' legal cultures like the Japanese one have been described quite frequently and that the *International Encyclopedia of Comparative Law*, vol. II offers many interesting insights in a comparison of legal cultures. Compare, also, a recent small brochure by E. Blankenburg and F. Bruinsma, *Dutch Legal Culture* (1991).

20 The possible contributions of these cultural comparisons to legal sociology are discussed in V. Gessner and A. Schade, 'Conflicts of Culture in Cross-Border Legal Relations: The Conception of a Research Topic in the Sociology of Law' (1990) 7 *Theory, Culture and Society* 253–77; V. Gessner, *'L'Interazione Giuridica Globale e le Culture Giuridichi'* (1993) 20 *Sociologia del Diritto* 61–78.

21 This is the programme of a textbook by Volkmar Gessner, Armin Höland, and Csaba Varga, *European Legal Cultures* (1995).

22 For an excellent critique of comparative law for its lack of complexity, compare I. Markovitz, op. cit., n. 13.

23 A. T. von Mehren, 'The Significance of Cultural and Legal diversity for International Transaction' in *Jus Privatum Gentiom – Festschrift für Max Rheinstein*, eds., E. von Caemmerer, S. Mentshikoff, and K. Zweigert (1969) 247–57; L. Cohen-Tanugi, *Le droit sans l'état* (1985); D. Zhang and K. Kuroda, 'Beware of Japanese Negotiation Style: How to Negotiate with Japanese Companies' (1989) 10 *Northwestern J. of International Law and Business* 195–212. The classical comparison is still D. Rüschemeyer, *Lawyers and their Society* (1973) whereas too few comparative insights are to be found in R.L. Abel and P.S. Lewis (eds.), *Lawyers in Society*, 3 vols. (1988).

24 N. Luhmann, 'The World Society as a Social System' (1982) *International J. of General Systems* 8.

25 J.W. Burton, *World Society* (1972); W.L. Hollist and J.N. Rosenau, 'World Society Debates' (1981) 31 *International Organisation* 1.

26 K. Tudyka, *'Weltgesellschaft Unbegriff und Phantom'* (1989) 30 *Politische Vierteljahresschrift* 503–8.

27 Sklair, op. cit., n. 10.

28 Luhmann, op. cit., n. 24.

29 Wallerstein, op. cit., n. 9.

30 Compare, for example, R. Robertson, *Globalization – Social Theory and Global Culture* (1992); A. Bergesen, 'Turning World-System Theory on its Head' (1990) 7 *Theory, Culture and Society* 67–81.

31 A. Giddens, *The Consequences of Modernity* (1990).

32 B. Badie and M.-C. Smouts, *Le retournment du monde – Sociologie de la scène internationale* (1992) 112.

33 A. Goldstajn, 'The New Law Merchant' (1961) 12 *J. of Business Law* 12; C.M Schmitthoff, *International Trade Usages* (1986), and 'The Unification or Harmonisation of Law by Means of Standard Contracts and General Conditions' (1968) 17 *International Comparative Law Q.* 551–70; O. Lando, 'The *lex mercatoria* in International Commercial Arbitration' (1985) 34 *International Comparative Law Q.* 747–68. Many authors either deny the legal quality of the *lex mercatoria* or reject assumptions about its effectiveness.

34 It seems to be a rare exception that the Hamburg district and family courts have created special sections for international matters.

35   Some first results in Y. Dezaley and D. Sugarman (eds.), *Professional Competition and the Social Construction of Markets: Lawyers, Accountants and the Emergence of a Transnational State* (1993).

36   R. Knieper, *Nationale Souveränität* (1991).

37   Badie and Smouts, op. cit., n. 32; J. Rosenau, 'Patterned Chaos in Global Life: Structure and Process in the Two Worlds of World Politics' (1988) *International Political Science Rev.* 357–94.

JOURNAL OF LAW AND SOCIETY
VOLUME 22, NUMBER 1, MARCH 1995
0263-323X

On Old and New Battles:
Obstacles to the Rule of Law in Eastern Europe

ANDRAS SAJO*

INTRODUCTION

After the collapse of communism the new political leaders promised democracy and the rule of law. Certain efforts were made to rewrite the codes and reform the administration of justice. Nevertheless, after five years of reshaping law, society, and economy, one wonders to what extent one can speak of a market-oriented, rule-of-law, efficient legal system in most post-communist countries. The radical transformation of a legal system is always part of the social transition. To the extent that a 'Western' legal system is related to a market economy and to a set of patterns of social interaction and cultural traditions, the incompleteness of the legal transformation will not surprise the sociologist of law. Even if the law in the books has been changed (with many shortcomings) into something non-communist, the impact of the official law on society is often different from the role which law plays in social control or conflict resolution in the West. This short essay will attempt to list a few social factors which contributed to the delays in transforming the legal systems in Eastern Europe, and particularly those which contributed to the lack of refashioning law into a rights-enforcing mechanism. Except otherwise stated, eastern Europe includes east-central Europe, although country-by-country differences might be enormous.

The non-accomplishment of a rights revolution is part and consequence of a set of interdependent factors. Perhaps it has to do with the non-revolutionary nature of the transition process. The lack of a rights-friendly political culture, the absence of good manners among the new élites, and the aggressiveness of the powerful, were important factors in these developments. These psychological factors are related to structural problems which are related primarily to the historical nature of the new emerging states.

* *Professor of Law, Central European University, Budapest 1021, Huvösvölgyi ut 54, Hungary*

First, in a number of cases, these states are the means to a new aggressive statehood for nations which were deprived of national identity, or at least for states which feel menaced by minorities. In the aftermath of communism, the existence of some new states is based on the denial of citizenship to many of those residents who were citizens under the previous regime for a considerable period of time. (Latvia and Estonia are the best known cases with regard to Russian minorities.)

Second, aggressive nationalism resulted in increased popular and, exceptionally, official or officially tolerated, unrepressed *anti-minoritarian aggression*. Anti-semitism is present in a fair number of the countries and anti-gipsy sentiments resulted in discrimination and violence nearly everywhere without strong official condemnation or intervention. Even if action is taken, it seems to be problematic from the rights perspective; generally the hate-speech prohibitions are cast aside, and therefore free speech and political freedoms are endangered. It is perhaps one of the great contradictions of post-communism that because of the legacy of the past, and because of the vulnerability of the emerging social and political structures which do not enjoy entrenched popular support, there is a general feeling that without *firm restrictive action* on the part of government, authoritarianism and racism cannot be stopped by government.

According to this approach, there is simply no time to allow the social menace to disappear, since history shows that the emerging societies do not yet have sufficient power or mechanisms of self-defence against intolerance. It may well be true that in other societies more speech is the remedy for false or even defamatory speech, but in eastern Europe, there is no time for more speech: we are sitting on a time bomb. The danger of this approach is that the insistence on quick solutions by government will perhaps perpetuate the *inability of society* to develop ways of immunizing itself against extremism.[1] The lack of autonomous social action has a certain disturbing impact even at the institutional level.

Traditional human rights, like freedom of religion, may suffer because of that. The churches were deprived of their property and their believers are short of the means to support the churches which have limited resources, especially for activities beyond religious services, particularly when it comes to education.[2] The churches may continue to be dependent on the government of the day which in turn seeks support in exchange for governmental subsidies. Moreover, and again as a continuation of previous practices, the more established churches will seek government support to combat emerging new churches labelled as 'sects'. So far as freedom of speech is concerned, the press and media are still subject to specific governmental restrictions. In some countries the newsprint is rationed by government, and the financial dependence of the press results in repeated compromises between the Russian government and Moscow dailies. The editorial offices of the major newspapers in Moscow were provided by the government, so that when it sequestered the building, the press accepted the intervention in exchange for further subsidies.

Third, the emerging post-Soviet states are unstable and sometimes *pre-modern* in the sense that they lack a proper bureaucracy in the Weberian sense. This shortcoming has negative impacts on the legal system, in particular, that the law will not be certain and predictable. No clear hierarchical structures exist in the legal system, the law is incoherent, and statutes are disregarded by unclear governmental regulations.[3] There is no rule of law, and, under these circumstances, fundamental rights remain ideological commitments. Lack of efficient bureaucracy means denial of rights through unlimited discretionary powers of the officials, as well as lack of enforcement of rights.

DEPENDENCE OF THE STATE

Fourth, the nature of the post-communist state does not favour the development of rights protection. The state which was inherited from state socialism remains overwhelmingly strong, with concentrated managerial and economic powers. The state and its organizations are interested in maintaining the economic and cultural monopolies, while the political parties and the emerging economic elites share that interest. Political parties may offer government jobs as booty, and the new business élite is interested in the use of an undifferentiated state property where control over state assets is obtained through personal networking, bribery, and political control. Lack of civil society means that the citizens are still *dependent* on the state for most services. According to Grazyna Skapska, social inertia inherited from communism and the passive society is 'marked by individual helplessness and dependence on the state'. In this system politically determined *privileges* survive:

> which differentiate social groups according to political criteria, instead of universal rights. In turn, the interests of these groups become tied to the former, communist structures. It is no accident, therefore, that a significant impediment to the introduction of a free market, but also to the changes of the system of rights by guaranteeing the formal equality or rights, is posed by depriving certain groups of their privileges and job security, i.e., the communist party *apparat*, but also workers in the heavy industry sector.[4]

The state is perceived by the general public not as a rule-bound partner but as a provider of welfare services. Such expectations have their counterpart in the public perception of law as a means of social guidance, change, and so on. Instrumentalism meets little resistance as it is inherited from the socialist concept of law. *Instrumentalism* is concerned with consequences; law, therefore, is not regarded as an autonomous element of social control. It follows that rights are not serious obstacles in achieving the desired goals of the government through administrative regulation. Given the enormous

99

task of socio-legal transition and the limited amount of available resources, our modern Saint Anthony cannot resist the temptation to use the law as an instrument of social change.

Of course, the anti-rights trend of communist privileges may well prevail in a number of east-European societies, particularly in most post-Soviet countries, and, according to Skapska, in Poland. But perhaps it is of equal importance how the new equality of rights (restrictive as they may be) helps to create *new privileges and dependencies*. It should be added that the demolition of the rights structures, which were entrenched by communism, runs the risk of undermining the rule of law system and the belief in rights itself. Although it is true that respect for these 'previous' rights (for example, pension rights of the privileged) may undermine respect for the new legal and political system by seeming to preserve the previous regime.[5] The rule of law, in the countries where it existed, became a protective device of the former ruling classes.[6] Where this was disregarded in the name of unique historical justice, it did undermine the rule of law and the concept of rights.

INTERESTS IN MAINTAINING A DISTORTED MARKET

Fifth, the *emerging market economy* is seriously *distorted*. This has a tremendous impact on the meaning of rights in transactions and on the foreseeability of transactions. Many legal rules remain under-enforced and the administration of justice is unable to guarantee the enforcement of business transactions. Consequently, the state is considered both illegitimate and powerless so that it is neither a moral nor a practical problem to disregard official norms.

Disregard of the law is often accompanied by reference to extra-legal norms, but there is little inducement in everyday life to observe moral norms, either. Rights are often referred to by the emerging entrepreneurial élite as absolute limits on legislation and its application to their activities. Such reference to rights may remind us of the historical eighteenth-century function of rights, namely, the restriction of government power. However, these arguments are based on the total denial of any normative structure: 'they [the government authorities] have no right whatsoever to impose duties on us'. Rights mean that all private action, including those which delimit governmental privileges of trade, physical violence, and taxation, can be defied. The consequence is anomie with emerging mafia and mafia-like, self-regulating private structures. Sometimes these self-regulating groups are respectable professional and other interest groups; at other times, the respectable face of a professional association helps only to disguise illegal pressure on government to grant and protect monopolies.

Partly related to the above 'extra-legal' structures, whole spheres of social interaction are based on the avoidance of contacts with official law. This phenomenon is well known in the legal sociology of developing societies

100

where whole sets of sub-legal systems (informal law) develop, from the Brazilian *favela* to neighbourhood law in Cairo districts. Since the rights of the weak remain unprotected, they have to seek remedies outside the official legal system, often at the cost of accepting local authoritarianism. Guarantees of rights in official criminal procedure mean very little if local order is maintained by uncontrolled local torture and informal summary justice.

The efficiency of the law is further undermined by the nature of economic transactions and the resulting disrespect for legal rights. Transactions are carried out without reliance and trust – 'take the money and run' – and there is no long term contractual planning. Promises are not considered to be sources of duties and therefore they cannot create rights. Perhaps the origins of this phenomenon are to be found in the rules of a command economy 'in which individuals are freed of any responsibility for the consequences of their acts'.[7] Under the circumstances of post-socialist capital accumulation, the denial of responsibility (that is, the sense of obligation) has a social function in that the denial of other people's rights helps the economically superior party to externalize its costs.

All the above-mentioned elements of the non-legal justice system are related to the structure of the emerging, distorted market economy. In such an economy, some of the main advantages of a modern, rights-based, foreseeable, and transactional law do not serve the interests of the dominant actors who are concerned with *replacing law with sub-legal arrangements*, including private law enforcement. The old/new entrepreneurial classes are much less interested in legally-secured, transparent markets and much more in an economy where networking, rather than price indicators, matters.

CULTURAL FACTORS

The above-mentioned structural shortcomings could have developed, at least in part, because there is little civic interest or a culture of rights, including civil and political rights. With the exception of Poland, the human-rights-based criticism of the communist regime was limited to a minority which became marginalized. Moreover, the development of a faith in human rights is hampered by daily reports of unpunished violations of human rights world wide. Events in Yugoslavia, and Bosnia particularly, contribute to growing disillusionment.

It is well known that rights protection and reliance on impartial and public conflict-resolution mechanisms is a matter of cultural and social values and traditions. Certain human rights and procedures are not particularly attractive (for example, procedural complications in criminal procedure) as they are seen as protecting those who are labelled as 'undeserving' (the criminals, the foreigners, the 'others'). The whole idea of rights which are to be protected by courts is problematical for at least two reasons. First,

101

neither social and political nor inter-subjective or business relations are conceived in terms of rights, that is, as unconditional claims. The tradition is that one expects *protection as a favour* from the authorities, while business and other everyday social relations are based on favouritism, privilege, power, or (due to a different tradition) goodwill, and fairness based on solidarity. Second, *courts* and other official institutions are not considered by the public to be efficient or reliable protectors of needs and claims. This is not surprising given the structural, legal, and mental resistance to rights enforcement in the administration of justice. In the ordinary legalism of the courts, rights do not receive privileged treatment. People do not consider themselves as having claims *vis à vis* the authorities with corresponding duties of the authorities towards them. As we noted earlier, law is seen as a means for achieving social goals. Given the enormous task of socio-legal transition and the limited amount of resources, the temptation to continue with the instrumental use of law is irresistible.[8] Moreover, instrumentalism offers great opportunities to create privileges for those who are in charge of shepherding the herd on the road to change.

The constitutional provision of social welfare rights are more shocking to Americans than Europeans. Some European constitutions have an abundance of welfare rights, but it is telling, however, that the Spanish constitution, for instance, recognizes these rights as state policy objectives. However, in most eastern European countries, they are formulated as being directly enforceable in court. Some constitutions institutionalize clearly non-market solutions, as is the case with the 'adequate salary' provision in the Slovak Constitution or the right to free housing in Russia. The expectation of rights as free state services has a noticeable impact on other rights too. Welfare rights are provided at the expense of classic individual rights.

Instead of legalistic, rights-based-arguments or reliance on fundamental concepts of civic dignity, there is a *culture of complaint*.[9] Of course, there was no tradition of an individualistic morality which would have created a social value system supporting the vindication of individual rights. On the contrary, litigation is sometimes considered as trouble-making. A most persistent peasant tradition in Hungary is to avoid contact with official authorities, since law is seen as the trick of the gentry. This is still quite understandable as courts are not particularly eager in responding to rights claims. (In five years of democracy, there is not a single case in which an ordinary Hungarian court grounded its decision on the fundamental rights provisions of the Constitution). The processes are slow and compensation is often inadequate, even in cases of violations of human rights. The level of social dependence naturally changes from country to country and depends also on the social strata within the country. Moreover, as democratic institutions begin to take shape, there were spectacular developments in people insisting on their rights. But the process is not unilinear. In a period of early capital accumulation, and under the pressure of state economic

102

monopolies, economic activities are carried out in a twilight zone. Under these circumstances of dependence it is not particularly helpful to antagonize the authorities.[10] Given the discretionary powers and the level of illegalities committed by ordinary citizens and businessmen, it is advisable to maintain good relations with the authorities.

CONCLUSION

There is an impressive reshaping of the legal system in eastern Europe. Rights receive a more central position, particularly through the protection of human rights in the form of entrenched fundamental rights, although the outburst of extreme nationalism has undermined this process in a fundamental way in certain countries. Notwithstanding the improvements, the post-communist legal system cannot always function in accordance with the normative expectations of a rule-of-law system. Democracy, nation-state building and the institutionalization of a market economy should take place at the same time.[11] The emerging economy is not, and cannot be, based on transparent, textbook-like, ideal market transactions. This may have struc-tural reasons (lack of self-regulating markets, competitive economy), but there are vested social interests in maintaining the semi-governmental economic structure.

NOTES AND REFERENCES

1 It is quite telling that the Hungarian constitutional court ruled that there is no need for criminal action in case of group defamation, because there is sufficient remedy in torts. The offending groups continue to criticize the government for lack of strong measures, yet not one single private action was taken under libel law.
2 It was common among the population in Poland to contribute to the expenses of the (Roman Catholic) Church as this was a gesture of defiance of communist power. In Hungary, however, there was no similar pattern and, therefore, believers expect the state to grant financial support from public funds.
3 G. Skapska, 'The Legacy of Anti-Legalism' (1994) 36 *Poznan Studies in the Philosophy of the Sciences and the Humanities* 214.
4 Compare id., p. 216.
5 It is remarkable that in Hungary as well as in Poland the *nomemklatura* pensions were abolished using equality arguments. The danger of that approach is obvious: it will encourage equality (social justice) considerations to the detriment of rights.
6 It was the rule of law argument which protected the oppressors in Hungary against retroactive justice.
7 Skapska, op. cit., n. 3, p. 216.
8 id., p. 217.
9 The Polish ombudsman received 92,000 complaints in her first year of office.
10 The Hungarian business community was outraged because the Foreign Trade Ministry reduced import quotas by 75 per cent for 1994. The applicants had to pay a high fee for the permits and the application fee was not returned for the refused quantities. According

to law, it seems at least probable that the applicants are entitled to this return which was denied by the Ministry. No one went to court to challenge the informal position of the Ministry because they felt that there might be revenge next year.

11 C. Offe, 'Capitalism by Democratic Design? Democratic Theory Facing Triple Transition in East Central Europe' (1991) 58 *Social Research* 865.

JOURNAL OF LAW AND SOCIETY
VOLUME 22, NUMBER 1, MARCH 1995
0263–323X

Being Social in Socio-Legal Studies

PETER FITZPATRICK*

INTRODUCTION: SOCIO-LEGAL STUDIES
AND THE FAILURE OF JUSTIFICATION

Although this may be an intensely secular occasion, I will begin with a seasonal text for Advent from the Gospel according to Luke. In chapter one, there is the rhapsodic prophecy of Zacharias on the birth of his son John the Baptist where, in a verse of piercing and now melancholy beauty, verse 78, he attributes all that the Baptist will achieve to 'the tender mercy of our God; whereby the dayspring on high hath visited us'.

It is the absence of such a visitation, the absence of transcendent origin, in the world of socio-legal studies that I want to talk about. To be more precise, the uncertainty of identity in socio-legal studies – is it social, or is it legal, or some mixture of these? – has not been relieved by the constant search for some resolving presence, for something that will enable us to say at last what it is. In my argument, the quest for identity is impelled, not by the experience of a presence which we assiduously seek to reveal, but by the intimation of an absence which we thereby seek to avoid.[1] The assumption and pursuit of a presence that is to be found or recovered serve to fill the void at the core of the social and the legal. Since this pursuit of presence is not to the point, it can never be successful. Debates about the social and the legal in, and out of, socio-legal studies are thence in-terminable.

Perhaps then a touch of ennui, even resignation, in recent assessments of the field becomes understandable. To draw on a survey by Thomas, some leading advocates of socio-legal studies now employ a strategy of confession and avoidance: the field is there but its 'definition' is attended with unspecific and unrelieved 'problems', 'difficulty', and a general absence of clarity in its 'lines of demarcation'.[2] There is also a kind of happy positivism which

* Darwin College, University of Kent at Canterbury, Canterbury, Kent CT2 7NY, England

Hans Mohr helped by indicating what an earlier version of the paper was about. Colin Perrin helped by providing crucial references at crucial times.

provides a more affirmative variation of this approach. Socio-legal studies is simply, and usually robustly, asserted to be an applied field and hence intrinsically valid and viable. Lacey's insight becomes apt here, and provides a leitmotif for the rest of this paper:

> ... thinking in terms of 'socio-legal' studies may encourage us to leave the concepts of the social and the legal – of society and law – underexamined, sidestepping questions such as whether the 'legal' can be meaningfully separated from 'the social', or of the extent to which either is unitary or unproblematically identifiable.[3]

In the region of the underexamined, it is the element of the legal that is most inviolate. To the large extent that socio-legal studies has been considered an applied field (without much regard to what is being applied) then, in the words of one practitioner, 'sociologists should be on tap but not on top'.[4] In this milieu, the integrity of law is given and questions asked about its effectiveness, about policy implementation, and such. The part of sociology in this is helpfully summarized by Travers:

> Socio-legal studies, whether these are conservative, liberal or radical in political orientation, tend to use sociological theories and concepts in a pragmatic, *ad hoc* and instrumental way, rather than as part of a commitment to a principled and systematic investigation of social life. They also tend to adopt ... an 'internal' lawyer's point of view of law and legal institutions, rather than the 'external' view afforded by different varieties of the sociological imagination.[5]

Nelken's redemptive thesis on socio-legal studies tends to confirm that stance. Although his thesis is cogent in showing that this applied, legal orientation is not 'necessarily theoretically barren', he also recognizes that 'some larger theoretical framework' is needed, one that socio-legal studies cannot provide but which the sociology of law can.[6] The redemption thence becomes ironic: socio-legal studies cannot be found wanting so long as it is based on the sociology of law to make up for its want. Sociologists should, after all, be on top as well as on tap.

Unfortunately for this consummation, the element of the social has proved no more successful than the legal in providing a focus. The 'social' in socio-legal studies itself has been remarkably underexamined, especially for a field that often took oppositional identity as social – that is, an identity in contraposition to positive, or merely posited, law. The sociology of law seems to be no more searching. It would claim to constitute law in terms of society or to show how law is essentially dependent on society. But society remains elusive. The inadequacies of the sociology of law are most often attributed to 'the theoretical and methodological underdevelopment of the field' in comparison to the virtues of sociology in general or of its other sub-disciplines.[7] I will now show, however, how the failure to grasp 'society' is both endemic to sociology and indicative of the impossibility of society as a self-generating entity. I will then argue that it is law which renders society possible, thus reversing the foundational claims of the sociology of law.[8] Although this resolution would support socio-legal studies in its focus on

106

the legal, the price for that support is a high one, as we shall see, involving as it does a reorientation of the whole field.

THE IMPOSSIBILITY OF SOCIETY

In a world without visitation, a world now denied exterior reference to endow it with meaning, modernity offers 'society' as a proudly profane substitute. Society has no need of external reference, says Lefort, because it is supposedly 'transparent to itself', or 'intelligible in itself'; there is 'an illusion which lies at the heart of modern society: namely, that the institution of the social can account for itself'.[9] This accounting takes place in terms of 'a discourse which carries a guarantee of an actual or virtual order and which tends to become anonymous in order to attest to a truth imprinted in things'.[10] This discourse is typified by 'the sciences of man and society'. Sociology, to ingenuously take an example, is a discourse with an intriguing inability to constitute its field of study. Frisby and Sayer find that the one constant thing that can be said about 'society' in sociology is that it is a problem.[11] Even when there is an attempt to escape society as a focus or foundation, it remains an operative 'absent concept' maintaining a presence in other guises – as adjectival or processual, 'social' and 'sociation', for example, or as a philosophy of history.[12] In a current tendency in sociology not to engage with society as a question, Frisby and Sayer discern the covert triumph of 'bürgerliche Gesellschaft', the consolidation of a particular occidental 'civil society' as the 'taken-for-granted obviousness' of the field, its domain assumption.[13]

Although 'society' has an ancient etymology, Lefort would locate beginnings of its modern usage in the late fourteenth and early fifteenth centuries, a usage in which society comes to be found in the social itself and is no longer derived from a realm beyond it.[14] Williams dates an English usage from the fourteenth century that would likewise accommodate the modern. After some intermediate 'strengthening', this usage acquires 'its most general and abstract sense' in the eighteenth century.[15] From the eighteenth century definitively, the order, the law, the reason of society can no longer be found beyond or prior to it.[16] A closure is often attempted around this self-elevation of society in the claim that society and its forms are only conceivable as such within a particular type of society or at a particular stage of society's development. For example, Frisby and Sayer have it that:

> ... the very possibility of abstractly conceptualizing society at all would seem to have been historically dependent upon the concrete development of bürgerliche Gesellschaft: market society, civil society, bourgeois society. Only then did the generality society become visible, a possible object of theory . . . .[17]

It is apparently not relevant that, on their own account, it seems to be impossible to discover the 'society' which that possibility makes visible.

107

Such a society has not been discovered because it cannot be. The persistent failure to encapsulate society attests to 'the impossible attempt to lodge the instituting moment within the instituted'.[18] The universal claims of modernity eliminate the godhead or any other external 'instituting moment'. The universal and scientific nature of those claims eliminate any enduring or certain moment of internal self-generation. Elevations of such moments – in such terms as economy, history, structure, language or psycho-sexual impulsion – have come and, eventually, gone.

Society is sustained in its universality, not by these precarious positivities, by what it is, but rather by what it is not.[19] Universality is constitutively matched by an illimitable negation. More specifically, being unable to assume identity in positive correspondences, society resorts to negative difference. It is constituted in its opposition to qualities antithetical to it and, in that sense, outside of it. Order naturally opposes the disordered, coherence opposes the incoherent, unity opposes the diverse, and so on. The exterior or disavowed qualities are embodied in terms of sexuality, racism, irrationality, and criminality. Given the universality of society, the sub-social carriers of these qualities must always be redeemable, always able to be brought into and become part of the properly, normally social. Universality thus imposes on society the convenient burden of a project, a civilizing mission. The carriers of difference have to be constantly worked on to make them the same. Although difference is a deviance, it is not confined in its relation to society. As always capable of being what society is not, and as always calling society into being in its whole range, difference is co-extensive, and in a way more than co-extensive, with society itself. Deviance is pervasive. All are born deviant – original sin survives – but some have more deviance thrust upon them. In order to assert the norm, we ask of its repository, conceived by Foucault with perhaps unintended aptness as male, 'how much of the child he has in him, what secret madness lies within him, what fundamental crime he has dreamt of committing'.[20] In all, to borrow a standard sociological definition from Dahrendorf, who also provides the apt emphasis, 'society *means* that norms regulate human conduct'.[21]

All of this provides society with some performative being as a project. With society being identified in this way, the exclusion constituting it comes to be lodged within society itself. This imports into society a necessary incompleteness which, in turn, provides a charter and *raison d'être* both for knowledge itself and for the operatives of the social who are to advance knowledge, to test and apply it. The project requires society continually to include that which it must exclude in order to be society. The very impossibility of society thence comes to reside in it. Society becomes its impossibility.[22] The bearers of society's impossibility are the excluded who take on the lineaments of that very impossibility. It is the excluded who are incoherent, unintegrated, obliged always to become other than what they are. They function, says Connolly, as the equivalent of evil in modernity.[23]

108

Law effects the possibility of society in a complex of compensations for its impossibility. Most immediately, law sustains society against the revelation of impossibility by containing recalcitrance among the excluded. Although the incubus of exclusion is a proper obsession of modern society, which develops minutely elaborated knowledges and tentacular disciplines to deal with it, the excluded are not always prepared to accept the uniform reign of reality. Short of a full discovery of social order, they cannot finally be contained by the factuality of society. Law enters as a necessary 'supplement' to contain what society, or social knowledge and discipline, cannot. In this process, law, as that which intervenes in society exceptionally and occasionally to correct aberration, confirms the ordered normality of society, and the marginality of the excluded. It also marks the ultimate bounds of those regulating norms which give 'meaning' to society.[24]

Law also compensates for the inadequacies of society by creating the very ground for its possibility. The point can be approached through a readily recognizable story of the creation by society of distinct law. In the same way that society in all its fullness is supposedly conceivable only with the advent of a certain form of modern society, so law as distinct and autonomous can only emerge when social forms became sufficiently 'specialized' and 'differentiated'.[25] As this comes to pass, law's ties with particular status and identities are broken and it finally assumes its essential, universal position, co-extensive with society itself. 'In the midst of strangers, law reaches its highest level'; 'the progress of law consists in the destruction of every natural tie, in a continued process of separation and isolation'; or Michelet, 'law, justice, is more reliable than all our forgetful loves, our tears so quickly dried'.[26]

Rather than seeing this apotheosis of law simply as the creation of modernity, it helps for my purposes to see it as the fusion of two pre-modern types of law. With one, law is explicitly tied to and represents what could retrospectively be called particular interests, and there is an element of endemic competition between the varied laws involved. With the other, law is in the ascendant, seeking to dominate and order particular interests. There were transcendent points of reference which would encompass or mediate between these positions, but never with a resolved outcome. The coming of secular society made resolution imperative and this was provided by the new transcendence, the unmediated claim to the universal. Both dimensions of law became coterminous with and joined in the universal. Law as representative of interests came to represent an encompassing general interest and was made to correspond with law as ascendant. Both now existed in the same dimension and an external resolution was no longer needed. This new combination of law, along with the consequent elevation and justification of a new sovereign authority, was only possible because of certain oblique relations between law and society. The social in modernity becomes a regulated realm in which the 'solitary individual', now divorced like law from particular interests, is trained not to challenge law unduly in its pretension to general rule. Furthermore, the coherence and completeness of law as monadic authority become possible because society, now occupying the field of factuality, relieves law of its previously integral connection to an order that contrarily accommodated not only what some authority thought things should be but also what things are, in all their irreducible diversity and division.

The purity and fullness of achieved law is affirmed in elaborations of the story I have just briefly interrupted. At an extreme, but a not uncommon extreme, law enters the scene only with the birth of civil society, where it surmounts, or always almost surmounts, a preceding state of lawlessness. Where law is accorded some prior presence, there it is incomplete or inchoate, having not yet broken its ties to an enveloping 'tradition' or to 'multiplex' social relations.

These tales of differentiation which recount law's coming-into-being also position it in relation to the particular interests from which it separates. Law is thence manifested and affirmed as general authority predominant over any particular or 'lesser' authority. These stories culminate inexorably in the assertion of law as pure generality opposed to but containing the particular, yet remaining in an ultimate way untouched by it.[27]

Law is thus enabled to deny all other authority any ultimate effect. Where the existence of this other authority is not prohibited outright by law, it has still to be exercised 'subject to' law and hence is always provisional. Law severs the connection between other authority and any order, natural or sacred, that could compete with itself. In so deracinating any alternative order, law frees society also from such competition. From its position of general dominance, law also renders any alternative order irredeemably particular. In these ways, law establishes the ground for the vacuous universality of a 'society' which, as we saw earlier, was created in negation. And this society is rendered capable of encompassing any order or authority within it.

Any order or authority, that is, except those of law. Because of its universal reach, society must claim to be able to explain law eventually; but to succeed and find at last that law is totally explicable in terms of economy or judicial viscera, and such, would entail the destruction of those qualities of law that confer universality on society and those qualities which, as we saw earlier, ultimately demarcate and enforce its reality. Society would then self-destruct, unless some other 'sacred game' were invented to sustain it.[28] In short, whilst society depends on law for its possibility, law has to remain apart from it, resisting reduction in terms of society. Law then also marks a point at which society fails in its universal sweep and becomes impossible. So, despite all the incantations about law being the product of society, about its having to change when society changes, and so on, law retains in its relation to society a resolute, 'positive' autonomy that has at least the virtue of maintaining

110

academic efforts to reduce it to something social. This orientation of the study of law and society also serves inherently to protect society against the revelation of law's necessity for its existence.

CONCLUSION

Returning to the seasonal theme, my account may not bring everyone 'good tidings of great joy' (Luke 2:10), but, given the occasion, I hope to have been sufficiently social by showing that socio-legal studies in its main orientation, its focus on the legal, does have theoretical point. In doing this, I have had to show how another type of being social, the explication of law in terms of society, is impossible. But accepting this line of argument involves yet another variant of being social, the acceptance of the excluded as integral to the constitution of society and to law in its relation to society. That has consequences for the starting point, the orientation, the 'truth' of socio-legal studies. Borrowing a summary, and some unfashionable advocacy from Zizek:

> Marx's great achievement was to demonstrate how all phenomena which appear to every bourgeois consciousness as simple deviations, contingent deformations and degenerations of the 'normal' functioning of society . . . , and as such abolishable through amelioration of the system, are necessary products of the system itself – the points at which the 'truth', the immanent antagonistic character of the system, erupts.[29]

In all this, I hope to have been social also in providing support for an initiative by the new director of this centre in exploring the prospect of a seminar series on law in the perspectives of the excluded.

NOTES AND REFERENCES

1   Compare J.W. Mohr, 'The Absence of Presence/The Presence of Absence' (manuscript).
2   P. Thomas, 'Socio-Legal Studies in the United Kingdom' in *Precaire Waarden*, ed. F. Bruisma (1994) 229–46.
3   N. Lacey, 'Conceiving Socio-Legal Studies', discussion paper for the ESRC Review of Socio-Legal Studies seminar, 28 April 1993.
4   As quoted in D. Nelken, 'The "Gap Problem" in the Sociology of Law: A Theoretical Review' (1981) 1 *Windsor Yearbook of Access to Justice* 35, at 36.
5   M. Travers, 'Putting Sociology Back into The Sociology of Law' (1993) 20 *J. of Law and Society* 438, at 443.
6   Nelken, op. cit., n. 4, pp. 39, 45.
7   Travers, op. cit., n. 5, p. 443 and generally.
8   The competition has supposedly been resolved in another way in burgeoning constitutive and relational theories of law where law and society have an indeterminate determining effect on each other: see, for example, A. Hunt, *Explorations in Law and Society: Toward a Constitutive Theory of Law* (1993) 174–5, 224–6.
9   C. Lefort, *The Political Forms of Modern Society: Bureaucracy, Democracy, Totalitarianism* (1986) 184, 201, 207.
10   id., p. 203.

111

11 D. Frisby and D. Sayer, *Society* (1986).
12 id., ch. 3.
13 id., p. 121; and on domain assumption, see A. Gouldner, *The Coming Crisis of Western Sociology* (1971) ch. 2.
14 Lefort, op. cit., n. 9, ch. 6.
15 R. Williams, *Keywords: A Vocabulary of Culture and Society* (1983) 292–3.
16 Compare E. Cassirer, *The Philosophy of the Enlightenment* (1955) 9.
17 Frisby and Sayer, op. cit., p. 121 (their emphasis). For another notable instance, see K. Marx, *Grundrisse: Foundations of the Critique of Political Economy* (1973) 83–111. A specific type of society thence becomes the exemplar of society in general: see, on this, the devastating critique in M. Strathern, 'Discovering "Social Control"' (1985) 12 *J. of Law and Society* 111, and *The Gender of The Gift: Problems with Women and Problems with Society in Melanesia* (1988).
18 Lefort, op. cit., n. 9, p. 202.
19 Something like this line of argument is presented more fully in my *The Mythology of Modern Law* (1992).
20 M. Foucault, *Discipline and Punish: The Birth of The Prison* (1979) 193.
21 R. Dahrendorf, 'On the Origin of Inequality among Men' in *Social Inequality*, ed. A. Béteille (1969) 38.
22 S. Zizek, *For They Know Not What They Do: Enjoyment as a Political Factor* (1991) 37.
23 W. Connolly, *Identity/Difference: Democratic Negotiations of Political Paradox* (1991).
24 Compare Dahrendorf, op. cit., n. 21, p. 38.
25 For such usage see, for example, E. Gellner, *Plough, Sword and Book: The Structure of Human History* (1988).
26 Respectively, D. Black, *The Behaviour of Law* (1976) 41; S. Diamond, 'The Rule of Law Versus The Order of Custom' in *The Social Organisation of Law*, eds D. Black and M. Mileski (1973) 326, quoting von Jhering; and J. Michelet, *Oeuvres Complètes de Jules Michelet* XXI (1982) 268.
27 See G. Gurvitch, *Sociology of Law* (1947) 72–96.
28 Compare F. Nietzsche, *The Gay Science* (1974) 181, para. 124.
29 S. Zizek, *The Sublime Object of Ideology* (1989) 128.

112

JOURNAL OF LAW AND SOCIETY
VOLUME 22, NUMBER 1, MARCH 1995
0263-323X

Contested Communities

RICHARD ABEL*

When I began teaching at Yale Law School twenty-five years ago, I was told that it had adapted *Annie Get Your Gun* for its theme song: 'Anything you can do, I can do meta/I can do anything meta than you'. This is a conference. about meta; but while acknowledging its charms, I will resist them. Rather than talk generally about the future of the field, I am going to sketch a particular path in the hope that others will find it worth further reflection.

A central challenge of the late twentieth century is the assault on community, by which I mean the sense of group membership and mutual responsibility.[1] Community can be measured both intensively – the strength of these feelings – and extensively – the number and diversity of those included. When I first lived in England in the mid-1960s and gave talks to local Labour and Conservative party meetings about the civil rights movement, I was assured that racial discrimination was a problem unique to the United States of America. Looking for a flat in London, therefore, I was startled by unembarrassed advertisements for 'whites only', just like those I had seen in Mississippi. Having recently read Enoch Powell's notorious 'rivers of blood' speech, I watched Asians flee Nairobi the night before England slammed the door on Commonwealth passport-holders in 1968. A decade later Margaret Thatcher warned that England was being 'overrun' and promised 'an end to immigration'.[2] A decade after that, Norman Tebbitt opposed immigration, declaring: 'I am an inhabitant of these islands, which are not very large, which have had the great gift of being islands and which have repelled those who wanted to come take them from us for the last 1000 years very successfully'. 'A large proportion' of Asian immigrants did not pass the 'cricket test', he complained. 'Which side do they cheer for?'[3] In June 1993, Winston Churchill Jr. denounced the 'relentless flow of immigrants' which was changing Britain irrevocably. Fifty years from now, he said, instead of 'spinsters . . . cycling to Communion on Sunday morning, the muezzin will be calling Allah's faithful to the high-street mosque'.[4] Three months later, the British National Party won a seat on Tower Hamlets local council, provoking street fights between neo-Nazis

* *UCLA Law School, Los Angeles, California, CA 90095–1476 United States of America*

113

and anti-racists.[5] And a recent poll indicated that two-thirds of British respondents did not want a gypsy neighbour, a third did not want Arabs or Pakistanis, and a fourth did not want West Indians or Africans.[6] Similar examples could be adduced about every industrialized country.

Although community is an essential ingredient of social life, it also is morally ambiguous, excluding as well as including, oppressing and fulfilling, degrading and elevating. Community can easily become pathological. Neo-fascist communities are organized around hate. Many South African whites continue to look to a homeland within a federal polity to perpetuate apartheid. Professions, including law, defend their homogeneity and anti-competitive practices. Criminal communities – Mafia, Camorra, Yakuza – violently enforce loyalty and silence to frustrate law enforcement. The prosecution of United States sailors for sexual harassment during the Tailhook Association convention in Las Vegas failed because real men don't blab. Youth gangs protect their turf and honour with drive-by shootings. Football fans become hooligans. Religious cults hide emotional and sexual abuse and commit mass suicide, as in Jonestown, Guyana, and recently Waco, Texas. Some of the most intense communities are the product of brutal oppression: prisons, mental hospitals, army boot camp. Fascist regimes in Germany and Japan suppressed conflict in the name of com-munity. Feminists have exposed that most basic community, the family, as a site of patriarchal oppression. And if community is so attractive, why is there mass flight: from marriage to divorce, rural villages to cities, the street life of vital slums to the isolation of suburban villas, the Third World to the first?

DEFINING INSIDERS AND OUTSIDERS

The first sociological question is: what boundaries divide insiders from outsiders?[7] With the end of the cold war, the Iron Curtain no longer separates the 'free world' from the 'evil empire'. Instead, the West displays contempt for the Arab world – I recently saw a California vanity license plate proclaiming 'NUK OPEC' – while Iran reciprocates with calls to destroy the 'Great Satan'. Israel's 'law of the return' may assure all Jews a home, but it has not been extended to the Falasha Mura of Ethiopia or Jews who recognize Jesus as the Messiah. The invidiousness of these boundaries was dramatically illustrated when a nineteen-year-old soldier killed by Palestinian gunmen was buried on the edge of a military cemetery because his father was Jewish but his mother Russian. Although this decision was eventually reversed, a Bedouin war hero who took a Hebrew name was barred entirely from a military cemetery.[8] Every language separates its speakers from others. Some states privilege the dominant language: the British state's prohibition of Welsh in schools (the 'Welsh Not'), French signs in Québec, English-only laws in the United States of America, the rejection of Russian in the Baltic

114

and other parts of the former Soviet Union, the prohibition on Kurdish in Turkey. Others seek to raise the status of subordinated languages: for instance, ballot pamphlets printed in Spanish, Chinese, Japanese, Vietnamese, and Tagalog in California. Accent can be a basis for discrimination or a protected status (because it is virtually ineradicable).[9] After more than a century of feminist protest, gender remains a major demarcation. The significance may be primarily symbolic, as when the Garrick voted 363–94 to continue barring women because they are not clubbable, or it may be a matter of life and death, as when ultrasound technology is abused to abort female foetuses, raising the male: female birth ratio to 1.144 in Haryana state (New Delhi) and 1.185 in China.[10] Homophobia is a central battle-ground. Parliament refuses to make the age of consent the same for homo-sexuals and heterosexuals. Churches debate whether to affirm or condemn homosexuality, celebrate homosexual unions, and ordain homosexual clergy. Employers must decide whether to extend benefits to homosexual partners. The American military has decided to accept closet homosexuality, which includes participation in a gay rights march or drinking at a gay bar but not holding hands. Russia and Ireland decriminalize homosexuality, while conservative local communities explicitly deny civil rights to homosexuals.[11] Disability is another arena. Reagan cut government spending by throwing 200,000 disabled people off Social Security. The Supreme Court has allowed an insurance company to refuse health benefits to an AIDS patient. AIDS has been the basis for denying health care, employment, even shelter. Shortly after Clinton repealed the ban on entry visas to the HIV positive, Congress voted by overwhelming majorities to deny their right to immigrate. At the other extreme, California has limited discrimination based on physical appearance and weight.[12]

Finally, as I mentioned earlier, many countries have restricted immigra-tion. Germany amended its constitution to place the first limitations on the right of asylum. After Valery Giscard d'Estaing condemned an immigrant 'invasion' and Jacques Chirac complained about the noise and smell of blacks, the French National Assembly overwhelmingly approved a bill allowing police to check the identity of those whose behaviour suggested they were foreign. Immigration Minister Charles Pasqua declared: 'When we have sent home several planeloads, even boatloads and trainloads, the world will get the message. We will close our frontiers.' In support of its goal of zero immigration, he has asked city officials to inform police and prosecutors whenever a French citizen marries a foreigner, many of whom are then deported. The United States of America is threatening to withdraw most-favoured-nation status from China for restricting emigration, while it deports Chinese who risked death to spend months on unseaworthy ships and swim to American shores. On the same day that Germany tripled its estimate of the number killed trying to cross the Berlin wall, California Governor Pete Wilson declared: 'If the Mexican government were to come in and simply shoo these people away and not permit them to start across,

115

it would greatly reduce the odds that are now faced by the Border Patrol. Here in this 14-mile sector alone, if they had law enforcement personnel, military personnel . . . they would make an enormous difference.' In 1993 the California legislature considered nearly two dozen anti-immigrant bills, which would ban children from school, deny drivers' licenses, allow hospitals to report the immigration status of patients, require proof of legality before emergency treatment, exclude from public housing, refuse workers' compensation, and build a prison in Baja to house the undocumented convicted of crimes in the United States of America. After the 1994 earthquake two legislators urged that all assistance should be denied to illegal immigrants: 'They should be relocated back to their home country – that's the humanitarian thing.' At the same time, the United States of America sells visas to those who invest $1 million; expecting 10,000 applicants, it was disappointed that only 177 applied (because of competition from Canada and Australia). Howard Ezell, former regional commissioner of the Immigration and Naturalization Service and now a middleman for potential applicants, commented: 'I believe we've done a great job with boat people, and I think that a few yacht people are not going to hurt America.' The United States also has begun charging $130 to process an application for asylum and denying work permits for half a year. At the end of 1989, Hungary ceremoniously removed the barbed-wire fence that had prevented its citizens from fleeing to Austria; less than a year later, Austria deployed 2,000 soldiers along the border to keep Hungarians out. When Ceausescu ruled Romania, the Federal Republic of Germany and Israel paid him millions to release ethnic Germans and Jews; since his overthrow, Germany has paid the post-communist regime $21 million to take back 40,000 Romanian refugees, 70 per cent of them gypsies.[13] These diverse forms of exclusion may constrict, petrify, and overlap, becoming increasingly difficult to reverse or transcend.[14]

NEGOTIATING BOUNDARIES

If the first question is where boundaries are drawn, the second is how and why they change. The global village is already a cliché. Local events can have instantaneous effects throughout the world, rippling through the media, trade, migration, epidemics, pollution, politics, and warfare. No man is an island: one of the 1993 Los Angeles fires, which destroyed hundreds of homes, was started by a homeless man trying to stay warm. But it is far more difficult to care about strangers thousands of miles away, or even next door, than about those who seem familiar and similar. Geographic and social mobility replace daily face-to-face contact among intimates with less frequent interaction through 'cooler' mediums – letters, phone calls, e-mail.

Many also have commented on the diminishing significance of the nation state, superseded by regional groupings while it simultaneously collapses beneath local animosities released by the decline of capitalist and communist empires. Nations are convulsed by internal strife: Northern Ireland, Yugoslavia, the Soviet Union, Czechoslovakia, Sri Lanka, Ethiopia, Angola, Somalia, 'South Africa, Liberia, Zaire, Burundi, India, Afghanistan, Iraq, Turkey. The sense of responsibility also erodes within more cohesive countries. After Hurricane Andrew devastated South Florida, the conservative Republican candidate for California Senator opposed federal disaster aid. 'It is not a shock that a hurricane hit Florida', he said. 'We all knew it could, and that it probably will in years to come, and the state itself has to accommodate itself to the kind of dangers that are imminent.'[15] This was a perverse comment from a resident of a region plagued by earthquake, fire, and flood. Indeed, the 6.8-strong earthquake in Northridge in January 1994 provoked a call that Californians be required to carry earthquake insurance so that the rest of the nation need not keep bailing them out.[16] Faced with the need to find sites for toxic waste, spent nuclear fuel, rubbish incinerators, prisons, mental hospitals, drug rehabilitation units, and low income housing the universal response is 'Nimby' – not in my back yard.[17]

There is a pervasive sense that social forces are destroying traditional communities, not just transforming them. In the city of strangers, public space offers a rare, if superficial, experience of community. This may explain why urban residents are so enraged by blatant selfishness: litter, dogs defecating and men urinating in the street, graffiti, road traffic, and noise (especially boom boxes). The new Los Angeles mayor just signed a law adding civil penalties to the year in jail and $50,000 fine that already threaten graffiti artists, declaring that they were 'the type of thing that destroys the spirit of our city', a 'constant assault on the psyche of Angelenos'. As a candidate he had advocated 'a month in boot camp for a first offense', defeating a city councilman who had suggested that we 'chop a few fingers off'.[18] Omnipresent homelessness induces most to grow a carapace of indifference, while a few explode in anger. In a confidential report Sir Bernard Ingham, Mrs. Thatcher's former press secretary, urged the Westminster City Council to address 'the moral blackmail and increasing menace of beggars' and 'end the blot on the domestic and tourist landscape'. Britain is 'the traditional home of the lost dogs of the world', he complained, and 'cannot continue to allow itself to be exploited'. New York City Parks Commissioner Betsy Gotbaum vowed to tear down the Naumberg Bandshell, built in Central Park in 1923: 'It is just awful to try to maintain. We can't keep people from sleeping in there. They set fires in it. It's a maintenance nightmare.' Memphis has required panhandlers to obtain a free permit, fining violators $50. Although the proportion of Americans who saw homelessness increasing rose from 36 per cent in 1986 to 58 per cent in 1991, fewer than half of all respondents were upset by it, least of all those from eighteen to twenty-nine years old. In April 1992 three sixteen to seventeen year-old Bronx boys set a homeless man on fire in the subway, the seventh such attack in three months, inspiring a copycat incident the next day.[19]

117

Crime, especially violence, is the most emotionally compelling symbol of lost community. Recorded crimes more than doubled in the United Kingdom between 1979 and 1990, the steepest increase in history, producing the highest crime rate in western Europe. Crime rates rose dramatically following the collapse of communism: five-fold in Prague between 1989 and 1991, a 50 per cent increase in burglaries in Russia during the first half of 1992. Trauma rose from the fifth to the third leading cause of death in Russia, as male life expectancy declined three years. Some crimes provoke particularly intense feelings of anger or despair: joyriding, racial attacks (such as the white Bronx youths who smeared whiteface on a black twelve-year-old boy), the two ten-year-old Liverpool boys who abducted a two-year-old and stoned him to death, the two seventeen-year-old girls who tortured and stabbed a seventy-year-old woman to death, the murder of their parents by Lyle and Erik Menendez, mass murders, and terrorist attacks. Racial tensions amplify reactions to crime, as shown by the Los Angeles trials of the white police officers who beat Rodney King and the black residents who beat Reginald Denny. The civil disorder following the first acquittal appeared to confirm the worst apprehensions of anarchy. A twenty-four-year-old mother sat in her car while her daughter and two nieces filled the back seat with videos and beauty care supplies. 'I'm not really like this', she insisted. But 'everybody else is grabbing and taking what they can take. Why not me? This ain't stealing. Ain't nobody in the store. It's free now.'

Society's response can be even more terrifying than crime itself. After the riots, gun sales rose 46 per cent in California and 64 per cent in Los Angeles. Los Angeles County is trying to ban gangs from public parks. The United States imprisonment rate is ten times that of the Netherlands or Japan; in 1995 its prison population will be three times that of 1970. In the District of Columbia, 42 per cent of black men between eighteen and thirty-five years old are imprisoned, paroled, on bail or being sought by the criminal justice system. Virtually every politician from the President down has acclaimed the 'three strikes and you're out' bills, mandating life sentences for a third felony conviction.

Vigilantism is glorified, in real life incidents, such as that involving Bernhard Goetz (who shot several black muggers in a New York subway) and endless media portrayals, epitomized by Clint Eastwood's *Dirty Harry*. Watching their city disintegrate in the movie *Falling Down*, Los Angelenos applauded when Michael Douglas beat up a Korean merchant for charging too much and then vandalized his store, shot a Mexican-American gang member, and terrorized a fast-food restaurant because a waiter refused to serve him breakfast. Shortly before the movie opened, eight Korean-American merchants were shot in Los Angeles, five fatally, and a white man shouting anti-Asian epithets was arrested for vandalizing a Korean store.[20]

Competition may create order at the expense of community. Pressure to win undermines sportsmanship. In 1992 an English team accused Pakistan's

118

two best bowlers of cheating; the accusers were sued for libel, and they, in turn, denounced the lawsuit. Political parties in Thailand openly buy votes. A Texas mother, determined that her daughter make the cheerleading squad, took out a contract to kill a thirteen-year-old competitor and neighbour. Tonya Harding's bodyguard sought to disable her rival, Nancy Kerrigan, from the 1994 Winter Olympics; the latter's agent estimated that a gold medal could be worth $10 million. More than a hundred students at the United States Naval Academy cheated on their final examination, 15 per cent of the graduating class. A primary school headmistress with nineteen years experience instructed her teachers to cheat to raise the school's test scores. A man shot up a primary school with two semi-automatic guns, distraught over his son's poor marks. Israeli kibbutzim, which long ago abandoned socialist principles by hiring Arab workers, now are selling shares. Lawyers, doctors, academics, and other professionals mourn the days before competition. The market's invisible hand inevitably fosters concentration, destroying the communities of producers and consumers constructed around small units: half of all food stores closed in Britain in the last twenty years. Tower blocks have replaced the ninteenth century's 'dark satanic mills' as the physical embodiment of alienation. The state periodically acknowledges this by blowing them up – to the cheers of neighbours.[21]

Intimate relationships are profoundly affected. Marriage declines and divorce rises. Few single mothers remarry, and fewer non-custodial fathers pay support. Unmarried women accounted for a fourth of all United States births in 1990, two-thirds of teenage births, and nine-tenths of black teenage births. Almost a fifth of British families are headed by single parents; only a quarter of households include a couple and dependent children; more than a quarter consist of a single person. The proportion of single mothers receiving support from their children's fathers declined from half to a third in the last ten years. The average household size shrank from 2.46 in 1971 to 1.9 in 1990. An increasing proportion of the elderly live alone, and many have no relatives. When the skeleton of a seventy-two-year-old man was found in a London house, police established that he had died more than three years earlier, but no neighbour had noticed. It took more than four years before neighbours discovered that a Massachusetts woman had died. Whereas half of Italians aged between twenty-five and forty-four see their mothers every day, only 12 per cent of British and 4 per cent of Dutch do so; nearly a third of Italians see their grandmothers two or three times a week but only 7 per cent of British and 4 per cent of Dutch. Following the 1990 San Francisco earthquake, relatives bitterly fought over custody of an orphaned child on whose behalf they had sought substantial damages for the death of his parents. When a Korean-American shopkeeper shot to death a fifteen-year-old African-American girl suspected of shoplifting a soft drink, the girl's father appeared to claim the $300,000 insurance payment, although he had abandoned his daughter nine years earlier and had spurned a relative's offer to pay his air fare from Chicago to attend her funeral in Los

119

Angeles. A Rhode Island father who had abandoned his daughter at five and owed his wife $69,000 in child support appeared ten years later to claim a $350,000 wrongful death settlement when the girl was killed in car crash. Several courts have recognized the right of children to 'divorce' their birth parents. One interpretation of these phenomena is increasing anomie. Nearly a third of American adolescents have considered suicide, one out of six has devised a plan, and one out of twelve has attempted it. The rate of successful teenage suicides rose more than four-fold between 1950 and 1988. Spousal and child abuse have been growing rapidly. When a wheelchair-bound Alzheimer's patient was abandoned by his daughter at a Greyhound terminal in 1991, hospital emergency rooms reported that there were 70,000 cases of 'granny-dumping' that year.[22]

Public services deteriorate while private producers cream off profitable sales. The postal service grows slower and more expensive as faxes, private express services, messengers, and e-mail proliferate. Public transport becomes less convenient, reliable, and affordable while automobile usage is subsidized through road construction and company cars. Fare avoidance increases. Park maintenance diminishes as shopping malls expand, Disneyland invades Europe, and fast-food restaurants add playgrounds. Private police come to outnumber public. Libraries close, shorten hours, and acquire fewer books as video rentals expand. States give parents vouchers to defray part of the cost of private schools. Rising university tuition is financed by student loans. More than 10,000 schools in the United States have accepted Whittle Communications' 'gift' of video monitors on condition that they require all students to watch a daily news broadcast including two minutes of commercials. Conscription is replaced by 'volunteer' armies. Private pension plans supplement Social Security. As the National Health Service is starved of money, private health insurance expands. Health Secretary William Waldegrave commented: 'It's just a fact of getting richer, so it's really nothing to do with me.' The state shifts responsibility for chronic care back to female relatives. Public housing starts in Britain declined from 79,600 in 1979 to 10,500 in the first half of 1991. Several hundred American judges have left the bench to become private arbitrators. American welfare benefits decreased an average of 43 per cent in real terms between 1970 and 1992; some states refuse to pay for additional children or limit the period of eligibility.[23]

Tax structures have become less progressive, reinforcing market tendencies to polarize income and wealth distributions. Former Conservative party chairman Chris Patten declared: 'We want to see a society in which people have the greatest encouragement and opportunity to build up wealth of their own they can pass on to their children.' John Major agreed: 'I want to see wealth cascading down the generations.' During the 1980s the poorest fifth of Americans lost 5 per cent of their pre-tax income while the richest fifth gained 20 per cent. The number of executives at the 800 largest publicly held companies earning at least $1 million annually increased from 386 to 401

120

between 1990 and 1991; the average pay of chief executives rose to 160 times that of the average employee. The proportion of full-time American workers earning less than $12,195 increased from 12.1 to 18 per cent in the 1980s. American families headed by a parent under thirty (to whom about half of all children are born) lost 32.1 per cent of their income from 1973 to 1990 (in real terms), while childless families gained 11.2 per cent. The top 1 per cent of American families increased their share of the national wealth from 31 to 37 per cent between 1983 and 1989, the first significant rise in concentration since the 1920s; they now own more than the bottom 90 per cent. Despite the myths, social mobility is severely limited. Children born to the bottom 20 per cent of families have a 30 per cent chance of ending in the bottom 10 per cent; those born to the top 5 per cent of families have the same chance of ending in the top 10 per cent.[24]

INSCRIBING COMMUNITY IN LAW

The assault on community is waged not only through social policies but also by means of legal rules, processes, and institutions. Let me start with torts examples. How do liability rules, damage awards, and access to law reproduce the distribution of risks and injuries? The Clinton administration has issued an executive order requiring all federal agencies to seek 'environmental equity' in the impact of their decisions. What encourages people to reduce risk or prevent injury to others, or discourages them from doing so? Do damages undermine sympathy for victims, inhibit care giving, or perversely provoke jealousy? What is the effect of damages for injury to intimate relationships (death, loss of consortium) – or, in the extreme case of Buffalo Creek, for the destruction of community? When do parties to a contract maximize short-term gain, and when do they value the stability and integrity of the relationship? Have recent changes in family law rendered families more egalitarian? democratic? contractarian? What are the obligations of property holders to the larger society, and how are these enforced? Examples include access by walkers, the construction of low-income housing or public facilities, and, of course, environmental protection of plants and animals, air and water quality. When does regulation constitute a taking and require compensation? How is society reconciling private exploitation and public enjoyment of new forms of property, such as cable television, telephone wires, computer networks, and the airwaves? The United States of America is about to sell unused frequencies to cellular phone companies for an estimated $200 billion. Does cable television's obligation to allow free access to programmes in the public interest extend to the Home Shopping Network, which generates $1 billion in sales a year? How are the former communist states privatizing public and party property? Should the United States of America allow a company to launch a half-mile long space satellite and sell advertising visible everywhere in the world? What makes people

121

deviate from or comply with legal regulations: health and safety, economic, environmental, tax, and criminal?[25]

CONSTRUCTING COMMUNITY

After we map and seek to understand the decline of community, we can turn to the forces that strengthen it, naturally or deliberately. Some of the very phenomena that erode community also foster it. Congestion created by population growth and urbanization makes it impossible for people to disregard each other, as they can in the idealized rural village. Technological development increases pollution and depletes natural resources, vividly demonstrating interdependence. Disasters, both natural and man-made, intensify feelings of mutual responsibility: the blitz in London, the earth-quakes, fires, and floods that beset California. The OPEC embargo temporarily produced almost total compliance with the 55 mph speed limit. Even my extremely individualistic fellow Angelenos overcomplied with water conservation during the six-year drought, cutting consumption 38 per cent instead of the requested 15 per cent. If Parisians jump turnstiles in the Metro, Amsterdamers punch their trolley tickets on the honour system, and most New Yorkers make 'suggested' contributions to museums.[26]

Societies reward altruistic behaviour in numerous ways. Donor names are engraved on buildings, reported in newspapers, announced during perform-ances and ceremonies, acknowledged on public radio and television, and lauded at Kol Nidre services. In New York, $10,000 buys your name on the back of an orchestra seat at the Metropolitan Opera; $10 million puts your name on the Guggenheim Museum. On designated holidays British donors sport ribbons proclaiming their good citizenship. The *New York Times* raises money twice a year by reproducing some of the letters accompanying gifts. American highways now display signs recognizing those who have 'adopted' a mile for clean-up and maintenance. Police and fire officials, lifeboat opera-tors, and civilians are rewarded for courage and self-sacrifice. Bar association journals record the law firms that have pledged to donate a minimum number of hours of *pro bono* service.[27]

Efforts to strengthen community through law or other forms of public or private coercion are more controversial, often provoking backlash. Some are readily accepted: laws compelling public accommodations to be wheel-chair-accessible, television sets to contain closed-caption decoders for the hearing-impaired, or schools to mainstream pupils with physical, mental, or emotional differences. Racial affirmative action in housing, employment, education, and government contracting, by contrast, has been strongly resisted. A Cleveland suburb subsidizes mortgages for purchasers who improve neighbourhood racial balance. But the United States Supreme Court struck down quotas adopted by Starrett City in Queens to prevent 'tipping'. That private housing development plans to build town houses,

122

condominiums, and a school to preserve integration. Lani Guinier was rejected as Assistant Attorney General for Civil Rights largely because she sought to increase minority electoral representation. A Richmond, Virginia, black primary school principal was ordered to stop 'clustering' the 12 per cent of white students in one classroom in each year to slow white flight. La Crosse, Wisconsin, has begun bussing pupils to promote economic integration in its schools. The campaign against 'political correctness' really represents opposition to cultural affirmative action.[28]

Resistance to coerced community can come from those previously excluded as well as those doing the excluding. Women have championed single-sex schools, like Mills College, arguing that they learn better and gain more confidence. Some historically black southern universities have opposed integration. British Muslims have sought voluntary-aided status for religious schools. Women, racial and religious minorities, and the physically disabled on university campuses have sought safe spaces, residences, courses, and research centres. Some urban United States school districts have created primary schools designed for African American or Hispanic boys, although they cannot exclude others. Born-again Christians have claimed a separate wing in a Texas prison.[29]

Efforts to compel altruism always provoke opposition Taxation has spawned revolution, revolt, and exile. Yet an increasing number of American high schools and colleges require public service before graduation. President Clinton has offered financial aid to university students in exchange for public service. Bar associations have discussed and law schools have imposed mandatory *pro bono* obligations.[30]

Finally, there are deliberate attempts to construct the simulacra of community. Many are transitory, superficial, or unconvincing: boot camp and basic training, fraternity hazing, cruise ships and guided tours, resort hotels and Billy Butlin camps, academic conferences, Disneyland and Colonial Williamsburg, nursing homes, football fans (and hooligans), even vacation cottages in artificially preserved villages. Some are ritual celebrations of lost communities: parades, the royal family, religious ceremonies, coronations, elections and inaugurations, school and university reunions, and family gatherings. Long after divorce was available on demand, states subjected couples to formalistic attempts at conciliation. Sometimes the state creates institutions in the vain hope that community will accrete around them (like the grain of sand in the oyster): neighbourhood justice centres, neighbourhood watches, Indian *panchayats*, local councils in South African townships, now even a 'community' court in that least communal of settings – Times Square.

These anecdotal observations on the fall and rise of community offer neither an elaborated theory nor a set of working hypotheses. But perhaps this Ripley's 'Believe It or Not' of *homo homini lupus* will provoke some readers to direct their research energies toward these pressing questions.

123

NOTES AND REFERENCES

1 See the revival of interest in 'republicanism' in political theory, for example, A. Fraser, *The Spirit of the Laws: Republicanism and the Unfinished Project of Modernity* (1990); from a very different perspective, see D. Bell, *Communitarianism and its Critics* (1993).

2 F.W. Reeves, *Race and Borough Politics* (1989) 101, 158.

3 *Observer* 6 October 1991, 22; *Guardian* 31 October 1991, 4; *Independent on Sunday* 3 November 1991, 12.

4 *New York Times* 1 June 1993, A2.

5 *New York Times* 19 September 1993, s. 1; *Los Angeles Times* 20 September 1993, A10.

6 *New York Times* 25 October 1993, A5.

7 See M. Minow, *Making All the Difference: Inclusion, Exclusion and American Law* (1990). A Durkheimian might argue that the contemporary passion for drawing boundaries and stigmatizing outsiders and deviants is an effort to reinvigorate community.

8 *Los Angeles Times* 14 August 1993, A3; *New York Times* 11 February 1993, A4; 11 January 1994, A5.

9 *New York Times* 18 January 1992, 5; 5 July 1993, s. 1, p. 9; 12 July 1993, s. 1, p. 10 (accent discrimination); *Los Angeles Times* 25 July 1992, A1; 3 July 1993, A23; *New York Times* 3 May 1993, A1; 19 October 1993, A3; *New York Times Magazine* 18 July 1993, 10 (elevating status of subordinate languages); A. Brumberg, 'Not So Free At Last' (1992) 39(17) *New York Review of Books* 60 (discrimination against Russian in the Baltics); *New York Times* 19 March 1993, B13; 19 May 1993, A8; 19 October 1993, A3; *Los Angeles Times* 29 January 1993, A22; 9 April 1993, A13 (privileging dominant language).

10 *New York Times* 23 July 1992, B1 (London clubs); *New York Times* 13 December 1991, A13, 21 July 1993, A1 (birth sex ratios).

11 *Los Angeles Times* 24 February 1992, D2; *New York Times* 10 March 1992, A13; 24 December 1992, A10; 2 March 1993, A15 (employee benefits); *New York Times* 25 March 1992; 5 April 1992, s. 1; 13 May 1992, A11; 11 June 1992, A16; *Los Angeles Times* 17 July 1992, A14; 24 July 1992, B4 (churches); *Los Angeles Times* 28 May 1993, A5; *New York Times* 16 June 1993, A1 (decriminalizing homosexuality); *New York Times* 14 July 1993, A1; 20 July 1993, A14 (American military policy); *New York Times* 30 July 1993, A8; 12 August 1993, A8; *Los Angeles Times* 25 August 1993, A1 (ordinances denying homosexuals civil rights).

12 *New York Times* 27 November 1991, A1 (insurer discrimination against AIDS patient); *New York Times* 10 December 1991, B13, B17 (employment, medical care, and shelter); *New York Times* 9 February 1993, A1; 19 February 1993, A7; 12 March 1993, A8 (immigration); *New York Times* 19 April 1992, s. 1 (social security); *Los Angeles Times* 24 January 1992, A3; 3 September 1993, A1 (California anti-discrimination laws).

13 *Los Angeles Times* 3 May 1993, A3 (California anti-immigrant bills); *Guardian* 24 September 1991, 8; *New York Times* 23 June 1993, A4; 7 January 1994, A5; 14 February 1994, A4 (France); *New York Times* 10 August 1993, A1 (German constitution); *Los Angeles Times* 12 August 1993, A3 (Berlin wall and Wilson speech); *New York Times* 22 December 1991, s. 1 (sale of visas); *New York Times* 6 June 1992, 2 (Austria-Hungary border); *New York Times* 19 September 1992, 1; *Los Angeles Times* 12 October 1992, A8 (payments to Romania); *Los Angeles Times* 29 January 1994, A24; 2 February 1994, A1 (earthquake aid for undocumented); *New York Times* 17 February 1994, A1 (asylum applications).

14 See Colin Turnbull's anthropological parable about the 'Ik' of Uganda, *The Mountain People* (1972). For an argument about contemporary America, see R.N. Bellah, R. Madsen, W.M. Sullivan, A. Swidler, and S.M. Tipton, *Habits of the Heart: Individualism and Commitment in American Life* (1985), and the sequel, *The Good Society* (1991).

15 *Los Angeles Times* 10 September 1992, A3.

16 *New York Times* 21 January 1994, C1.

124

17 Alabama, Oklahoma, and Texas have refused New York City sludge as fertilizer. *New York Times* 25 January 1993, A1, C11. But the impoverished Mescalero Apache of southern New Mexico are conducting studies preliminary to accepting nuclear waste storage. *New York Times* 6 August 1993, A6.

18 *Los Angeles Times* 29 June 1993, B3; 9 July 1993, B1.

19 *Independent on Sunday* 3 November 1991, 8 (Ingham); *New York Times* 20 December 1991, B1; 19 January 1992, s. 1 (Gotbaum); *New York Times* 20 January 1992, A1 (attitudes); *New York Times* 23 April 1992, A15 (attacks); *Los Angeles Times* 15 February 1994, A5 (Memphis).

20 *Observer* 15 September 1991, 4; 22 September 1991, 3 (United Kingdom crime rates); *New York Times* 18 December 1991, A21; *Los Angeles Times* 29 July 1992, A4 (post-communist crime rates); *Los Angeles Times* 1 May 1992, A1; 4 June 1992, A3; *New York Times* 29 March 1993, A7 (*Los Angeles riots*); *New York Times* 14 January 1992, B14 (racist crimes); *Los Angeles Times* 2 November 1993, A6 (ten-year-old English accused); *New York Times* 11 March 1993, A4 (seventeen-year-old English accused); *Los Angeles Times* 15 January 1992, A13; 23 January 1992, A1; *New York Times* 11 February 1992, A12; 18 April 1992, 1 (imprisonment rates); *Los Angeles Times* 15 January 1992, B4 (Los Angeles gangs); *New York Times* 20 February 1994, s. 1 (Russian life expectancy); G.P. Fletcher, *A Crime of Self-Defense: Bernhard Goetz and the Law on Trial* (1988).

21 *New York Times* 13 September 1992, s. 1 (decline of sportsmanship in cricket); *New York Times* 13 September 1992, s. 1 (vote buying in Thailand); *New York Times* 17 March 1991, s. 1 (contract for killing cheerleader); *New York Times* 1 January 1992, 36 (cheating by elementary school principal); *New York Times* 19 September 1992, 5 (man distraught over son's grades); *New York Times* 8 July 1993, A1 (kibbutz); *Independent on Sunday* 3 November 1991, 19 (economic concentration); *New York Times* 13 January 1994, A1 (Naval Academy); *Los Angeles Times* 14 January 1994, A1 (Tanya Harding's bodyguard); *New York Times* 16 January 1994, s. 4 (worth of gold medal).

22 *Times* 16 September 1991, 7 (elderly alone); *New York Times* 7 February 1994, A1 (child support); *Guardian* 20 September 1991, 6 (British household size); *Observer* 22 September 1991, 16 (contact among relatives); *Observer* 22 September 1991, 11 (child support); *New York Times* 4 December 1991, A20 (unmarried motherhood); *Los Angeles Times* 29 July 1992, B3 (father claiming money for daughter's death); *New York Times* 26 September 1992, 1 (children 'divorcing' parents); *Guardian* 21 September 1991, 9 (teenage suicide rate); *New York Times* 26 March 1992, A1 ('granny-dumping'); *Los Angeles Times* 3 November 1993, B1 (child abuse rates); *New York Times* 28 October 1993, A8 (Massachusetts body discovered); *Guardian* 16 December 1993, 9 (London body discovered); *New York Times* 17 January 1994, A7 (absconding father's wrongful death claim).

23 *Guardian* 7 October, 1991, 12 (libraries); *New York Times* 13 January 1992, A13 (fare dodging); *Guardian* 19 September 1991, 21; 23 September 1991, 4; 7 October 1991, 12; 22 October 1991, 1; 18 November 1991, 4 (British health care, housing and education); *Los Angeles Times* 28 July 1992, A3 (adjudication); *New York Times* 23 April 1992, A8 (American education); *Los Angeles Times* 2 April 1992, A1, A16; 28 August 1992, A3; *New York Times* 18 December 1991, A1 (American welfare benefits); M. Kaus, *The End of Equality* (1992) (welfare benefits).

24 *Guardian* 30 September 1991, 2; 12 October 1991, 6 (British wealth inheritance); *New York Times* 5 March 1992, A1; 15 April 1992, A19; 21 April 1992, A1; 11 May 1992, C1, C5; 12 May 1992, A7; 18 May 1992, A1; 22 May 1992, A11; 16 August 1992, s. 4 (American income and wealth distribution); D.C. Bok, *The Cost of Talent: How executive and professionals are paid and how it affects America* (1993) (income disparities).

25 K.T. Erikson, *Everything In Its Path: Destruction of Community in the Buffalo Creek Flood* (1976); G.M. Stern, *The Buffalo Creek Disaster* (1977) (destruction of community); S. Mottley, *Tough Cookie* (1991) (effect of compensation on family of thalidomide victim); S. Macaulay, 'Non-Contractual Relations in Business: A Preliminary Study' (1959) 28 *Am. Sociological Rev.* 55–67; D. Kennedy, 'Form and Substance in Private Law Adjudication'

125

(1976) 89 *Harvard Law Rev.* 1685; J. Cable and S. Charles, *Reciprocity in the Prisoners Dilemma* (1989); D. Collard, *Altruism and Economy: A Study in Non-Selfish Economics* (1978); R. Dore, 'Goodwill and the Spirit of Market Capitalism' (1983) 34 *Brit. J. of Sociology* 459–82; A. Fox, *Beyond Contract: Work, Power and Trust Relations* (1974); F.E. Olsen, 'The Family and the Market: A Study of Ideology and Legal Reform' (1983) 96 *Harvard Law Rev.* 1497; *Guardian* 27 September 1991, 4; *New Statesman and Society* 27 September 1991, 24 (ramblers); *New York Times* 19 January 1992, s. 4 (obligation to preserve shade trees); *New York Times* 20 January 1992, A1 (tension between regulation and taking); *New York Times* 23 June 1993 (advertising satellite); *New York Times* 3 July 1993, 1 (cable television access); *New York Times* 9 August 1993, C10 (sale of radio frequencies); 10 February 1994, A1 (environmental equity); J.A. Roth, J.T. Scholz, and A.D. Witte (eds.), *Taxpayer Compliance* (2 vols., 1989); K. Hawkins and J.M. Thomas (eds.), *Enforcing Regulation* (1984).

26 *Guardian* 25 October 1991, 31; *Los Angeles Times* 19 February 1991, A1, A3 (water consumption).

27 For social scientific and historical studies of altruism, see R.G. Simmons, 'Altruism and Sociology' 1991) 32 *Sociological Q.* 1–22; F. Prochaska, *The Voluntary Impulse: philanthropy in modern Britain* (1988); S. Yeo (ed.), *New Views of Co-operation* (1988); D. Sills, *The Volunteers: means and ends in a national organization* (1957); R. Titmuss, *The Gift Relationship: from human blood to social policy* (1971). The Carnegie Hero Fund Commission has honoured heroism since 1904. *Los Angeles Times* 27 December 1991, A4. On the price of philanthropic recognition, see *New York Times* 24 January 1994, B1.

28 *New York Times* 11 July 1993, s. 2 (hearing impaired); *New York Times* 4 December 1991, B16; 14 December 1991, 1; 23 December 1991, A1; 30 December 1991, A1; 3 August 1992, A12; 2 February 1993, A9; 9 July 1993, A7; 27 October 1993, B12 (racial affirmative action); *New York Times* 22 January 1992, A13; *Los Angeles Times* 23 March 1992, A1 (economic integration); R. Cotterrell, 'Law's Images of Community and Imperium' (1990) 10 *Studies in Law, Politics and Society* 3–27.

29 *Guardian* 5 November 1991, 29; *New York Times* 26 April 1992, s. 1; 24 December 1992, A7; 11 February 1993, A10; 11 July 1993, s. 4 (self-segregation).

30 *New York Times* 29 July 1992, A1; 23 September 1993, A8 (mandatory service for high school and college students).

126

JOURNAL OF LAW AND SOCIETY
VOLUME 22, NUMBER 1, MARCH 1995
0263–323X

The Future of Socio-Legal Research with respect to Environmental Problems

MICHAEL FAURE*

If one thinks about the difficult question what is or what should be the future of socio-legal research, one could do so in two different ways. One could either look at the method to be applied for further socio-legal research or look at the contents of the research agenda, focusing on what topics should be examined in the future in the various disciplines.

Taking up the first idea, regarding the method of socio-legal research, a researcher inevitably sticks to his or her own hobbies. One of my hobbies is, and has been for a long time, the economic analysis of law. Anthony Ogus has already indicated the importance of the economic analysis of law for socio-legal research and I would very much like to support his plea for an increasing emphasis on the economic methodology in future socio-legal research.

LAW AND ECONOMICS AS A METHOD FOR INTERDISCIPLINARY RESEARCH

Looking at the method of socio-legal research more generally, I would suggest that future research should anyway be increasingly multidisciplinary. It is clear that the trans-boundary problems the world confronted with nowadays, some of which have been discussed in the paper by Richard Abel, are so complex that any attempt to solve them can only be successful if the joint efforts of various disciplines are combined. One major advantage of the economic analysis of law, as has been indicated by Ogus[1] and Cooter[2] is that this methodology allows for such an interdisciplinary approach. Positive economic analysis especially shows how certain legal rules come into being and what the influence of legal institutions will be on the incentives of the various market participants. Economic analysis of law can also judge the efficiency of a certain set of legal rules. Obviously efficiency is not the

* Attorney at Law, Academic Director of METRO, the Institute for Transnational Legal Research, and Professor of Comparative and International Environmental Law, University of Limburg, P.O. Box 616, 6200 MD, Maastricht, The Netherlands

Since 1988 Michael Faure has been secretary of the European Association of Law and Economics.

only criterion by which the value of legal rules should be measured, but it is certainly a criterion that can be taken into account when legal rules are examined from a normative point of view. Moreover, in many cases, there is no conflict with other values such as justice, although this has often wrongly been argued.[3] Moreover, by combining neo-classic economic analysis of law and public choice theory, the economic analysis of law can explain why in some cases inefficient legal rules come into being by showing that they provide returns to certain interest groups.

The economic analysis of law has had great success in the United States of America. Law and economics courses are taught in all the major law schools, and law and economics is gaining importance in legal practice. Landes and Posner argue from a quantitative study that law and economics undoubtedly has been the most influential movement within legal theory in the 1980s in the United States. The influence on legal practice also follows from the fact that leading scholars such as Richard Posner, Frank Easterbrook, and Robert Bork are judges at appellate court level and can thus turn their ideas into practice. Even the Supreme Court of the United States quotes law and economics literature, for instance, to decide on issues arising from a hostile takeover bid.

The law and economics approach is indeed a good example of how interdisciplinary research can contribute to a better explanation of the complex real world. One may, by the way, also note that law and economics research itself has become even more interdisciplinary over the last few years. Whereas, originally, United States scholars such as Posner, Calabresi, and Shavel used neo-classic economic models and applied those to legal problems, law and economic scholars now increasingly introduce the results of social and political sciences in their research as well. Good examples of this new trend away from the narrow neo-classic models towards a broader socio-legal approach can be found in the work of Cooter and Ogus. In this respect, reference can also be made to the public choice school which is now widely introduced in the law and economics community.

An important aspect of the methodology of socio-Legal research is that the outcome of an analysis should also be empirically tested. In that respect, the work performed at the Oxford Centre for Socio-Legal Studies has been of a great value. Indeed, many scholars like Don Harris, Roger Bowles, Paul Fenn, Allister McGuire, and Neil Rickman have shown how to combine good modelling with empirical work in order to test the results of theory. The law and economics approach is likely to be accepted widely within the European legal community only when the outcomes of theoretical models can be supported by convincing empirical research.

ENVIRONMENTAL PROBLEMS

I believe that the multi-disciplinary method, which I strongly defend, should focus on one of the most important problems of today, namely, the deteriorating state of the environment. This brings me to a second topic on which I would like to reflect: environmental problems and environmental policy in general. Indeed, I believe that given the social and political priority that this topic has, it should stand high on the agenda for future socio-legal research. In this respect excellent work has been done by the centre as well, by Bridget Hutter, Keith Hawkins, and Paul Fenn, on environmental policy. But everyone familiar with this area will agree that a lot of research has still to be done. Let me go over a number of issues which I consider merit further research. Some of those might be of interest for areas of socio-legal research outside the environmental field.

1. *Standard setting*

A first research topic is the very basic question of how much pollution should be allowed. Let me explain. The way in which most legal systems provide environmental protection or, in other words, allow environmental pollution is not by a general prohibition of all pollution, but by introducing a licensing system. In most cases the licence sets specific standards which have to be complied with and which are enforced through administrative or criminal sanctions. A basic question is how the standards are set. Obviously, the quality of the environmental standards will have a considerable influence on the quality of the environment itself. Economists have argued that one of the ways to fix these standards is by introducing an economic marginal cost-benefit test. A standard should be set where the marginal costs of pollution abatement equal the marginal benefit in reduction of environmental damage. This, or another technological kind of standard setting approach, could be used to determine how standards should be set in the public interest. However, political scientists and the public-choice scholars have often stressed that these standards will fail to be efficient because the bureaucrats who set the standards might be captured by the regulated industry. The influence of private interests will, of course, be larger if democratic control of the standard-setting process through, for instance, environmental groups, is smaller. In the words of an economist: when the information costs for the public at large to discover the *rent seeking by the interest group are larger*, one can expect a higher degree of success of the private interest group. Obviously, the success of interest groups will be smaller when the public can identify that standards are favouring certain groups. It is noteworthy that information problems are probably the highest when standards are set by international organizations. These are most likely to intervene for large trans-frontier environmental problems, such as nuclear accidents and oil pollution. In those cases, standards are set by, for instance, the international maritime organization (with respect to oil pollution) or the nuclear energy agency of the Organization for Economic Co-operation and Development (OECD), for nuclear accidents. So the paradox is that the more important the environmental problem seems to be (since it becomes global or at least trans-boundary), the more likely it is that private interest groups will influence

129

the standard-setting process and, hence, that inefficiencies will follow since the amount of control on international organizations is relatively low.

The same can be said about the standard-setting process at the European level. It is very difficult to control, for instance, how European directives are made, since the influence of powerful lobby groups in Brussels is substantial. This might be one of the reasons why many member states have difficulties implementing European directives correctly and on time. Another reason for the implementation problems might be connected to an issue addressed by Ogus, namely, whether local differences should be taken into account in the standard-setting process. It might well be inefficient to require the same emission standards in Portugal with totally different environmental circumstances compared with Belgium. Moreover, the Portuguese might have different preferences with respect to environmental pollution. If one accepts the idea that these differences can play a role, one might question whether it was such a good idea for the European union to focus merely on a harmonization of standards in order to avoid market distortion, as it has done so far.

In sum, I think research into the standard setting process should certainly be high on the future agenda for socio-legal research. This obviously involves various disciplines, for instance, to determine what is the best available technology without incurring excessive costs, as has been discussed by Keith Hawkins.[4]

2. *Catastrophic risks*

A second topic that merits special attention are the catastrophical risks and, especially, the large environmental risks, such as nuclear accidents. In the legal system,one can note the influence of interest groups which lead to a serious limitation of the compensation due to victims in case of an accident. Indeed, most of the international conventions regulating the liability for damage caused by oil pollution or nuclear accidents have introduced financial caps on liability. In these cases, there is, in the language of economics, no full internalization of the risk. For instance, in the case of nuclear accidents, this lack of internalization means that energy and the price for nuclear power do not reflect the true social costs. In that respect, many important legal and economic, but also political questions arise, such as: is a compensation for these large-scale risks at all possible? If not, because these risks are uninsurable as is often argued, does society want to accept the risks at all? In addition, complicated political issues will arise, such as: will the whole community be prepared to share these large risks or will one community be reluctant to contribute to the compensation of victims of another community? Since the question whether we are willing to accept these large risks has already long been answered affirmatively, as can be seen from the existence of nuclear power plants, I believe that we need thorough interdisciplinary research into the institutional arrangements that

130

can lead to an optimal prevention and compensation for these large risks. There again, combined use of law, economics, and also risk management, political science, and psychology concerned with decision making under uncertainty, can help to provide answers to these complex questions.

3. *Regulation of global pollution*

Finally, I think that socio-legal research focusing on environmental policy should look at the specific problems that trans-boundary pollution and especially global pollution pose. The classic problem with trans-frontier pollution is that it is very tempting for states to export their externalities to another state. We can see all kinds of examples of this behaviour. Nuclear power stations are usually located close to a border; the Walloon government seems to allow the old industry to keep polluting the river Maas because the effects are mostly felt in the Netherlands. This problem arises in almost every case of trans-boundary river pollution. Here again, the question arises how institutional arrangements could react to these negative externality problems. One obvious solution would be to make use of liability law, but, in many cases, this will not be very effective. This can be illustrated by the problem of the cutting down of tropical rain forests in Brazil and on the island of Calimantan in Indonesia. This destruction allegedly contributes to the greenhouse effect. These effects are felt mostly by other victims, situated in the northern countries. Moreover, the priorities and preferences in Indonesia could be set differently. However, I do not think that a liability suit against the states of Brazil or Indonesia will prove to be effective remedies. With respect to these large-scale problems, totally different questions arise such as: should the victims pay the polluter in the form of development aid, for instance, in order to avoid the pollution? But if we accept this idea of investing in environmentally sound technologies in developing countries, will the local polluters still have sufficient incentives to invest in additional abatement measures?

A similar set of questions can also be asked with respect to a topic that has also been discussed at the conference, namely, the transition in eastern Europe. The role of environmental policy in this transition process poses special problems. Many eastern European countries are now drafting new environmental legislation, but there is a lot of scepticism about whether this legislation is actually going to be implemented and enforced. The question of the development of environmental policy in eastern Europe is another topic that should be of interest for future socio-legal research. Here, once more, one can point not only at altruistic reasons, such as that everyone should care about the state of the environment in other countries, including eastern Europe, but research into environmental problems in eastern Europe might well be interesting for western researchers for simple, selfish reasons as well. Environmental pollution in eastern Europe, for instance, the well-known emission of sulphurdioxide, clearly harms western European

131

countries. In addition, one might also wonder whether it is useful to have probably the safest nuclear power plants in the world in Germany if, just a short distance away, nuclear power plants in Bulgaria pose serious risks. Therefore, socio-legal research into the institutional framework that needs to be built to guarantee environmental protection in eastern Europe should be high on the research agenda as well.

CONCLUSION

In this brief overview, I have indicated a few topics which I consider merit further research. I have indicated that these topics could be of interest to the various social sciences: law, economics, political, and social sciences. It was not possible to discuss within the scope of these brief remarks how this interdisciplinary research should be built. Should it be on the basis of co-operation between the various disciplines, or should all the scholars approach environmental problems from their own perspective first, only comparing the research results later? This is a different methodological discussion that has been dealt with by other contributors to this volume. My only goal was to formulate a few thoughts on possible topics for future socio-legal research with respect to environmental problems.

NOTES AND REFERENCES

1 See Ogus's contribution to this volume, (p. 26).
2 See, for example, Cooter's paper in this volume, (p. 50) and his handbook with Tom Ulen, *Law and Economics* (1988).
3 See C.G. Veljanovski, 'The Economic Theory of Tort Liability – Toward a Corrective Justice Approach' in *The Economic Approach to Law*, eds. P. Burrows and C.G. Veljanovski (1981).
4 K. Hawkins, *Environment and Enforcement* (1982).

132

JOURNAL OF LAW AND SOCIETY
VOLUME 22, NUMBER 1, MARCH 1995
0263-323X

Looking to the Future: A Psychologist's Comments on Richard Abel's *Contested Communities*

GEOFFREY M. STEPHENSON*

LAW, PSYCHOLOGY, AND COMMUNITY

I would like first to pay tribute to the notable achievements of psychology and law at this centre. Last year the Third European Conference in Psychology and Law was held at Oxford following those at Maastricht and Nuremberg in previous years. There is no doubt that these European conferences are a direct descendent of the many conferences on law and psychology initiated here at the centre in the 70s and the 80s. Those earlier Oxford conferences established a European focus for collaboration between the two disciplines, attracting scholars from many different countries. The European Association of Psychology and Law that was newly formed last year at the Oxford conference owes a great deal to the initiatives taken here in the early days of the centre's existence. Encouragement has been given to the full range of social science disciplines in the Oxford Centre, and I can say that the investment in psychology has proved very fruitful. The potential, indeed, necessity for psychological input into the centre's proposed future programme is considerable, and I hope will be welcomed and fulfilled in future years.

Psychology's active concern with law has a long history, going back to the last century, and one might ask why it has not exerted more influence on the recent development of socio-legal studies. The application of psychology to law has not been without influence in relation to policy making; for example, the use of identification evidence and, more recently, in relation to the acceptability of children's evidence. Psychology has played a useful role in policy making in those, and other instances. There remains, however, a strong feeling that psychology's theoretical role in the development of socio-legal studies has been less then it should have been.

Richard Abel's essay shows how certain core areas of social psychology may have a fundamental influence on our approach to the development of a research programme required to address socio-legal issues emanating from

* *Professor of Social Psychology, Institute of Social and Applied Psychology, University of Kent at Canterbury, Canterbury, Kent CT2 7NP, England*

the rise and fall of communities. There are two currently flourishing areas of social psychology – attribution theory, and social identity theory – that are, in my view, especially relevant.

On first reading 'Contested Communities', I thought that the term 'community' was being used in a number of significantly different ways. Clearly there are important distinctions to make, for example, between the very different types or categories of communities – professional, neighbourhood, 'law-abiding', and so on – that one individual may perceive him or herself as belonging to. Perhaps this does not matter, because the important point being made by Abel is that there seems to be a general movement towards individual self-interest, and away from communal responsibilities, epitomized, for example, in Margaret Thatcher's notorious assertion that there is no such thing as society.

One characteristic by which members of a community, or that 'society' which is said not to exist, may be judged is the responsibility taken by each for another member's misfortune. Groups have to fight against what Melvin Lerner, a social psychologist, called the 'just world theory'.[1] Those who believe in a just world, and evidence suggests that we generally tend that way, albeit some more than others, will believe, for example, that victims of misfortune have deserved their misfortune. Clinical psychologists, for example, David Smail,[2] have observed the emergence in the 1980s of a new kind of unhappiness or depression in those who suffered economic misfortune, or problems in adapting to changing demands at work, but who, in the peculiar moral and political climate then prevailing, found no one to blame but themselves. In the 1980s, as Abel's paper aptly demonstrates, many remote governmental and business decisions were taken which profoundly and adversely affected people's lives. Smail's argument is that evidence from clinical and social psychological studies suggests that the distressed victims of those decisions were more inclined than in previous years to blame themselves for their misfortune; in other words, the political and moral climate endorsed 'just world' reasoning by victims, and failure was attributed to deficiencies in 'self', and not, more appropriately, blamed on those more remotely responsible for the changes being implemented.

The detrimental effects of blaming the victim, and victims' tendency for self-blame are pervasive processes. They create problems which have been amply demonstrated in the field of law and psychology in relation to particular crimes, like the crime of rape.[3] Conclusions from these studies might well have more general application in relation to the individual/society interface. We need more understanding of the circumstances in which victims of misfortune are inclined or not to accept responsibility for their fate. Work in this field by Sally Lloyd-Bostock[4] has revealed much about the response of accident victims, but a plethora of problems is suggested by the trends towards societal victimization that are documented by Abel in his paper.

A model for the introduction of community variables into victimization studies may be found in Lerner's valuable work[5] on the 'justice motive' in human relations. Lerner points out that the acceptability of a given distribution of resources within a community depends on an individual's perception of their personal relation to others in the community in question. We must ask, are the relations between individuals one of *identity* (the 'same'), *unit* ('similar') or *non-unit* ('different')?

The problems which arise in communities when the perception of others is *non-unit* loom quite large in Abel's analysis of contested communities, and the social psychological literature on inter-group behaviour has something to contribute to our understanding of the many varied, and sometimes paradoxical observations and reports listed by him. Individuals' perceptions of their social identifications – the groups with which they identify – are malleable, and may be manipulated in self-serving, expedient, and contradictory ways.[6] Delinquency and crime, and disruptive and subversive activity, for example, may have attractive symbolic meaning for the social identities of the protagonists, so that the picture of uncontrollable if not quite random disorder and disintegration portrayed by Abel may be less alarming than the whole suggests. The British government's present desperate proposals to build more penal institutions for ten to sixteen-year-olds might be better abandoned in favour of research designed to explore the personal significance of juvenile crime in order appropriately to address the social and community needs of those involved.

I have indicated, however briefly, the potential contribution that just two areas of social-psychological analysis – attribution theory and intergroup relations – might make in the research programmes required to address the problems and paradoxes listed by Abel in his account of changing community life. Let me move on to consider briefly the question of why psychology has perhaps not entered the mainstream of socio-legal studies more convincingly.

IMPLICATIONS OF RESEARCH

There has been a tendency for psychologists to examine *procedural* rather than *distributive* aspects of justice, and to do this in piecemeal fashion, independently of systematic social influences. Nonetheless, a great deal of multi-disciplinary evidence about how 'the system' works in practice has now accumulated, and it is time to reflect on some of the implications of all this knowledge. Whereas psychologists in the past have generally thought in terms of tinkering with this or that aspect of the system with a view to improving somewhat the performance of actors within the existing system – making witnesses remember more, improving police interviewing techniques, educating the judges, and so on – there is a clear need now to explore the possibility that more fundamental reforms are required.[7]

Psychologists have shared with others the pervasive admiration for the adversarial system. Although they might have suggested minor adjustments to the system, they have not thought seriously of trying to challenge it. This is odd, because much psychological evidence confirms what isolated sceptics, like Ludovic Kennedy in this country, have consistently said, that the adversarial system has outlived its usefulness. Of course, changes are being made, albeit slowly, but the rhetoric in its favour abounds. This is in spite of research which shows that decisions at all stages in criminal processing are adversely influenced by the estimates and the prospects of winning in court. Victims fear to report crimes; witnesses fear the consequences of becoming involved; criminal stereotypes of what a criminal is are carefully nurtured for maximum courtroom effect, and have been shown to influence decision making at all stages by judges and jurors alike. Police cook the evidence; lawyers seek to pervert and manipulate evidence and destroy witnesses' confidence and credibility. Judges take little responsibility for the outcome of trials, and juries who have the responsibility, frequently have no competence and, of course, they have no accountability. Psychologists, amongst others, have demonstrated all this, but nobody seems to be practically concerned about it, and psychologists are loath to suggest remedies for the deficiencies their research has highlighted.

As an example of their reticence, consider psychological studies of juries. In particular, consider the conclusions of Strasser, Kerr, and Bray, three highly distinguished American social psychologists, who have reviewed the state of the art, noting that 'the large body of research we have reviewed provides input into procedural and policy debates'. However, they recoil from making recommendations for reform from fear of:

> unwanted side effects of remedial, procedural or policy changes. For example, one important function of the jury may be to bolster community confidence in our system of justice. We would be ill-advised to implement procedures which ensure more equal participation or which reduce the power of the majority if these procedures also materially erode public confidence and satisfaction with the process of jury decision making.
>
> In summary, the social scientist's task is to clarify the processes by which juries make decisions . . . The policy maker's task is to use the empirical literature judiciously, carefully noting its limitations, to guide the development and revision of policy and procedure.[8]

According to these authors, it seems not to matter that the evidence consistently highlights the unreliability of jury decision making: psychologists, the authors say, must leave it to politicians to judge the significance of research. Such deference is touching and academically cosy, but it is feeble, and discourages constructive debate of basic jurisprudential issues of lively interest in the community.

REFORMING THE CRIMINAL JUSTICE SYSTEM

Despite the extensive criticism to which our adversarial, or accusatorial criminal justice system has been subjected in recent years, the recent Royal

136

Commission on Criminal Justice avoided a serious consideration of alternatives to adversarial procedures. Let me quote the penultimate paragraph, characterizing the commission's conclusions on a matter considered by them within the space altogether of six paragraphs. In the preceding paragraphs, they note, without drawing conclusions, that they have examined other jurisdictions and alternative 'inquisitorial' procedures:

> Our reason for not recommending a change to an inquisitorial system as such is not simply fear of the consequences of an unsuccessful cultural transplant . . . We believe that a system in which the critical roles are kept separate offers a better protection for the innocent defendant, including protection against the risk of unnecessarily prolonged detention prior to trial. Moreover, there are 'inquisitorial' jurisdictions in which the system is moving, or being urged to move, in an 'adversarial' direction. For example, Italy has sought to introduce a more adversarial approach, and in France there has been widespread criticism of the role of the *juge d'instruction*.[9]

This statement of simple faith in the superiority of all things English is not exactly the high point of the Royal Commission's reasoning, and we may note that they get this comforting conclusion out of the way right at the beginning of the report, before the evidence has been considered. One can sense the relief engendered by the realization that no fundamental changes were required to address adequately the problems underlying the gross miscarriages of justice that had led to the establishment of the commission in the first place.

The performance of the police was one aspect of the Criminal Justice System which the Royal Commission did address in some depth, and which was, of course, the subject itself of an earlier report leading to the influential Police and Criminal Evidence Act of 1984. The behaviour of the police has in some ways radically changed since that Act was passed, and the movement towards ethical and investigative (rather than confession-seeking) interviewing is well under way.[10] Adrian Zuckerman suggests that police misconduct is at the root of miscarriages of justice, and that reform of the investigatory process will purify the system as a whole.[11] Rather, the evidence seems to me to suggest that police misconduct is, and certainly was, more a symptom of problems that are inherent in the adversarial system.

Addressing the symptoms rather than the core complaint, can have unexpected consequences. One is that expectations of other protagonists in the system are not fulfilled and their performance is undermined. For example, the metropolitan police, in line with the results of research showing the inefficiency of collaborative testimony,[12] have recently required the officers who have witnessed an event to write separate reports. These might then reveal discrepancies in their evidence.[13] This is, not surprisingly, unnerving for prosecuting lawyers, subject to traditional onslaughts from the defence who happily seek, in such circumstances, to cast doubt on the substance of the police evidence as a whole. There is, of course, a possibility that a more even-handed, evidence-orientated inquisitorial approach by the police may shame lawyers generally into less extravagantly partisan ways in

137

court. It is more likely, however, that fewer cases will be brought to court and/or brought to a successful conclusion.

Another possibility is that the police may discover different ways of achieving their ends within the adversarial framework. For example, one study for the Royal Commission indicated that conversations between police and suspects outside the designated interview room were related to the decision of the suspect to confess when the tape-recorded interview was later conducted inside the station.[14] Specifically, the tape-recorded admission or confession rate inside the station rose from 48 per cent to 62 per cent to 64 per cent to 82 per cent, as 'non-offence-related' conversations outside the station ranged from 'none' to 'minimum necessary for politeness', to 'limited' to 'extensive'. Such an association may be one reason why the confession rate seems to have remained steady over the last decade or so, despite changes in procedure making it more difficult for the police to exert undue pressure on suspects.[15]

The Royal Commission retains its faith in adversarial procedures, but we have little knowledge of what citizens and communities think of our system of criminal justice. The faith which different communities have in the criminal justice system is an area which would repay intensive comparative study. There is little cross-cultural comparative data on community attitudes.[16] The work of Tyler in the United States of America suggests that the mechanics of the system ('adversarial' v. 'inquisitorial') are less important than the quality of our inter-personal encounters with police and legal personnel in forming our attitudes to law and our willingness to co-operate with its procedures.[17] We do, however, need good comparative data from different legal systems, especially throughout Europe, on perceptions of justice, and on the fairness of the outcomes of trials, on the assessment of fairness of procedures, and on the influence of stereotypes at different stages throughout decision making in this criminal justice system. Our willingness to report crimes, our willingness to participate as witnesses, our attitudes towards police and other protagonists in the system are related issues that also need investigating within the framework of an international comparative study of criminal justice systems.

NOTES AND REFERENCES

1 M.J. Lerner and D.T. Miller, 'Just world research and the attribution process: looking back and ahead' (1978) 85 *Psychological Bull.* 1031.

2 D. Smail, *The Origins of Unhappiness: a new understanding of personal distress* (1993).

3 G.M. Stephenson, *The Psychology of Criminal Justice* (1992).

4 S. Lloyd-Bostock, *Law in Practice* (1988).

5 M.J. Lerner, 'The justice motive in human relations: some thoughts on what we know and need to know about justice' in *The Justice Motive in Social Behaviour: adapting to times of scarcity and change*, eds. M.J. Lerner and S.C. Lerner (1981) 11–35.

6 M.A. Hogg and D. Abrams, *Social Identifications* (1988).

7 Stephenson, op. cit., n. 3.

8   G. Stasser, N.L. Kerr, and R.M. Bray, 'The social psychology of jury deliberations: structure, process and process, and product' in *The Psychology of the Courtroom*, eds. N.L. Kerr and R.M. Bray (1982) 253.

9   *Report of the Royal Commission on Criminal Justice* (1993; Cm. 2263; Chair, Lord Runciman) para. 14.

10   T. Williamson, 'Reflections on Current Police Practice' in *Suspicion and Silence: the Right to Silence in Criminal Investigations*, eds. D. Morgan and G.M. Stephenson (1994).

11   A.A.S. Zuckerman, 'Miscarriage of justice – a root treatment' (1992) *Crim. Law Rev.* 323.

12   G.M. Stephenson, 'Should collaborative testimony be permitted in courts of law?' (1990) *Crim. Law Rev.* 302.

13   N.K. Clark and G.M. Stephenson, 'Social Remembering: Individual and collaborative memory for social information' (1995) *European Rev. of Social Psychology*.

14   S. Moston and G.M. Stephenson, 'The Changing Face of Police Interrogation' (1993) 3 *J. of Community and Applied Social Psychology* 101–15.

15   id., pp. 3, 101.

16   L.H. Leigh and L. Zedner, *A Report on the Administration of Criminal Justice in the Pre-Trial phase in France and Germany* RCCJ research study no. 1 (1992).

17   T.R. Tyler, *Why people obey the law* (1990).

139

JOURNAL OF LAW AND SOCIETY
VOLUME 22, NUMBER 1, MARCH 1995
0263-323X

What Socio-Legal Scholars Should Do When There is Too Much Law to Study

ROBERT A. KAGAN*

INTRODUCTION

Twenty-one years ago, as the Oxford Centre for Socio-Legal Studies was taking form, I was working on my Ph.D. dissertation in sociology of law. It was a time of intellectual optimism, of hope for collective development of theoretically and empirically grounded understanding of how legal systems really worked. Each new empirical study cast a beam of light into a little-known, often humble province of law's empire, illuminating relationships between the law in action and the law on the books. The learning curve slanted upward sharply.

These days, on the other hand, I feel a certain frustration. In the last twenty-one years, socio-legal studies have accomplished a great deal. But we are failing, I feel, to keep up with developments in the legal systems that surround us. The problem is this: in contemporary democracies, positive law, the law on the books, proliferates extremely rapidly – so rapidly that it confounds our attempts to find out, in any systematic way, what is actually going on. Like Lewis Carroll's Red Queen, we seem to run faster and faster only to keep from falling further behind. The ecological outlook in the Amazon may be troubled, but the number of species in the legal rainforest keeps multiplying.

LEGAL PROLIFERATION

The growth of law is proceeding along several dimensions. First, law has become far more ambitious. It attempts to regulate or even extirpate scores of behaviours that it virtually ignored twenty-five years ago: sexual harrassment in the workplace, leakage from underground fuel storage tanks, medical malpractice, the incidental taking of birds and marine mammals by fishing boats, the education of handicapped children, the management of

* Professor of Political Science and Law, and Director, Center for the Study of Law and Society, University of California, Berkeley, CA 94720, United States of America

140

pension plans, treatment of the mentally ill, intellectual property in computer software. The list could be extended for pages.

Second, within each policy domain or traditional subject matter category, law has become more dense, more complex,[1] more politically-charged, and most importantly, more changeable. Prodded by the media and by political controversy, legislators, administrators, lawyers, and judges have become perpetual legal reformers. Criticizing the status quo, they continuously articulate new legal goals and theories. They establish new agencies and techniques for implementing or enforcing the law. Each is consciously designed to improve upon, and hence to differ from, its predecessors. But change stimulates additional legal and political conflict; hence, it also stimulates demands to strengthen, weaken, or revise the recently enacted law as soon as possible. Third, law has spread laterally across the globe, expanding its domain geographically. The collapse of communism has led to the creation of new constitutional courts and legal regimes, raising new questions about the conditions under which law might come to matter, or how law works in societies undergoing radical political and economic change. Finally, law also has spread vertically. Supra-national regulatory regimes and rulings have multiplied, interacting in complex ways with domestic ones.

Amidst these proliferating legal regimes, institutions, and practices, our little community of socio-legal scholars resembles a band of near-sighted detectives, stooping to search for evidence concerning one event while a crime wave is breaking behind our backs. Once we do turn to examine the territory behind us, we look back over our shoulders to find that a new legal structure has been built in the portion of the legal landscape we thought we had figured out. In the years to come, moreover, the gap between socio-legal research and the dynamism of the phenomena to be studied is likely to grow wider. The basic trends that have generated the modern world's legal explosion are not likely to abate.

WHY HAS LAW PROLIFERATED?

We now dwell (and will continue to dwell) in a world shaped by four powerful, law-generating factors:

(i)   more intense international economic competition;
(ii)   extremely rapid technological change;
(iii) mounting environmental stress; and
(iv)   greater geographical mobility.

These engines of change erode older forms of social control. They batter down tariff barriers and protected monopolies. They undermine the religious authority and the old-boy networks that managed conflict in socially homogeneous, stratified communities. While technological change, competi-

141

tion, and mobility promote higher aggregate levels of health, wealth, and freedom, they also generate entirely new forms of fraud and new kinds of inequality. They stimulate a constantly changing array of threats to economic security, new fears of environmental degradation, new cultural challenges to traditional community norms. Most distressingly, as Professor Abel reminds us elsewhere in this volume, they also bring us more social disorganization, crime, and ethnic tension.

These recurrent disruptions and tensions all give rise to intense demands for new legal rules and controls. Indeed, the fifth and perhaps the most important law-generating trend of the late twentieth century, I would argue, is occurring in the realm of political culture. One might call it the decline of fatalism. Lawrence Friedman refers to it as rising popular expectations of 'total justice'[2] – the belief that because sophisticated modern societies *can* afford to provide compensation for victims of unfair treatment, personal injury, and sudden economic loss, they *should* enact laws that do so. Because modern governments *can* provide prophylactic regulatory protections against identifiable sources of harm, against economic insecurity, and against unfair treatment, they *should* enact laws that do so.

The culture of total justice, moreover, expands the notion of 'unfairness'. Groups that for generations fatalistically accepted subordinate status now feel justified in demanding legal equality. Spurred by modern communications, individuals throughout the world more often see themselves as rights-bearing, rights-demanding citizens. They demand new legal protections against construction projects that threaten their neighbourhoods. They demand more aggressive legal efforts to combat discrimination. They demand legal rights even for the voiceless, for dolphins, owls, trees, and marshes. Democratic governments tend to supply what the citizens demand. Some citizens, riding the waves of change, demand new rights of inclusion, equality, political access, and control. Others, threatened by change and disruption, demand legal protection from harm and loss of control. Democratic governments pass laws responsive to both.

In all likelihood, therefore, the decades to come will see an accelerated rate of change, disruption, and political demands for more law. New legal rules, institutions, jurisdictions, remedies, and enforcement methods will continue to proliferate, as will political controversy about law. For socio-legal scholars, these developments will be very interesting. But the relentless proliferation of law will make it even more difficult to develop systematic, empirically-validated knowledge and coherent theories of legal processes.

WHAT, THEN, ARE WE TO DO?

When the phenomena in a field of scholarly attention seem beyond the ken of the existing cohort of scholars, ideally they would make concerted choices about which phenomena, which problems, are most important to address.

142

Scholars being scholars, however, they rarely want anyone else to tell them what is most important. One time-tested response is to clarify the division of scholarly labour, encouraging individual scholars to congregate in the subdivision which they think most important. As new sub-universes within the universe of living things have been discovered, the biology department at the University of California at Berkeley established separate divisions of molecular and cell biology, biochemistry, genetics, immunology, and neurobiology.

Institutes of socio-legal studies are hardly large enough to establish separate divisions. And I surely do not recommend any division of labour that would entail a retreat into separate academic disciplines, for it is precisely the collaboration of sociologists, economists, political scientists, psychologists, and legal scholars that have made socio-legal studies vital and interesting. I do suggest, however, that we should be quite clear about which portion of the legal universe we are working on. Let me attempt to illustrate.

THREE RESEARCH AGENDAS

At a very general level, three research agendas have dominated socio-legal studies. In the first research agenda, law and institutional design are the phenomena to be explained, the 'dependent variables'. The goal is to analyse the social, political, cultural, and economic forces that shape the formulation of law and the design and function of legal institutions. What political and intellectual conditions account for the formation and maintenance of independent judiciaries?[3] Why do Japanese methods of compensating motor vehicle accident or pollution victims differ from those in the United States of America?[4] What accounts for historical or cross-national variations in the business of courts?[5] Professor Abel's remarks can be interpreted as urging scholars to analyse the forces that lead to legal policies that bolster (or erode) community cohesion and mutual responsibility, that draw the boundaries of community tightly or loosely, that promote (or discourage) law that guarantees tolerance and compassion.

In the second research agenda, the focus is on the behaviour of legal institutions. One might call it the 'legal process' agenda. Its premise is the famous 'legal realist' aphorism: 'Rules don't decide cases, men do.' But the question then arises, what influences the men? Thus, United States social scientists code cases and perform statistical analyses to determine whether the policy thrust of judicial decisions is best explained by individual judges' political party membership, their prior career experience, the status, wealth or race of the parties, and so on.[6] Students of regulation have sought to determine which organizational, political and economic factors induce regulatory law enforcers to be aggressive and legalistic rather than conciliatory or lenient.[7] Numerous scholars have studied how lawyers' incentives, attitudes, and fees affect the disposition of civil cases.[8]

143

The third research agenda treats law and legal decisions not as dependent but as 'independent variables'. Its goal is not to explain why laws and legal decisions vary, but to discover and assess what effect legal processes, in all their variations, actually have on social life. We can call that the 'social effects' agenda. Scholars working on this agenda explore the limits of the sociologist William Graham Sumner's overly pessimistic dictum that 'law ways cannot change folk ways.'[9]

As I see it, the socio-legal studies movement, with many individual exceptions, of course, especially at the Oxford Socio-Legal Centre and among law-and-economics scholars, has been far more preoccupied with explaining the provenance of legal institutions and legal decisions than with examining their impact. We have been more concerned with legal process, in short, than with social consequences. This is quite understandable. Socio-legal scholars have been influenced by traditional legal scholarship's focus on the decisions of official legal actors and the ideas that influence them. Even more importantly, it is easier and far less expensive to study a small number of legal decision-makers or the records of their decisions than to study the far-flung individuals and organizations who are the subjects of law.

CONCERNING THE SOCIAL EFFECTS AGENDA

Nevertheless, I do think it would be desirable to intensify our efforts to assess the actual consequences of legal institutions and interventions, to look at law and legal institutions from a 'consumer perspective'.[10] A focus on the consequences of law teaches us about the strengths as as well the limits of legal interventions, while reminding us that law is not the only factor influencing behaviour.[11] It directs us to consider the unintended costs as well as the intended benefits of legal interventions, to look beyond their first order 'effectiveness' and examine their impact on fundamental social values, such as equality and efficiency, co-operation and conflict, security and creativity.

Many of the most useful contributions to our understanding of legal life have explored this terrain. The Oxford Centre's survey of accident victims and similar studies elsewhere revealed the extent to which victims of misfortune fail to invoke the remedies provided by law.[12] Detailed studies of the lawyering costs in tort cases in the United States have exposed how woefully inefficient and inadequate the liability law system is in providing compensation to injured persons.[13] The Kansas City police study showed the limited impact that intensified patrols actually had on crime.[14] The Minneapolis spousal violence study, on the other hand, indicated that when police arrested offenders – rather than mediating – violence was reduced.[15] Research in Maine showed that court orders following adjudication yielded lower subsequent compliance rates than dispositions reached via mediation.[16]

144

These were all expensive, labour-intensive studies. But their intellectual pay off was great.

Still, it is unfortunate how little really is known about the impact of some of the most controversial legal changes of our time. Has enhanced liability for product-caused injuries produced discernible changes in product design, injury levels, or prices? How do affirmative action or 'positive discrimination' laws affect organizational efficiency and morale? How does medical malpractice liability affect hospital practice, positively as well as negatively? How do police practices change, if at all, when courts are aggressive in excluding illegally seized evidence?

Socio-legal researchers, as far as I know, have hardly begun to research those kinds of questions,[17] much less provide answers. Work on such a impact agenda, however, would be of great importance both practically and theoretically.

BEYOND PAROCHIALISM

By and large, socio-legal studies have been rather parochial, focused on legal processes in a single country. Yet dollar for dollar, scholar for scholar, the greatest contributions to understanding legal processes, in my view, come from cross-national comparative studies. Traditional comparative law scholarship tells us how law differs, or sometimes how legal institutions and legal processes differ. But it rarely tells us how much those differences actually matter and for whom. That is a task for comparative socio-legal studies, which can examine how cross-national differences in law or legal institutions affect relatively similar social functions or types of enterprise.

To provide an example from my own experience, for several years I intensively studied seaports in the United States of America, northern Europe, and China, asking how differences in legal regimes affected port operations. Dutch and American labour law, it turned out, created different incentives for dockworkers' unions. In consequence, stevedoring operations in Rotterdam, compared to American ports, were more efficient, 25 per cent less costly, and resulted in a more equitable sharing of productivity gains.[18] I learned, too, that United States environmental and land use law slowed port expansion, but without producing greater environmental benefits.[19] One could employ a similar methodology to examine the social consequences of other kinds of laws and institutions. To what extent do producers change their products (and prices, warnings, and warranties) when they sell them in jurisdictions with weaker (or tougher) product liability laws? How do multi-national manufacturers alter their pollution abatement methods in countries with different environmental laws or enforcement systems?

Economic competition and instantaneous communications have made cross-national differences in law and legal methods much more politically relevant than they used to be. The more we ask law to do in society, the

145

more it costs. Increasingly, policy-makers want to know 'what works', whether the laws and legal methods used by other nations are more or less effective, more or less efficient, more or less fair. This, in my view, is all to the good. It is more likely to produce a virtuous circle, an emulation of the best, than to produce a vicious circle, a race to the bottom. By responding to this demand, socio-legal scholars can do good while learning more.

Finally, cross-national comparative legal impact studies require cross-national scholarly collaboration. The problems of access and in-depth interpretation always are best dealt with by natives. The often startling insights that come from comparison, on the other hand, flow from intensive interaction between two or more sets of natives. I am gratified by the steps toward cross-national collaboration I see being undertaken by the Oxford Centre, for I am confident that along that path lies the most exciting and meaningful future for socio-legal studies.

NOTES AND REFERENCES

1　See Peter Schuck, 'Legal Complexity: Some Causes, Consequences, and Cures' (1992) 42 *Duke Law J.* 1.

2　L.M. Friedman, *Total Justice* (1985).

3　P. Nonet and P. Selznick, *Law and Society in Transition: Toward Responsive Law* (1978); H.J. Berman, *Law and Revolution: The Formation of the Western Legal Tradition* (1983); M. Shapiro, *Courts: A Comparative and Political Analysis* (1981); P. Van Koppen, 'The Dutch Supreme Court and Parliament: Political Decisionmaking versus Nonpolitical Appointments' (1990) 24 *Law and Society Rev.* 745; M. Krygier, 'Marxism and the Rule of Law' (1990) 15 *Law and Social Inquiry* 633.

4　T. Tanase, 'The Management of Disputes: Automobile Accident Compensation in Japan' (1990) 24 *Law and Society Rev.* 651; F. Upham, *Law and Social Change in Post-War Japan* (1987); V.L. Hamilton and J. Sanders, *Everyday Justice: Responsibility and the Individual in Japan and the United States* (1992).

5　E. Blankenburg and R. Rogowski, 'German Labour Courts and the British Industrial Tribunal System: A Socio-Legal Comparison of Degrees of Judicialisation' (1986) 13 *Brit. J. of Law and Society* 67; E. Blankenburg and J. Verwoerd, 'The Courts as Final Resort? Some Comparisons Between the Legal Cultures of the Netherlands and the Federal Republic of Germany' (1988) 35 *Netherlands International Law J.* 9–28; I. Markovits, 'Pursuing One's Rights Under Socialism' (1986) 38 *Stanford Law Rev.* 689; D.S. Clark, 'Civil Litigation Trends in Europe and Latin American Since 1945' (1990) 24 *Law and Society Rev.* 549; M. Galanter, 'Case Congregations and Their Careers' (1990) 24 *Law and Society Rev.* 371; R.A. Kagan, 'The Routinization of Debt Collection' (1984) 18 *Law and Society Rev.* 323.

6　C.K. Rowland and R.A. Carp, 'The Relative Effects of Maturation, Period, and Appointing President on District Judges' Policy Choice' (1983) 5 *Political Behaviour* 109; S. Wheeler et al., 'Do The "Haves" Come Out Ahead? Winning and Losing in State Supreme Courts, 1870–1970' (1987) 21 *Law and Society Rev.* 403; C. Spohn et al., 'The Sentencing Decisions of Black and White Judges' (1990) 24 *Law and Society Rev.* 1197 and 'The Effect of Race on Sentencing' (1981–82) 16 *Law and Society Rev.* 72; S. Wheeler, K. Mann, and A. Sarat, *Sitting In Judgment: The Sentencing of White Collar Criminals* (1988).

146

7 B. Hutter, 'Variations in Regulatory Enforcement Styles' (1989) 11 *Law and Policy* 153; K. Hawkins and J. Thomas (eds.), *Enforcing Regulation* (1984); J.T. Scholz and Feng Heng Wei, 'Regulatory Enforcement in a Federalist System' (1986) 80 *Am. Political Science Rev.* 1249; G.D. Wood and R. Waterman, 'The Dynamics of Political Control of the Bureaucracy' (1991) 85 *Am. Political Science Rev.* 801.

8 H. Genn, *Hard Bargaining: Out of Court Settlement in Personal Injury Cases* (1987); H.M. Kritzer, *The Justice Broker: Lawyers and Ordinary Litigation* (1990); A. Sarat and W. Felstiner, 'Law and Strategy in the Divorce Lawyers Office' (1986) 20 *Law and Society Rev.* 93; J. Griffiths, 'What Do Dutch Lawyers Actually Do in Divorce Cases?' (1986) 20 *Law and Society Rev.* 135.

9 W.G. Sumner, *Folkways* (1906). See, also, T.R. Tyler, *Why People Obey the Law* (1990); W.K. Muir Jr., *Law and Attitude Change* (1973); G.N. Rosenberg, *The Hollow Hope: Can Courts Bring About Social Change?* (1991); L.M. Friedman, *The Legal System: A Social Science Perspective* (1975) chaps. IV and V, 'When Is Law Effective?'; J. Skolnick and R.A. Kagan, 'Banning Smoking: Compliance Without Enforcement' in *Smoking Policy: Law, Politics, and Culture*, eds. R. Rabin and S. Sugarman (1993).

10 This phrase is meant to echo a similar call made over thirty years ago by E. Cahn, 'Law in the Consumer Perspective' (1963) 112 *Pennsylvania Law Rev.* 1.

11 Economists tend to approach law-related behaviour in this way. In their models, markets for goods, services, reputation, and information are at the heart of social life; this provides a starting point for studying what impact variations in law and in enforcement will actually have. There is no a priori assumption that law will matter lot, or that 'compliance' is a good thing, or at least a costless thing. Business firms are not treated merely as parties who win or lose cases, but as economic entities through which legal wins and losses are transmitted to the public via price changes or signals for the redirection of investment.

I would not suggest that political scientists and sociologists adopt economists' methods, especially in so far as they rely on restricted assumptions rather than on detailed data collection. Nor do I think it desirable to focus on economic efficiency as the sole benchmark for assessing outcomes. Indeed, those characteristic limitations make it all the more important for other disciplines to work on the impact agenda.

12 D. Harris et al., *Compensation and Support of Illness and Injury* (1984). See, also, the replication of the Oxford study, D. Hensler et al., *Accidents and Injuries in the U.S. Costs, Compensation and Claiming Behavior* (1991); the Wisconsin Civil Litigation Project, J. Miller and A. Sarat, 'Grievances, Claims and Disputes: Assessing the Adversary Culture' (1980–81) 15 *Law and Society Rev.* 537; and California and Harvard medical accident studies, summarized in M. Saks, 'Do We Really Know Anything About the Behavior of the Tort Litigation System?' (1992) 140 *Pennsylvania Law Rev.* 1147, 1183–7.

13 J.S. Kakalik and N.M. Pace, *Costs and Compensation Paid in Tort Litigation* (1986); L. Brickman, 'The Asbestos Litigation Crisis: Is There a Need for an Administrative Alternative?' (1992) 13 *Cardozo Law Rev.* 1819 ; S. Sugarman, *Doing Away With Personal Injury Law* (1989); K. Abraham and L. Liebman, 'Private Insurance, Social Insurance and Tort Reform: Toward a New Vision of Compensation for Illness and Injury' (1993) 93 *Columbia Law Rev.* 75–188.

14 G. Kelling et al., *The Kansas City Preventive Patrol Experiment* (1974).

15 L. Sherman and R. Berk, 'The Specific Deterrent Effects of Arrest for Domestic Assault' (1984) 49 *Am. Sociological Rev.* 261. But see F. Dunford et al., 'The Role of Arrest in Domestic Assault: The Omaha Police Experiment' (1990) 28 *Criminology* 183; S. Miller, 'Unintended Side Effects of Pro-Arrest Policies and Their Race and Class Implications for Battered Women' (1989) 3 *Crim. Justice Policy Rev.* 299.

16 C. McEwen and R. Maiman, 'The Relative Significance of Disputing Forum and Dispute Characteristics for Outcome and Compliance' (1986) 20 *Law and Society Rev.* 439. See also N. Vidmar, 'Assessing the Effects of Case Characteristics and Settlement Forum on Dispute Outcomes and Compliance' (1987) 21 *Law and Society Rev.* 155; P. Van Koppen and M. Malsch, 'Defendants and One-Shotters Win After All, Compliance with Courts

147

Decisions in Civil Cases' (1991) 25 *Law and Society Rev.* 803.

17 See, for example, P. Huber and R. Litan (eds)., *The Liability Maze* (1991); L. Edelman et al., 'Internal Dispute Resolution: The Transformation of Civil Rights in the workplace' (1987) 43 *University of Chicago Law Rev.* 1016.

18 R.A. Kagan, 'How Much Does Law Matter? Labor Law, Competition, and Waterfront Labor Relations in Rotterdam and U.S. Ports' (1984) 24 *Law and Society Rev.* 35.

19 R.A. Kagan, 'The Dredging Dilemma: Economic Development and Environmental Protection in Oakland Harbor' (1991) 19 *Coastal Management* 313.

JOURNAL OF LAW AND SOCIETY
VOLUME 22, NUMBER 1, MARCH 1995
0263–323X

The Last Word

STEWART MACAULAY*

INTRODUCTION

When I was asked to speak, I was told that I would have 'the last word'. A long-serving director's retirement might tempt us to think that the Centre for Socio-Legal Studies had accomplished its mission. However, the last word at this conference is not the last word about socio-legal studies. We must remember how relieved Gertrude Stein was when she discovered that she never would read all the books in the Oakland Public Library. We too can be relieved: we will never read all the books to be written in socio-legal studies, no matter how long we continue to work in the field. Just as a favour to the field of socio-legal studies, the powers that be fashioned the European Community and the North American Free Trade Area (NAFTA). This alone will spawn enough law and society questions to keep generations of researchers occupied. Of course, not everyone in power will want to read their reports. But, as they say, what else is new? In short, the last word is: there is not one. It is impossible to foresee the future, but let me briefly sketch one possible direction for our field.

GLOBALIZATION COMPETES WITH LOCALIZATION

We face a paradoxical expansion of globalization, but, at the same time, we witness increasing withdrawal into localization. We all know that there is an increasing internationalization of culture: as we travel around the world, we cannot hide from McDonalds, Levi jeans, CNN and the BBC, Schweppes tonic water, Japanese cars and cameras as well as miniature toiletries cloned in miniature factories and provided in hotels that look the same in Dakar and London. Music is international. Rock and roll is played wherever young people can plug in instruments. Also, I recently bought a recording of music written by a Hungarian, played by a young Japanese violinist appearing with a German orchestra conducted by an Indian.[1]

* Malcolm Pitman Sharp Hilldale Professor and Walter T. Brazeau Bascom Professor of Law, University of Wisconsin-Madison, The Law School, 975 Bascom Mall, Madison, Wisconsin 53706, United States of America

149

And we cannot hide from each other. Indeed, one of my Japanese colleagues told me that we can all rest easy because all the great sites/sights in Europe are guarded by large groups of Japanese tourists armed with Canons. They will have pictures of anyone who might try to steal or deface these treasures! They are buttressed by other armies of Germans, Americans, and even citizens of the United Kingdom roaming the world armed with Nikons and Minoltas. Business has long been international, but more and more we are seeing business conducted by major corporations that exist beyond the structures of any one nation. These are truly global companies that do business where they see opportunities and staff their organizations with talented citizens of many nations. Such corporations are a potent force for the globalization of culture.

The globalization of law has followed this spread of Western and Japanese culture. At the outset, we must recall that we are in the second wave of this phenomenon. India has long had both its versions of the English language and the common law; countries as diverse as Japan and Chile have adaptations of the German legal tradition. This first wave was the result of colonialism, both economic and intellectual. Today other processes are also at work.

International groups are working to create supranational law dealing with such things as contracts and human rights through the United Nations, the European Community, and other international organizations. There also are more subtle forces. For example, nations that offer major market opportunities for international corporations often have their own regulations dealing with such things as safety, environmental protection, the quality of food, and the like. Those selling in these markets must cope with the law they meet there. One strategy is to comply with the most restrictive regulation. They hope that when they do this, they will also comply with the regulations of less restrictive markets. For example, United States regulation of automobile design influences how cars are built around the world. Its regulations about passenger aircraft design apply to any plane that serves the United States of America. Few manufacturers would design a plane that could not serve this vast market. They modify their designs to please United States regulatory officials. In other situations, manufacturers must meet multiple sets of overlapping if not conflicting standards. Even a small producer of automobiles such as SAAB, must modify some of its cars to meet the special regulations of the state of California and other cars to satisfy conflicting Canadian demands.

International corporations have created a transnational law that governs their operations through standardized contracts that all of those in a given trade use. Even with standardized norms, there are disputes. Most are settled, but some require dispute resolution. Several countries, including the United Kingdom, have long sold judicial services to multinational ventures, and many kinds of private arbitration structures exist as well. Multinationals not only create their own structures for dealings with other multinationals, they also make contracts with governments. The governments in these trans-

150

actions do not act as sovereigns. They are just another contracting party, and they may not be as powerful as a multinational corporation.

This multinational environment has characteristics that stem from the spread of American culture since the end of the Second World War. Students from around the world have been studying at United States law schools, and they have been returning home with their interpretation of United States law and United States legal culture. Volkmar Gessner points out:

> [T]he world market dominated by the English language, American capital and common law reasoning is a home-match for American lawyers who in addition are organized much more in the entrepreneurial form needed for worldwide activities.'[2]

Bryant Garth notes that transnational lawyers preach an ideology of free market and stability that may sound apolitical but undercuts the power of a nation to protect workers, consumers or its environment.[3]

We now have not only supranational private legal systems, but multinational governments such as the European Community and NAFTA. Moreover, there are still other transnational institutions that we might call legal. Maureen Cain has asked, 'Are the Olympic Games an international state form, or the European Court of Human Rights, or UNESCO, or Interpol, or the IMF, or the Red Cross . . .?'[4] However we categorize these structures, such institutions increasingly affect human behaviour. There are even more complex examples of the interplay of public and private governments on the world stage. Alison Brysk has detailed the tangled mixture of public-and-private as well as national-and-international actors involved in the Argentinean human rights crisis.[5] Multinational legal pluralism has come to characterize the institutions that govern more and more of our lives. As always, legal pluralism presents the potential for inconsistent, overlapping, and conflicting rules, procedures, and practices.

At the same time, there is an increasing pressure for particularism, usually well mixed with nationalism or regionalism. Smaller and smaller units demand their own language, flag and, perhaps, law. We can look to Northern Ireland, the former Yugoslavia as well as to the former Soviet Union for case studies of this phenomenon. Even in nations that seem historically stable, we can see this counter-trend. We must remember demonstrations by French farmers against rulings of the European Community, and the campaign against NAFTA by the Ralph Nader organization. These examples remind us that there will be many instances of resistance to the brave new world of globalization.

WHAT HAS THIS TENSION DONE, AND WHAT WILL IT DO, TO LAW?

On the symbolic level, we can expect pressure for one world and the globalization of law and legal institutions in the name of order and harmony. We

151

will see private and supranational entities that govern larger and large spaces. The information highway will extend the span of control. It may be harder for organizations to hide without leaving an electronic trail. Evasion may require greater skill. However, powerful multinational organizations too will be able to use transnational law as a tool to fight regulation.[6] Local authorities may face the threat of defending their actions before the legal bodies of the European Community, NAFTA or other similar organizations.

International capital may seek to cut transaction costs and rationalize regulation in the name of minimizing the competitive advantage of nations that impose little effective governance. Privatization and deregulation are songs still being sung to admiring audiences throughout the world although Prime Minister Thatcher and President Reagan have left office.[7] Socio-legal scholars should remember that the law-and-economics movement preaches that everything has costs. After more than a decade of market-oriented policies, it might be profitable to assess the costs of law and economics teaching which was put in place by governments around the world.

We may find new opportunities for particularism in many forms. We must ask how the new transnational law will affect the law in action, how people will cope with the absence of familiar legal rules or with the presence of unwanted regulation, and how street level bureaucrats will respond to the demands of individuals and the commands coming down from above. Those officials who must apply the rules and policies of the larger units to those who are the targets of regulation may be caught in a web of conflicting reward and punishment systems. Inevitably there will be a counter-movement, advocating decentralization and delegation to regional and local units. Local officials will justifiably claim to know local conditions and to command the knowledge needed to make necessary adjustments at the local level. The experiences of the planned economies of the old Soviet Union and the nations of eastern Europe will be held up as examples to be avoided. Then, as effective control is delegated downward, planners at the transnational level will tend to lose control and exert only influence.

Moreover, an important principle of the sociology of law is that people cope; they are not puppets controlled from above. People will fashion ways to use a mixture of multinational and local law in unanticipated ways to further their own ends rather than those of the distant law-givers. We should expect what Doreen McBarnet has called 'creative compliance' as well as out-and-out evasion. As she notes, those who can afford to hire lawyers can use law against law. All such people need is a plausible argument so that the burden of taking legal action falls on those who would implement the transnational law. Often, knocking down plausible arguments will not be worth the cost.

We can expect, moreover, that the costs of the transition to a global market will affect different regions and different industries unevenly. We can expect local political officials to focus parochial discontent on the face-less bureaucrats in Brussels, the United Nations or other agencies of

152

globalization. The result often may be symbolic transnational law with a reality of local patterned evasion.

We can expect, then, less than 100 per cent compliance with the brave new globalized legal system. We can also expect the resulting mixture of multinational and local law plus patterns of creative compliance and evasion to produce something very different from we would have found ten to twenty years ago.

CHALLENGES AND OPPORTUNITIES

The new patterns that will be provoked by the countervailing pressures for globalization and localism will open an opportunity for a truly comparative study of the law-in-action. Donald Black had a vision, perhaps utopian, of scientific laws about law that hold true everywhere.[8] My proposal is more modest. We must seek a payoff from comparative empirical work as the world system changes. Today we know something about the reality of legal systems in the United States of America, the United Kingdom, western Europe and even Japan. We are beginning to look elsewhere, particularly in Asia. Perhaps in ten or twenty years we may conclude that the more things change, the more they stay the same. However, this is not what I expect. As we read studies of, say, how authorities in Northern Spain deal with Basque reactions to the directives of the European Community, we should look for patterns that may be found in similar situations elsewhere.

For example, about twenty-five years ago I spent a year and a half in Chile. I was surprised to discover that outside Santiago few legal officials had up-to-date accurate copies of much of the Chilean law. Large Santiago law firms viewed their copies of the law as a major asset, and lawyers in smaller cities had to make major efforts to stay current. Chile lacked all the competing law book publishers that we take for granted in the United States and the United Kingdom.

However, when I returned to Madison, I started asking what legal materials were, as a practical matter, available to Wisconsin lawyers outside the two largest cities in the state.[9] Once I thought to ask, the answer was not surprising. A lawyer in Racine, Wisconsin has no greater access to all legal materials than a Chilean lawyer in Antofagasta. Much as classical pianists, lawyers around the world have repertoires of things they play constantly, and most of the time they have sufficient sheet music – the statutes, administrative regulations and cases – to practice. However, if they meet a problem out of their repertoire, they are likely to lack the legal resources to cope with it. Perhaps I could have recognized that legal materials were not uniformly available to lawyers throughout the state without spending time abroad, but my experience in another legal system made me sensitive to the point. Comparative law at its best will help us see what we have long failed to notice about our own legal systems.

153

IN CLOSING

The Centre for Socio-Legal Studies has solid achievements and world-wide fame. All of us from around the world can say 'well done' to Donald Harris and his colleagues. Not only have they done memorable work, but they have kept an institution alive in the face of budget cuts and the opinions of those who did not see the impact of law as problematic. Nonetheless, I am sure that Don Harris would be the first to say there is still important work to be done. The legal world is changing. This means that the challenges for the law and society community have changed too. Just as the social structures of the cold war seem to be dead or dying, the optimistic world of progressive reform through law seems a bit of history. Perhaps the eras of Thatcher and Reagan also are passing into history. If globalization matched by nationalistic or religious localization is what comes next, we can expect the functioning legal systems of the world to change as well. Charting and challenging that change should keep us busy. Those of us in the United States law and society community are eager to continue our long and valued association with those at the Oxford Centre. Again, there is not a last word; only new challenges. Would we have it any other way?

NOTES AND REFERENCES

1 The compact disk features Midori with Zubin Mehta conducting the Berlin Philharmonic playing Bartok's Violin Concertos 1 and 2 (Sony SK 45941).
2 Personal communication from the author.
3 B.G. Garth, 'Transnational Legal Practice and Professional Ideology' (1985) 7 *Issues of Transnational Legal Practice* 3.
4 M. Cain, 'Introduction: Towards an Understanding of the International State' (1983) 11 *International J. of the Sociology of Law* 1.
5 A. Brysk, 'From Above and Below: Social Movements, the International System, and Human Rights in Argentina' (1993) 26 *Comparative Political Studies* 259.
6 R. Rawlings, 'The Eurolaw Game: Some Deductions from a Saga' (1993) 20 *J. of Law and Society* 309.
7 See, for example, H. De Soto, *The Other Path* (1989).
8 D. Black, 'The Boundaries of Legal Sociology' (1972) 81 *Yale Law J.* 1086.
9 See S. Macaulay, 'Lawyers and Consumer Protection Laws' (1979) 14 *Law and Society Rev.* 115.

Bibliography

R. Abel, *The Legal Profession in England and Wales* (1988) at 465.

R. Abel, 'Law Books and Books About Law' (1975) 26 *Stanford Law Rev.* 175–228.

R. Abel and P.S. Lewis (eds.), *Lawyers in Society* 3 vols. (1988).

B. Abel-Smith and R. Stevens, *Lawyers and the Courts* (1967) 352–3, 365–75.

K. Abraham and L. Liebman, 'Private Insurance, Social Insurance and Tort Reform: Toward a New Vision of Compensation for Illness and Injury' (1993) 93 *Columbia Law Rev.* 75–188.

H. Allen, *Justice Unbalanced* (1987).

N. Annan, *Our Age* (1990).

P.S. Atiyah, *Accidents, Compensation and the Law* (1st ed., 1970).

M. Bach, *Eine leise Revolution durch Verwaltungsverfahren – Bürokratische Integrationsprozesse in der Europäischen Gemeinschaft* (1990) 21 *Zeitschrift für Soziologie* 16–30.

B. Badie and M.-C. Smouts, *Le retournment du monde – Sociologie de la scène Internationale* (1992) 112.

D. Baird, R. Girtner, and R. Picker, *Game Theory and the Law* (1994).

J. Baldwin, N. Wikeley, and R. Young, *Judging Social Security* (1993).

R. Baldwin, *Regulating the Airlines* (1985).

A. Barron and C. Scott, 'The Citizen's Charter Programme' (1988) 55 *Modern Law Rev.* 526.

L.A. Bebchuk (ed.), *Corporate Law and Economic Analysis* (1990) (sections by F.H. Easterbrook and D.R. Fischel, and H. Hansmann).

T. Becher, *Academic Tribes and Territories* (1989).

G. Becker, 'Crime and Punishment: An Economic Approach' (1968) 76 *J. of Political Economy* 169.

H. Becker, *Outsiders* (1963).

M.E. Becker, 'Four Faces of Liberal Legal Thought' (1988) 34 *University of Chicago Law School Record* at 11.

Bela-Muhle v. *Grows Farm* (1977) E.C.R. 1211.

D. Bell, *Communitarianism and its Critics* (1993).

R.N. Bellah et al., *Habits of the Heart: Individualism and Commitment in American Life* (1985).

R.N. Bellah et al., *The Good Society* (1991).

A. Bergesen, 'Turning World-System Theory on its Head' (1990) 7 *Theory, Culture and Society* 67–81.

H.J. Berman, *Law and Revolution: The Formation of the Western Legal Tradition* (1983).

R. Bhaskar, *The Possibility of Naturalism* (1979).

W. Bishop, 'Negligent Misrepresentation through the Economists' Eyes' (1980) 96 *Law Q. Rev.* 369.

W. Bishop, 'Economic Loss in Tort' (1982) 2 *Oxford J. of Legal Studies* 1.

E. Bittner, *The Functions of the Police in Modern Society* (1970).

E. Bittner, 'The Police on Skid Row' (1963) 28 *Am. Sociological Rev.* 699–715.

D. Black, 'The Boundaries of Legal Sociology' (1972) 81 *Yale Law J.* 1086.

D. Black, *The Behaviour of Law* (1976) 41.

E. Blankenburg and R. Rogowski, 'German Labour Courts and the British Industrial Tribunal System: A Socio-Legal Comparison of Degrees of Judicialisation' (1986) 13 *Brit. J. of Law and Society* 67.

E. Blankenburg and J. Verwoerd, 'The Courts as a Final Resort? Some Comparisons Between the Legal Cultures of the Netherlands and the Federal Republic of Germany' (1988) 35 *Netherlands International Law J.* 9–28.

E. Blankenburg and F. Bruinsma, *Dutch Legal Culture* (1991).

P. Bohannan, *Justice and Judgement Among the Tiv* (1979).

D. Bok, *The Cost of Talent* (1993).

R. Bowles and P. Jones, *Professional Liability* (1989).

R. Bowles and J. Phillips, 'Solicitors' Remuneration: A Critique of Recent Developments in Conveyancing' (1977) 40 *Modern Law Rev.* 639.

R. Bowles and C. Whelan, 'The Currency of Suit in Actions for Damages' (1979) 25 *McGill Law J.* 236.

R. Bowles and C. Whelan, 'Law Commission Working Paper No.80: Private International Law Foreign Money Liabilities' (1982) 45 *Modern Law Rev.* 434.

J. Braithwaite, *Crime, Shame and Reintergration* (1989).

L. Brickman, 'The Asbestos Litigation Crisis: Is There Any Need for an Administrative Alternative" (1992) 13 *Cardozo Law Rev.* 1819.

L. Bridges, 'ESRC Review Surveys of Socio-Legal Studies' (1993) 10 *Socio-Legal Newsletter* 1.

A. Brysk, 'From Above and Below: Social Movements, the International System, and Human Rights in Argentina' (1993) 26 *Comparative Political Studies* 259.

P. Burrows, P. *The Economic Theory of Pollution Control* (1979) chs. 4–5.

P. Burrows, 'Getting a Stranglehold with the Eminent Domain Clause' (1989) 9 *International Rev. of Law and Economics* 129.

J.W. Burton, *World Society* (1972).

J. Cable and S. Charles, *Reciprocity in the Prisoners' Dilemma* (1989).

E. Cahn, 'Law in the Consumer Perspective' (1963) 112 *Pennsylvania Law Rev.* 1.

M. Cain, 'The Policing of Culture in Trinidad and Tobago and the Caribbean: Transcending the "modern" vs "post-modern" divide'. Paper presented to the Law and Society Association, Phoenix, Arizona, June 1984.

M. Cain, 'Introduction: Towards an Understanding of the International State' (1983) 11 *International J. of the Sociology of Law* 1.

M. Cain (ed.), *Growing Up Good* (1989).

M. Cain, 'Realism, feminism, methodology, and law' (1986) 14 *International J. of the Sociology of Law* 384.

M. Cain, 'Realist philosophy and standpoint epistemologies OR feminist criminology as a successor science' in *Feminist Perspectives in Criminology*, eds. L. Gelsthorpe and A. Morris (1990).

M. Cain, 'Foucault, feminism, and feeling: what Foucault can and cannot contribute to feminist epistemology' in *Up Against Foucault*, ed. C. Ramazanoglu (1993).

M. Cain, *Society and the Policeman's Role* (1974).

G. Calabresi, *The Costs of Legal Accidents: A Legal and Economic Analysis* (1970).

P. Carlen, *Women's Imprisonment* (1983).

W.G. Carson, 'Symbolic and Instrumental Dimensions of Early Factory Legislation' in *Crime, Criminology and Public Policy*, ed. R. Hood (1974).

W.G. Carson, 'White Collar Crime and the Enforcement of Factory Legislation' (1970) 10 *Brit. J. of Criminology* 393.

J. Carswell, *Government and Universities in Britain* (1985).

E. Cassirer, *The Philosophy of the Enlightenment* (1955) 9.

D. Chapman, *Sociology and the Stereotype of the Criminal* (1968).

M. Chatterton, 'Police Work and Assault Charges' in *Control in the Police Organization*, ed. M. Punch (1983).

M. Chesney-Lind, 'Judicial paternalism and the female status offender' (1977) 23 *Crime and Delinquency* 121–30.

A. Cicourel, *The Social Organization of Juvenile Justice* (1968).

D.S. Clark, 'Civil Litigation Trends in Europe and Latin America Since 1945' (1990) 24 *Law and Society Rev.* 549.

N.K. Clark and G.M. Stephenson, 'Social Remembering: Individual and collaborative memory for social information' (1995) *European Rev. of Social Psychology*.

Criminal Law Revision Committee (CLRC), *Eleventh Report: Evidence (General)* (1972; Cmnd. 4991).

R.H. Coase, 'The Problem of Social Cost' (1960) 3 *J. of Law and Economics* 1.

L.J. Cohen, *The Probable and the Provable* (1977).

S. Cohen, introduction to *Images of Deviance* (1971) 19.

L. Cohen-Tanugi, *Le droit sans l'état* (1985).

D. Collard, *Altruism and Economy: A Study in Non-Selfish Economics* (1978).

W. Connoley, *Identity/Difference: Democratic Negotitatons of Political Paradox* (1991).

T.D. Cook and D.T. Campbell, *Quasi-Experimentation: Design and Analysis Issues for Field Settings* (1979).

Coopers & Lybrand Europe, *Handling of Cross-Border Consumer Disputes, Final Report for the Commission of the European Communities 1990* (1990).

R. Cooter, 'Lapses, Conflict, and Akrasia in Torts and Crimes: Towards an Economic Theory of the Will' (1991) 11 *International Rev. of Law and Economics* 149–64.

R. Cooter, 'Structural Adjudication and the New Law Merchant: A Model of Decentralized Law' (1994) 14 *International Rev. of Law and Economics* 215–31.

R. Cooter and T. Ulen, *Law and Economics* (1994).

R. Cotterrell, 'Law's Images of Community and Imperium' (1990) 10 *Studies in Law, Politics and Society* 3–27.

K.C. Crabb, 'Providing Legal Services in Foreign Countries: Making Room for the American Attorney' (1983) 83 *Columbia Law Rev.* 1767–823.

S. Craig, *Smiles and Blood* (1988).

R. Cranston, *Regulating Business* (1979) 169.

E. Cummings et al., 'Policeman as Philosopher, Friend and Guide' (1965) 12 *Social Problems* 276–86.

R. Dahrendorf, 'On the Origin of Inequality among Men' in *Social Inequality*, ed. A. Beteille (1969) 38.

R. David, *Les Grands Systèmes de Droit Contemporains* (1950).

R. David, 'The International Unification of Private Law' in *International Encyclopedia of Comparative Law*, vol. II (1971) ch. 5.

R. David and J.E.C. Brierly, *Major Legal Systems of the World Today* (1978).

R.M. Dawes, D. Faust, and P.E. Meehl, 'Clinical Versus Actuarial Judgment' (1989) 243 *Science* 1668.

R. Delgado and J. Stefancic, 'Critical Race Theory: An Annotated Bibliography' (1993) 79 *Virginia Law Rev.* 461.

J. Derrida, *Grammatology* (1974).

H. De Soto, *The Other Path* (1989).

Y. Dezalay, *Marchands de droit – La restructuration de l'ordre juridique international par les multinationales du droit* (1992).

Y. Dezalay, 'The Big Bang and the Law: The Internationalization and Restructuration of the Legal Field' (1990) 7 *Theory, Culture and Society* 1–14.

Y. Dezalay and D. Sugarman (eds.), *Professional Competition and the Social Construction of Markets: Lawyers, Accountants and the Emergence of a Transnational State* (1993).

A. Diamond (ed.), *The Victorian Achievement of Sir Henry Maine* (1991).

S.S. Diamond, 'Foreword' in *Handbook of Psychology and Law*, eds. D.K. Kagehiro and W.S. Laufer (1992).

S. Diamond, 'The Rule of Law Versus the Order of Custom' in *The Social Organisation of Law*, eds. D. Black and M. Mileski (1973).

158

S. Domberger and A. Sherr, 'The Impact of Competition on Pricing and Quality of Legal Services' (1989) 9 *International Rev. of Law and Economics* 41.

A.N. Doob and J.V. Roberts, 'Social Psychology, Social Attitudes, and Attitudes Toward Sentencing' (1984) 16 *Canadian J. of Behavioural Science Rev.* 269.

R. Dore, 'Goodwill and the Spirit of Market Capitalism' (1983) 34 *Brit. J. of Sociology* 459–82.

C. Douzinas, R. Warrington, and S. McVeigh, *Post-modern Jurisprudence* (1991).

F. Dunford et al., 'The Role of Arrest in Domestic Assault: The Omah Police Experiment' (1990) 28 *Criminology* 183.

E. Durkheim, *The Division of Labour in Society* (1964 ed., originally published 1893).

N. Duxbury, 'Law and Economics and the Legacy of Chicago' in University of Hull, *Studies in Law* (1994).

F.H. Easterbrook, 'Federalism and European Business Law' (1994) 14 *International Rev. of Law and Economics* 125.

M. Eaton, *Justice for Women* (1986).

L. Edelman et al., 'Internal Dispute Resolution: The Transformation of Civil Rights in the Workplace' (1987) 43 *University of Chicago Law School* 1016.

H.T. Edwards, 'The growing disjunction between legal educaton and the legal profession' (1992) 91 *Michigan Law Rev.* 34.

H.T. Edwards, 'Symposium on Legal Education' (1993) 91 *Michigan Law Rev.* 1921–2219.

J. Eekelaar, *Regulating Divorce* (1991).

J. Eekelaar and M. Maclean, *Maintenance After Divorce* (1986).

R.C. Ellickson, 'Bringing culture and human frailty to rational actors: A critique of classical Law-and-Economics' (1989) 65 *Chicago–Kent Law Rev.* 23–55.

R.C. Ellickson, *Order Without Law: How Neighbours Settle Disputes* (1991).

R. Emerson, *Judging Deliquents* (1969).

K.T. Erickson, *Everything in its Path: Destruction of Community in the Buffalo Creek Flood* (1976).

ESRC, *Review of Socio-Legal Research* (1994).

ESRC, *Review of Socio-Legal Studies: Final Report* (1994).

W. Evan, *Social Structure and Law* (1990).

P. Fenn, A. McGuire, and D. Prentice, 'Information Asymmetry and the Securities Market' in *European Insider Law*, eds. K. Hopt and E. Wymeersch (1991) ch. 1.

P. Fenn and C.G. Veljanovski, 'A Positive Theory of Regulatory Enforcement' (1988) 98 *Economics J.* 1055.

M. Fineman, 'Implementing equality: ideology, contradiction and social change' (1983) *Wisconsin Law Rev.* 789.

159

S. Fiske, 'Attention and Weight in Person Perception: The Impact of Negative and Extreme Behaviours' (1980) 38 *J. of Personality and Social Psychology* 889.

P. Fitzpatrick, *Mythology of Modern Law* (1992).

J. Flax, 'Remembering the selves: is the repressed gendered?' (1987) 26 *Michigan Q. Rev.* 92–110.

G.P. Fletcher, *A Crime of Self-Defense: Bernhard Goetz and the Law on Trial* (1988).

C. Foster, *Privatization, Public Ownership and the Regulation of Natural Monopoly* (1992).

M. Foucault, *The Archaeology of Knowledge* (1972).

M. Foucault, *The History of Sexuality, Volume 1: An Introduction* (1978).

M. Foucault, *Discipline and Punish: The Birth of the Prison* (1979) 193.

A. Fox, *Beyond Contract: Work, Power and Trust Relations* (1974).

A. Fraser, *The Spirit of the Laws: Republicanism and the Unfinished Project of Modernity* (1990).

S. Freud, *The Ego and the Id*, trans. J. Riviere, revised and edited by J. Strachey (1962).

L.M. Friedman, *The Legal System: A Social Science Perspective* (1975) 202.

L.M. Friedman, *Total Justice* (1985).

L.M. Friedman, 'The Law and Society Movement' (1986) 38 *Stanford Law Rev.* 763.

D. Frisby and D. Sayer, *Society* (1986).

J. Froud, R. Boden, A. Ogus, and P. Stubbs, 'Toeing the Line: Compliance Cost Assessment in Britain' (1994) 22 *Policy and Politics* 313.

M. Galanter, 'Case Congregations and Their Careers' (1990) 24 *Law and Society Rev.* 371.

D. Galligan, *Discretionary Powers* (1986).

D.J. Galligan, 'Introduction' in *Readings in Socio-Legal Studies: Administrative Law* (1995).

B.G. Garth, 'Transnational Legal Practice and Professional Ideology' (1985) 7 *Issues of Transnational Legal Practice, 1985 Michigan Yearbook of International Studies* 3.

H. Gavelle, 'The Efficiency Implications of Cost-Shifting Rules' (1993) 13 *International Rev. of Law and Economics* 3.

E. Gellner, *Plough, Sword and Book: The Structure of Human History* (1988).

E. Gemmette, 'Law and Literature: An Unnecessarily Suspect Class in the Liberal Arts Component of Law School Curriculum' (1989) 23 *Valparaiso Law Rev.* 267.

H. Genn, *Hard Bargaining: Out of Court Settlement in Personal Injury Cases* (1987).

H. and Y. Genn, *The Effectiveness of Representation Before Tribunals* (1992).

V. Gessner, *Der Richter im Staatenkonflikt-Eine Untersuchung am Beispiel des Völkerrechtsverkehrs der Amerikanischen Republiken* (1969).

V. Gessner and A. Schade, 'Conflicts of Culture in Cross-Border Legal Relations: The Conception of a Research Topic in the Sociology of Law (1990) 7 *Theory, Culture and Society* 253–77.

V. Gessner, '*Wandel europäischer Rechtskulturen*' in *Lebensverhältnisse und soziale Konflikte im neuen Europa – Verhandlungen des 26 deutschen Soziologentages*, ed. B. Schäfers (1993).

V. Gessner, '*L'Interazione Giuridica Globale e le Culture Giuridichi*' (1993) 20 *Sociologia del Diritto* 61–78.

V. Gessner, A. Höland, and C. Varga, *European Legal Cultures* (1994).

A. Giddens, *The Consequences of Modernity* (1990).

C. Gilligan, *In a Different Voice: The Psychology of Women's Development* (1982).

H.P. Glenn, 'Private International Law and the New International Legal Profession' in *Conflits et Harmonisation – Mélanges en l'honneur d'Alfred von Overbeck*, eds. W.A. Stoffel and P. Volken (1990).

M.C. Gluckman, *The Judicial Processes Among the Barotse of Northern Rhodesia* (1958).

R.J. Goebel, 'Professional Qualification and Educational Requirements for Law Practice in a Foreign Country: Bridging the Cultural Gap' (1989) 63 *Tulane Law Rev.* 443–523.

Lord Goff, 'The Search for Principle' (Maccabean Lecture) (1983) LXIX *Proceedings of the Brit. Academy* 169.

A. Goldstajn, 'The New Law Merchant' (1961) 12 *J. of Business Law* 12.

P. Goodrich, *Reading the Law: A Critical Introduction to Legal Method and Techniques* (1986).

A. Gouldner, *The Coming Crisis of Western Sociology* (1971) ch. 2.

A. Gouldner, 'Anti-Minotaur: The Myth of a Value-Free Sociology' (1962) 10 *Social Problems* 209.

C. Graham and T. Prosser, *Privatizing Public Enterprises – Constitutions, the State and Regulation in Comparative Perspective* (1991).

J. Griffiths, 'What Do Dutch Lawyers Actually Do in Divorce Cases?' (1986) 20 *Law and Society Rev.* 135.

M. Gruter, *Law and Mind: Biological Origins of Human Behavior* (1991).

G. Gurvitch, *Sociology of Law* (1947) 72–96.

A.H. Halsey, *Decline of Donnish Dominion: The British Academic Professions in the Twentieth Century* (1992).

J.L. Hamilton and J. Sanders, *Everyday Justice: Responsibility and the Individual in Japan and the United States* (1992).

D. Haraway, 'Situated Knowledges: The Science Question in Feminism and the privilege of partial perspective" (1988) 14 *Feminist Studies* 3.

A. Harding, *A Social History of English Law* (1966).

S. Harding, 'Why has the sex-gender structure become visible only now?' in *Discovering Reality*, eds. S. Harding and M. Hintikka (1983).

S. Harding, *The Science Question in Feminism* (1986).

161

S. Harding, 'Conclusion: epistemological questions' in *Feminism and Methodology*, ed. S. Harding (1987).

D. Harris et al., *Compensation and Support for Illness and Injury* (1984).

D. Harris, A. Ogus, and J. Phillips, 'Contract Remedies and the Consumer Surplus' (1979) 95 *Law Q. Rev.* 581.

M. Harris, *The Rise of Anthropological Theory* (1968).

P. Harris and S. Bellerby, *A Survey of Law Teaching* (1993).

M. Hartsock, 'The feminist standpoint: developing the ground for a specifically feminist historical materialism' in *Discovering Reality*, eds. S. Harding and M. Hintikka (1983).

K. Hawkins, *Environment and Enforcement* (1984).

K. Hawkins and J. Thomas (eds.), *Enforcing Regulation* (1984).

K. Hawkins, 'The Use of Legal Discretion: Perspectives from Law and Social Science' in *The Uses of Discretion*, ed. K. Hawkins (1993).

K. Hawkins and J. Thomas, 'Making Policy in Regulatory Bureaucracies' in *Making Regulatory Policy*, eds. K. Hawkins and J. Thomas (1989) 10–11.

Heads of University Law Schools, *Law as an Academic Discipline* (1983).

F. Heidensohn, *Women in Control* (1992).

C.M. Heimann, 'Project: The Impact of Cost-Benefit Analysis on Federal Administrative Law' (1990) 42 *Administrative Law Rev.* 545.

D. Hensler et al., *Accidents and Injuries in the U.S. Costs, Compensation and Claiming Behaviour* (1984).

K. Hindell and M. Sims, *Abortion Law Reformed* (1971).

L. Hoebel, *The Law of Primitive Man* (1964).

M.A. Hogg and D. Abrams, *Social Identifications* (1988).

S. Holdaway, *Inside the British Police* (1983).

W.L. Hollist and J.N. Rosenau, 'World Society Debates' (1981) 31 *International Organisation* 1.

b. hooks, *Ain't I a Woman: Black Women and Feminism* (1982).

P. Huber and R. Litan (eds.), *The Liability Maze* (1991).

A. Hunt, *Explorations in Law and Society: Toward a Constitutive Theory of Law* (1993) 174–5, 224–6.

B. Hutter, *The Reasonable Arm of the Law?* (1988).

B. Hutter, 'Variations in Regulatory Enforcement Styles' (1989) 11 *Law and Policy* 153.

B. Jackson, *Semiotics and Legal Theory* (1985).

V. Johnston and J. Shapland, *Developing Vocational Legal Training for the Bar* (1990).

J. Jowell and A. Lester, 'Proportionally: Neither New Nor Dangerous' in *New Directions in Judicial Review*, eds. J. Jowell and D. Oliver (1988) 51.

JUSTICE, *Breaking the Rules* (1980).

R.A. Kagan, 'How Much Does Law Matter? Labor Law, Competition, and Waterfront Labor Relations in Rotterdam and U.S. Ports' (1984) 24 *Law and Society Rev.* 35.

R.A. Kagan, 'The Routinizaton of Debt Collection' (1984) 18 *Law and Society Rev.* 323.

R.A. Kagan, 'The Dredging Dilemma: Economic Development and Environmental Protection in Oakland Harbour' (1984) 19 *Coastal Management* 313.

D. Kagehiro and W.S. Laufer (eds.), *Handbook of Psychology and Law* (1991/92).

O. Kahn-Freund, 'Reflections on Legal Education' (1966) 29 *Modern Law Review* 121, at 127.

D. Kairys (ed.), *The Politics of Law: A Progressive Critique* (1982).

J.S. Kakalik and N.M. Pace, *Costs and Compensation Paid in Tort Litigation* (1986).

L. Kaplow and S. Shavell, 'The Efficiency of the Legal System versus the Income Tax in Redistributing Income', Harvard working paper no. 130 (1993).

M. Kaus, *The End of Equality* (1992).

D.Kaye, 'The Law of Probability and the Law of the Land' (1979) 47 *University of Chicago Law Rev.* 34.

G. Kelling, et al., *The Kansas City Preventive Patrol Experiment* (1974).

L. Kelly, *Surviving Sexual Violence* (1988).

D. Kennedy and K. Klare, 'A Bibliography of Critical Legal Studies' (1984) 94 *Yale Law J.* 461.

D. Kennedy, 'Form and Substance in Private Law Adjudication' (1976) 89 *Harvard Law Rev.* 1685.

D. Kennedy, 'How the Law School Fails: A Polemic' (1970) 1 *Yale Rev. of Law and Social Action* 71.

V. Kerruish, *Jurisprudence as Ideology* (1991).

R. Kneiper, *Nationale Souveränität* (1991).

J. Koehler and D.M. Shaviro, 'Verdicial Verdicts: Increasing Verdict Accuracy Through the Use of Overtly Probablistic Evidence and Methods' (1990) 75 *Cornell Law Rev.* 247.

L. Kohlberg, 'Moral Stages and Moralization: The Cognitive-Developmental Approach' in *Moral Development and Behavior: Theory, Research, and Social Issues*, ed. T. Lickona (1976).

L. Kohlberg, 'Stage and Sequence: The Cognitive-Development Approach to Socialization' in *Handbook of Socialization Theory and Research*, ed. D.A. Goslin (1969).

L. Kohlberg, *The Philosophy of Moral Development: Moral Stages and the Idea of Justice* (1981).

L. Kohlberg, 'Appendix. The Six Stages of Moral Judgement' in *The Philosophy of Moral Development: Essays on Moral Development*, vol. 1 (1981) 409–12.

S. Krislov, 'The Concept of Families of Law' in *Legal Systems and Social Systems*, eds. A. Podgorecki, C.J. Whelan, and D. Koshla (1985) 25–38.

H.M. Kritzerr, *The Justice Broker: Lawyers and Ordinary Litigation* (1990).

163

M. Krygier, 'Marxism and the Rule of Law' (1990) 15 *Law and Social Inquiry* 633.

N. Lacey, 'Conceiving Socio-Legal Studies', paper for the ESRC Review of Socio-Legal Studies Seminar (1993).

W.M. Landes and R. Posner, 'The Influence of Economics on Law: A Quantitative Study' (1993) 36 *J. of Law and Economics*.

B. Landheer, *On the Sociology of International Law and International Law and International Society* (1966).

O. Lando, 'The *lex mercatoria* in International Commercial Arbitration' (1985) 34 *International Comparative Law Q.* 747–68.

J.H. Langbein, 'The German Advantage in Civil Procedure' (1983) 52 *University of Chicago Law Rev.* 823–86.

H. Laski, *Holmes-Laski Letters* vol. 1 (1953) 763 (13/7/1925), compare vol. 2, at p. 1156.

Law Society, submissions to the Universities Funding Council and the Polytechnics Funding Council, nos. 0228R and 0234R (1991).

S. Lees, *Losing Out* (1988).

C. Lefort, *The Political Forms of Modern Society: Bureaucracy, Democracy, Totalitarianism* (1986) 184, 201, 207.

L.H. Leigh and L. Zedner, *A Report on the Administration of Criminal Justice in the Pre-Trial Phase in France and Germany* RCCJ research study no. 1 (1992).

M.J. Lerner, 'The justice motive in human relations: some thoughts on what we know and need to know about justice' in *The Justice Motive in Social Behaviour: adapting to times of scarcity and change*, eds. M.J. Lerner and S.C. Lerner (1981) 11–35.

M.J. Lerner and D.T. Miller, 'Just world research and the attribution process: looking back and ahead' (1978) 85 *Psychological Bul.* 1031.

E.A. Lind and T.R. Tyler, *The Social Psychology of Procedural Justice* (1988).

E.A. Lind et al., 'Individual and Corporate Dispute Resolution: Using Procedural Fairness as a Decision Heuristic' (1993) 38 *Administrative Science Q.* 224.

S. Lloyd-Bostock, *Law in Practice* (1988).

S. Lloyd-Bostock, 'Psychology and the Law: Their Theoretical and Working Relationship' (1993, unpublished).

S. Lloyd-Bostock, 'Fault and Liability for accidents: the Accident Victim's Perspective' in *Compensation and Support for Illness and Injury*, ed. D. Harris et al. (1984).

N. Luhmann, 'The World Society as a Social System' (1982) *International J. of General Systems* 8.

J.F. Lyotard, *The Post-Modern Condition: a Report on Knowledge* (1984).

S. Macaulay, 'Non-Contractual Relations in Business: A Preliminary Study' (1959) 28 *Am. Sociological Rev.* 55–67.

S. Macaulay, 'Lawyers and Consumer Protection Laws' (1979) 14 *Law and Society Rev.* 115.

G. Majone, 'Market Integration and Regulation: Europe After 1992' (1992) 43 *Metroeconomica* 131.

P. Manning, *Police Work* (1977).

I. Markovitz, 'Pursuing One's Rights Under Socialism' (1986) 38 *Stanford Law Rev.* 689.

I. Markovitz, 'Hedgehogs or Foxes?: A Review of Westinghouse and Schleider's *Zivilrecht im Systemvergleich*' (1986) 34 *Am. J. of Comparative Law* 113–35.

K. Marx, *Grundrisse: Foundation of the Critique of Political Economy* (1973) 83–111.

L. Mather and B. Yngvesson, 'Language, Audience, and the Transformation of Disputes' (1981) 12 *Law and Society Rev.* 775–821.

U. Mattei, 'Efficiency in Legal Transplants: The Foundations of Comparative Law and Economics' (1994) 14 *International Rev. of Law and Economics* 3.

D. Matza, *Becoming Deviant* (1969).

M.L. May and D.B. Stengel, 'Who Sues Their Doctors? How Patients Handle Medical Grievances' (1990) 24 *Law and Society Rev.* 105.

D. McBarnet, *Conviction, State, Law and Order* (1978).

D. McBarnet, 'False Dichotomies in Criminal Justice Research' in *Criminal Justice: Selected Readings*, ed. A.K. Bottomley (1978).

M.W. McConnell, 'Four Faces of Conservative Legal Thought' (1988) 34 *University of Chicago Law School Record* 12.

C. McEwen and R. Maiman, 'The Relative Significance of Disputing Forum and Dispute Characteristics for Outcome and Compliance' (1986) 20 *Law and Society Rev.* 439.

A.T. von Mehren, 'The Significance of Cultural and Legal Diversity for International Transaction' in *Jus Privatum Gentiom – Festschrift für Max Rheinstein*, eds. E. von Caemmerer, S. Mentshikoff, and K. Zweigert (1969) 247–57.

S. Merry, *Getting Justice and Getting Even* (1990).

J. Michelet, *Oeuvres Complètes de Jules Michelet* (1982) 268.

J. Miller and A. Sarat, 'Grievances, Claims and Disputes: Assessing the Adversary Culture' (1980–1) 15 *Law and Society Rev.* 537.

S. Miller, 'Unintended Side Effects of Pro-Arrest Policies and Their Race and Class Implications for Battered Women' (1989) 3 *Crim. Justice Policy Rev.* 299.

G. Minda, 'Jurisprudence at Century's End' (1993) 43 *J. of Legal Education* 27.

M. Minow, *Making All the Difference: Inclusion, Exclusion and American Law* (1990).

J.W. Mohr, 'The Absence of Presence/The Presence of Absence' (unpublished).

S. Moston and G.M. Stephenson, 'The Changing Face of Police Interrogation' (1993) 3 *J. of Community and Applied Social Psychology* 101–15.

S. Mottley, *Tough Cookie* (1991).

W.K. Muir Jr., *Law and Attitude Change* (1973).

G. Neave, in *Lawyers in Society: Comparative Theories*, eds. R. Abel and P. Lewis (1989).

D. Nelken, 'The "Gap Problem" in the Sociology of Law: A Theoretical Review' (1981) *Windsor Yearbook of Access to Justice* 35, 36.

M. Nicholson (ed.), *Feminism/Post Modernism* (1990).

F. Nietzsche, *The Gay Science* (1974) 181, para. 124.

R.E. Nisbett and T.D. Wilson, 'Telling More Than We Can Know: Verbal Reports on Mental Processes' (1977) 84 *Psychological Rev.* 231.

P. Nonet and P. Selznick, *Law and Society in Transition* (1978).

S. Noonan, 'Theorizing connection' (1992) 30 *Alberta Law Rev.* 719–37.

Sir H.W. Norman, *Correspondence Respecting the Recent Coolie Disturbances in Trinidad at the Mohurrum Festival with the Report Thereon by Sir H.W. Norman KCB* (1885).

C. Offe, 'Capitalism by Democratic Design? Democratic Theory Facing Triple Transition in East Central Europe' (1991) 58 *Social Research* 865.

A.I. Ogus and G.M. Richardson, 'Economics and the Environment: A study of Private Nuisance" (1977) 36 *Cambridge Law J.* 284.

A.I. Ogus, 'The Trust as Governance Structure' (1986) 30 *University of Toronto Law J.* 186.

F.E. Olsen, 'The Family and the Market: A Study of Ideology and Legal Reform' (1983) 96 *Harvard Law Rev.* 1497.

C.R. Ottley, *An Historical Account of the Trinidad and Tobago Police Force from the Earliest Times* (1964).

F. Pearce and S. Tombs, 'Ideology, Hegemony, and Empiricism: Compliance Theories of regulation' (1990) 30 *Brit. J. of Criminology* 423–43.

J. Phillips, K.O. Hawkins, and J. Flemming, 'Compensation for Personal Injury' (1975) 85 *Economics J.* 129.

J. Phillips and K.O. Hawkins, 'Some Economic Aspects of the Settlement Process: A study of Personal Injury Claims' (1976) 39 *Modern Law Rev.* 497.

A. Podgorecki, C.J. Whelan, and D. Koshla, 'Social Systems and Legal Systems – Criteria for Classification' in *Legal Systems and Social Systems* (1985) 1–24.

R.A. Posner, *Economic Analysis of Law* (1970).

R.A. Posner, 'The decline of law as an autonomous discipline: 1962–87' (1987) 100 *Harvard Law Rev.* 761.

R. Posner, *Law and Literature: A Misunderstood Relation* (1988).

R. Posner, *The Problems of Jurisprudence* (1990).

R. Posner, *Sex and Reason* (1992).

G.L. Priest, 'The Common Law Process and the Selection of Efficient Rules' (1977) 6 *J. of Legal Studies* 65.

F. Prochaska, *The Voluntary Impulse: Philanthropy in modern Britain* (1988).

D. Pyle, *The Economics of Crime and Law Enforcement* (1983).

166

R. Rawlings, 'The Eurolaw Game: Some Deductions from a Saga' (1993) 20 *J. of Law and Society* 309.

F.W. Reeves, *Race and Borough Politics* (1989).

R. Reiner, *Chief Constables* (1991).

A. Reiss, *The Police and the Public* (1971).

G. Richardson et al., *Policing Pollution* (1984).

R. Robertson, *Globalizatiõn – Social Theory and Global Culture* (1992).

P. Rock, *Making People Pay* (1973).

P. Rock, 'The Social Organization of British Criminology' in *The Oxford Handbook of Criminology*, eds. M. Maguire et al. (1994)

G. Rohlehr, *Calypso and Society in Pre-Independence Trinidad* (1990).

J. Rosenau, 'Patterned Chaos in Global Life: Structure and Process in the Two Worlds of World Politics' (1988) *International Political Science Rev.* 357–94.

G.N. Rosenberg, The Hollow Hope: Can Courts Bring About Social Change? (1991).

J. Roth, J. Scholz, and A. Witte (eds.), Taxpayer Compliance 2 vols. (1989).

V. Rothschild, *The Organisation and Management of Government Research and Development* (1971; Cmnd. 4814).

J. Rowan-Robinson, P. Watchman, and C. Barker, *Crime and Regulation: A Study of the Enforcement of Regulatory Codes* (1990).

C.K. Rowland and R.A. Carp, 'The Relative Effects of Maturation, Period, and Appointing President on District Judges' Policy Choice' (1983) 5 *Political Behaviour* 109.

P.H. Rubin, *Business Firms and the Common Law: The Evolution of Efficient Rules* (1983).

J. Rubinstein, *City Police* (1973).

D. Rüschemeyer, *Lawyers and their Society* (1973).

Report of the Royal Commission on Criminal Justice, chair, Viscount Runciman of Doxford (1993; Cm. 2263).

M.J. Sacks and R. Hastie, *Social Psychology in Court* (1978).

M. Saks, 'Do We Really Know Anything About the Behaviour of the Tort Litigation System?' (1992) 140 *Pennsylvania Law Rev.* 1147, 1183–7.

A. Sanders, 'Research for the Royal Commission on Criminal Justice: Implications for Education and Training' (1993) 10 *Socio-Legal Newsletter* 2.

U. Santino, 'The Financial Mafia: The Illegal Accumulation of Wealth and the Financial-Industrial Complex' (1988) 12 *Contemporary Crises* 203–43.

A. Sarat and W. Felstiner, 'Law and Strategy in the Divorce Lawyer's Office' (1986) 20 *Law and Society Rev.* 93.

P. Scales, 'Towards a Feminist Jurisprudence' (1981) 56 *Indiana Law J.* 375.

C.M. Schmitthoff, 'The Unification or Harmonisation of Law by Means of Standard Contracts and General Conditions' (1968) 17 *International Comparative Law Q.* 551–70.

C.M. Schmitthoff, *International Trade Usages* (1986).

167

J.T. Scholz and Feng Heng Wei, 'Regulatory Enforcement in a Federalist System' (1986) 80 *Am. Political Science Rev.* 1249.

P. Schuck, 'Legal Complexity: Some Causes, Consequences, and Cures' (1992) 42 *Duke Law J.* 1.

P. Scott, *The Crisis of the University* (1984).

M. Shapiro, *Courts: A Comparative and Political Analysis* (1981).

J. Shapland, V. Johnston, and R. Wild, *Studying for the Bar* (1993).

J. Shapland and J. Vagg, *Policing by the Public* (1988).

C. Shearing and P. Stenning (eds.), *Private Policing* (1987).

L. Sherman and R. Berk, 'The Specific Deterrent Effects for Arrest for Domestic Assault' (1984) 49 *Am. Sociological Rev.* 261.

P. Siegelman and J. Donohue III, 'Studying the Iceberg from its Tip: A Comparison of Published and Unpublished Employment Discrimination Cases' (1990) 24 *Law and Society Rev.* 113.

D. Sills, *The Volunteers: means and ends in a national organisation* (1957).

R.G. Simmons, 'Altruism and Sociology' (1991) 32 *Sociological Q.* 1–22.

K. Singh, *Bloodstained Tombs: The Mohurram Massacre of 1884* (1988).

G. Skapska, 'The Legacy of Anti-Legalism' (1994) 36 *Poznan Studies in the Philosophy of the Sciences and the Humanities* 214.

L. Sklair, *Sociology of the Global System* (1991).

J. Skolnick and R.A. Kagan, 'Banning Smoking: Compliance Without Enforcement' in *Smoking Policy: Law, Politics, and Culture*, eds. R. Rabin and S. Sugarman (1993).

J. Skolnick, *Justice Without Trial* (1966).

D. Smail, *The Origins of Unhappiness: a new understanding of personal distress* (1993).

C. Smart, *Feminism and the Power of Law* (1989).

C. Smart and S. Sevenhuijsen, *Child Custody and the Politics of Gender* (1989).

Smith v. *Rapid Transport* (1945) 317 Mass. 469, 58 N.E. 2d 754.

F. Snyder, 'Anthropology, Dispute Processes and Law'' (1981) 8 *Brit. J. of Law and Society* 141.

C. Spohn et al., 'The Sentencing Decisions of Black and White Judges' (1990) 24 *Law and Society Rev.* 1197.

C. Spohn et al., 'The Effect of Race on Sentencing' (1981–2) 16 *Law and Society Rev.* 72.

Society of Public Law Teachers, *Newsletter* (Summer, 1984).

L. Stanley and S. Wise, *Breaking Out* (1983).

G. Stasser, N.L. Kerr, and R.M. Bray, "The social psychology of jury deliberations: structure, process and process, and product' in *The Psychology of the Courtroom*, eds. N.L. Kerr and R.M. Bray (1982) 253.

F. Stephen, J. Love, D. Gillander, and A. Patterson, 'Testing for Price Discrimination in the Market for Conveyancing Services' (1992) 12 *International Rev. of Law and Economics* 397.

G.M. Stephenson, 'Should collaborative testimony be permitted in courts of law?' (1990) *Crim. Law Rev.* 302.

G.M. Stephenson, *The Psychology of Criminal Justice* (1992).

G.M. Stern, *The Buffalo Creek Disaster* (1977).

W.A.C. Stewart, *Higher Education in Post-war Britain* (1989).

A. Stinchcombe, 'Institutions of Privacy in the Determination of Police Administrative Practice' (1963) 69 *Am. J. of Sociology*.

M. Strathern, 'Discovering "Social Control"' (1985) 12 *J. of Law and Society* 111.

M. Strathern, *The Gender of the Gift: Problems with Women and Problems with Society in Melanesia* (1988).

S. Sugarman, *Doing Away With Personal Injury Law* (1989).

W.G. Sumner, *Folkways* (1906).

T. Tanase, 'The Management of Disputes: Automobile Accident Compensation in Japan' (1990) 24 *Law and Society Rev.* 651.

I. Taylor, 'The International Drug Trade and Money-Laundering: Border Controls and Other Issues' (1992) 8 *European Sociological Rev.* 181–93.

G. Teubner, *Autopoietic Law: A New Approach* (1988).

P. Thomas, 'The Poverty of Students' (1993) 27 *The Law Teacher* 152.

P. Thomas, 'Socio-Legal Studies in the United Kingdom' in *Precaire Waarden*, ed. F. Bruisma (1994).

S.M. Tipton, N. Bellah, R. Madsen, W.M. Sullivan, and A. Swidler, *Habits of the Heart: Individualism and Commitment in American Life and The Good Society* (1985).

R. Titmuss, *The Gift Relationship: From Human Blood to Social Policy* (1971).

M. Travers, 'Putting Sociology Back into the Sociology of Law" (1993) 20 *J. of Law and Society* 438, at 443.

L.H. Tribe, 'Trial by Mathematics: Precision and Ritual in the Legal Process'(1971) 84 *Harvard Law Rev.* 1329.

D. Trotman, *Crime in Trinidad* (1986).

M. Trow, 'Comparative Perspectives on Higher Education Policy in the UK and US' (1988) 14 *Oxford Rev. of Education* 81.

K. Tudyka, '*Weltgesellschaft Unbegriff und Phantom*' (1989) 30 *Politische Vierteljahresschrift* 503–8.

R. Tur and W. Twining (eds.), *Essays on Kelsen* (1986).

C. Turnbull, *The Mountain People* (1972).

A. Tversky and D. Kahnman, 'Evidential Impact of Base Rates' in *Judgement under Uncertainty: Heuristics and Biases*, eds. D. Kahnman, P. Slovic, and A. Tversky (1982).

W. Twining, 'Reading Bentham' (Maccabean Lecture) (1989) LXXV *Proceedings of the Brit. Academy* 97.

W. Twining, 'Reading Law' (1989) 24 *Valparaiso Law Rev.* 1.

W. Twining, *Rethinking Evidence* (1990) ch. 10.

W. Twining, 'Decision and Interference in Litigation' (1991) 13 *Cardozo Law Rev.* at 295–302, 713–15.

W. Twining, 'The Initial Stage': Notes on the Context and a Search for Consensus', LCAC First Consultative Conference, 9 July 1993.

W. Twining, *Blackstone's Tower: The English Law School* (1994).

W. Twining and E. Quick (eds.), *Legal Records in the Commonwealth* (1994).

T.R. Tyler, *Why People Obey the Law* (1990).

R. Unger, *Knowledge and Politics* (1975).

University of London, *LLM Review: second Interim Report* (1992).

F. Upham, *Law and Social Change in Post-War Japan* (1987).

P. Van Koppen, 'The Dutch Supreme Court and Parliament: Political Decision Making versus Non-Political Appointments' (1990) 24 *Law and Society Rev.* 745.

P. Van Koppen and M. Malsch, 'Defendants and One-Shotters Win After All' (1991) 25 *Law and Society Rev.* 803.

T. Veblen, *The Higher Learning in America* (1918) 211.

C.G. Veljanovski, 'The Economic Approach to Law – A Critical Introduction' (1980) 7 *Brit. J. of Law and Society* 158.

C.G. Veljanovski, 'Wealth Maximisation, Law and Ethics – on the Limits of Economic Efficiency' (1981) 1 *International Rev. of Law and Economics* 5.

C.G. Veljanovski and C.J. Whelan, 'Professional Negligence and the Quality of Legal Services – An Economic Perspective' (1983) 46 *Modern Law Rev.* 700.

C.G. Veljanovski, 'The Coase Theorem and the Economic Theory of Markets and Law' (1982) 35 *Kylos* 53.

C.G. Veljanovski, *The New Law-and-Economics: A Research Review* (1983).

C.G. Veljanovski, *The Future of Industry Regulation in the UK* (1993).

C.G. Veljanovski, "The Economic Theory of Tort Liability — Toward a Corrective Justice Approach' in *The Economic Approach to Law*, eds. P. Burrows and C.G. Veljanovski (1981).

J. Vickers and G. Yarrow, *Privatisation: An Economic Analysis* (1988).

N. Vidmar, 'Assessing the Effects of Case Characteristics and Settlement Forum on Dispute Outcomes and Compliance' (1987) 21 *Law and Society Rev.* 155.

W. Von Quine, 'Two Dogmas of Empiricism' in *From a Logical Point of View* (1953).

I. Wallerstein, *The Modern World-System* (1974).

M. Weber, *The Protestant Ethic and the Spirit of Capitalism*, tr. T. Parsons (2nd ed., 1976).

M. Weber, *Wirtschaft und Gesellschaft* (1956) 346 ff.

G. Wells, 'Naked Statistical Evidence of Liability: Is Subjective Probability Enough?' (1992) 62 *J. of Personality and Social Psychology* 739.

C. Werthman and I. Piliavin, 'Gang Members and the Police' in *The Police: Six Sociological Essays*, ed. D. Bordua (1967).

W. Westley, 'Violence and the Police' (1953) *Am. J. of Sociology* 59.

S. Wheeler et al., 'Do the "Haves" Come Out Ahead? Winning and Losing in State Supreme Courts, 1870–1970' (1987) 21 *Law and Society Rev.* 403.

S. Wheeler, K. Mann, and A. Sarat, *Sitting in Judgement: The Sentencing of White-collar Criminals* (1988).

J.B. White, *The Legal Imagination* (1973).

R. Williams, *Keywords: A Vocabulary of Culture and Society* (1983) 292–3.

T. Williamson, 'Reflections on Current Police Practice' in *Suspicion and Silence: the Right to Silence in Criminal Investigations,* eds. D. Morgan and G.M. Stephenson (1994).

J. Wills, 'Thieves, drunkards, and vagrants: defining crime in colonial Mombasa, 1902–1932' in *Policing the Empire*, eds. D. Anderson and D. Killingray (1991) 219–35.

R. Wollheim, 'The Last Phase' in *Sigmund Freud* (1971) ch. 7.

J. Wilson, *Varieties of Police Behavior* (1968).

G.D. Wood and R. Waterman, 'The Dynamics of Political Control of the Bureaucracy' (1991) 85 *Am. Political Science Rev.* 801.

A. Woodiwiss, *Social Theory After Post-Modernism* (1990).

A. Worral, *Offending Women: Female Law Breakers and the Criminal Justice System* (1990).

S. Yeo, *New Views of Co-operation* (1988).

D. Zhang and K. Kuroda, 'Beware of Japanese Negotiation Style: How to Negotiate with Japanese Companies' (1989) 10 *Northwestern J. of International Law and Business* 195–212.

S. Zizek, *The Sublime Object of Ideology* (1989) 128.

S. Zizek, *For They Know Not What They Do: Enjoyment as a Political Factor* (1991) 37.

A.A.S. Zuckerman, "Miscarriage of justice — a root treatment' (1992) *Crim. Law Rev.* 323.

K. Zweigert and H. Kötz, *An Introduction to Comparative Law* (1977).

171

INDEX

AUTHORS

172

Stephen, F., 29
Stephenson, G., 7, 10–11, 13, 133–9
Sumner, W.S., 144
Thomas, J., 19
Twining, W., 1, 35–49
Tyler, T., 138
Unger, R., 69

Veljanovski, C., 27, 29, 30
Warrington, R., 69
Wells, G., 81
Whelan, C., 28
Williams, R., 107
Wilson, J., 19
Zuckerman, A., 137

SUBJECTS

173

and, 109; pre-modern types of, 109; proliferation of, 140–2
legal aid, 4
legal concepts, socio-legal study of, 6
legal education, development of, 35–49; relationship with socio-legal studies, 35–49
modernity, society in, 107
Oxford Centre for Socio-Legal Studies: compensation projects, 4; contribution to socio-legal research, 2–7, 14–15; creation of a discipline, 18; discretion, 5; economic analysis of law, 7, 26–34; family policy, 4–5; foundation, 1; multi-disciplinary approach, 7; psychology of law, 7, 42–4; relationship to legal education, 35–49
postmodernism: emergence of, 69–70; Horatio's Mistake, 74; social relations in, 74; understanding of colonial experience, 71
post-modernity, 69–70
psychology of law: attribution theory, 134–5; community as a concept within, 134; contribution of Oxford Centre, 43–4, 133; criminal justice system as research area, 137; decision making, 81–3; impact of research, 135–8; place in socio-legal studies, 42–4, 135–8; role of, 10–11; social identity theory, 134–5
Royal Commission on Criminal Justice, 137–8
social science, importance in socio-legal research, 7
social theory, law and, 50–67; development of unified, 60–5

society, concept of, 106–11; impossibility of, 107–8; law as constitutive of, 106–11; nature of, 9; norms as defining feature of, 108–11
socio-legal studies: comparative approach, 11, 145–6; compliance theory, see compliance theory; concept of community in, 13, 113–23; concept of the social, 105–11; coping with high volume of law, 12, 140–4; economic analysis, see economic analysis of law; environment as area of research, 128–32; family law, 13; future directions, 10–14; globalization as area of research, 85–97, 149–53; impact of law on people and institutions, 12, 144–5; interdisciplinary approach, 75; methodology, 10–11; more than the sum of its parts, 8; nature of the discipline, 8–10; policy, 14, 42; proliferation of law, see law; psychology of law, see psychology of law; relationship with legal education, 41–4; research agendas, 143; statistics, role of, 80–2; theory, meaning of, 8; theory of social-legal research, 9; transition, study of societies in, 13–14, 97–104
transition: cultural factors, 101–3; distorion of market, 100–1; fear of law in transition, 98–9; rights, 102 (constitutional), 99–100 (in post-communist states), 99 (in societies in transition); socio-legal study of, 97–104